Herschelle

A Biography

Colin Bryden

SPEARHEAD

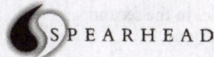

Published by Spearhead
An imprint of New Africa Books (Pty) Ltd.
99 Garfield Road
Claremont 7700
South Africa
(021) 674 4136
newafrica@newafricabooks.co.za

Copyright in text © Colin Bryden
Copyright in published edition © Spearhead 2003

All rights reserved. No part of this publication may be reproduced or transmitted in any form or by any means without prior written permission from the publisher.

First edition, first impression 2003

ISBN: 0-86486-520-1

EDITING AND PRODUCTION BY Integrated Publishing Solutions (IPS)
PROOFREADING BY Chris Whales
DESIGN AND LAYOUT BY Damian Gibbs

STATISTICS BY Andrew Samson, official statistician of the United Cricket Board of South Africa

Set in Minion 10 on 12.5pt

FRONT AND BACK COVER PHOTOGRAPHS BY
Tertius Pickard/Touchline Photo
COVER DESIGN BY Peter Bosman
ORIGINATION BY House of Colours
PRINTING AND BINDING BY ABC Press, Epping

COVER PICTURE: A career highlight as Herschelle Gibbs acknowledges the applause for a century against the West Indies in the second one-day international in Antigua, May 2001.

Contents

Preface 4
From Bonteheuwel to Bishops 6
Centuries, broken windows and records 18
More than just cricket 29
Tough going – and a tour 38
Too much, too soon? 50
Unexpected fatherhood 62
A step onto the world stage 65
The meeting in Mumbai 78
Back to earth 86
The big breakthrough 100
Dropping the World Cup 115
The captain makes a deal 126
Triumph and corruption 133
Scandal and suspension 144
The Cronjé factor 157
Back from the wilderness 162
Smoking in the West Indies 172
The runs flow 177
Outsmarted and outplayed in Australia 184
A career in progress 193
Career record 197
Bibliography 205
Index 206

Preface

Herschelle Gibbs has packed an extraordinary number of experiences into his first 28 years, many of which have caused him to be on the front pages of newspapers.

He is one of cricket's entertainers. One of the most revealing comments in this biography is by his former Western Province team-mate, John Commins, who says he doesn't watch much cricket since retiring from the game but he does watch Herschelle Gibbs. A Gibbs cover drive is one of the game's most exquisite sights and he has an array of strokes beyond the scope of most good players.

Being an entertaining cricketer, though, is not enough to justify a biography of a young man whose career is likely to have many more highlights.

When I was approached to write this book by Luke Alfred, who is now a colleague on the *Sunday Times*, my initial reaction was one of scepticism. It is, though, an intriguing story and the idea became more appealing, provided it could be an honest story about much more than cricket.

Herschelle has been involved in cricket's match-fixing scandal, fathered a child out of wedlock and smoked marijuana in the West Indies. He was suspended from a schoolboy cricket week after a late night out. As a Test player, he was caught sneaking back into a hotel in New Zealand after sunrise by a convenor of selectors who was already up and about after a good night's sleep. He is not one of cricket's angels.

His background as a player of colour in race-conscious South Africa is fascinating, although race is not an issue which troubles him.

All of these strands had to be pulled together and woven into a coherent tapestry.

Herschelle's business is handled by the Octagon company and at an early meeting with Donné Commins, of Octagon, it was quickly agreed that an account of the life of Herschelle Gibbs could not gloss over controversial issues.

Herschelle himself was a wonderful subject. Meetings with him were invariably informative and often highly entertaining. He is a young man with a zest for life and a natural warmth. He was disarmingly forthcoming about events which have kept him in the headlines and others which were not previously public property.

His father, Herman, was one of the prime movers for this book. He was a rich source of information and seldom short of a trenchant view.

Many people gave freely of their time. Fellow players and coaches, without exception, spoke about Herschelle with enthusiasm and affection.

Among those who made valuable contributions were: HD Ackerman, Hylton Ackerman, Basil Bey, Selborne Boome, Naas Botha, Lauren Collier, Donné Commins, John Commins, Gerald de Kock, Mike Demaine, Morné du Plessis, Robbie Fleck, Duncan Fletcher, John Gardener, Barbara Gibbs, Herman Gibbs, Lucinda Gibbs, Mike Haysman, Robert Houwing, Robin Jackman, Mark Keohane, Gary Kirsten, Peter Kirsten, Gert le Roux, Brian McMillan, Percy Montgomery, Richard Morris, Professor Tim Noakes, Grant Norton, Professor André Odendaal, Richard Parker, Shaun Pollock, Eric Simons, Michael Owen-Smith, Dan Retief, Keith Richardson, Gawie Swart, Pat Symcox, Gill Taylor, Melvyn Wallis-Brown, Bob Woolmer, Carol van Vuuren, John Young.

No-one, though, was more helpful than my wife, Romi, an accomplished writer herself, who conducted several interviews on my behalf and made many constructive suggestions after checking the early drafts of the manuscript.

Colin Bryden
Cape Town, January 2003

CHAPTER **ONE**

From Bonteheuwel to Bishops

It is a 12-kilometre journey from St Joseph's College to the Cape Town suburb of Elfindale. At the end of Herschelle Gibbs's first day at school there was no sign of his lift home. His mother had told him to look out for a neighbour's blue BMW. He spotted what he thought was the car but a stranger was in the driver's seat. Crestfallen but undaunted, the skinny five-year-old decided to walk.

It was a long, hot journey. About a third of the way along, there is a small park where a model train is a familiar landmark. It was time for a pitstop. Opposite the park was a corner shop. Temptingly displayed on a table on the pavement were chunks of juicy, pink watermelon. He had no money and nothing to drink. When no-one was looking he helped himself to some melon and played engine driver in the park while he ate it.

At the family flat in Elfindale, Barbara Gibbs was distraught. Her son had gone missing. She telephoned her husband, Herman. He called the police.

Herschelle finished his watermelon and carried on walking. His journey took him five hours. 'I walked into the flat to find my mom was in tears,' he remembers. Neighbours had rallied round. 'I told them there was nothing to worry about. On my way home from school I'd just stopped a bit, to play in the park.'

In the years to come, there would be many challenges, some remarkable achievements and more than a measure of anguish for the family, friends and supporters of Herschelle Gibbs as the intrepid five-year-old grew up to be a famous sports star, sometimes foolish, often controversial but never bland.

That he was at St Joseph's was because Herman Gibbs wanted his son to have a better start in life than his own.

Herman, the child of a third marriage, never had the chance to go to a good school or even to play sport with his own father. 'He was 60 when I was 13. He couldn't play soccer with me. I was determined that wouldn't happen when I became a parent.'

Handsome Herman, a star sportsman, was spotted by young Barbara Crayenstein when they travelled on the bus from the run-down area of Bonteheuwel to Athlone. 'He was attractive, with broad shoulders and an eye for every pretty girl. I thought he was very full of himself.' That opinion softened when they met for the first time at a beauty competition in Bonteheuwel. Barbara won second prize and Herman was augmenting a teacher's salary by working as a photographer.

Bonteheuwel, bordered by the Epping industrial estate, the Langa township for black Africans and the N2 highway into Cape Town, was infested by gangs. Herman's family, classified as 'coloured', were forcibly moved there when he was 13. They had been evicted from smarter Mowbray when the suburb was declared a 'white' area.

Herman's sprinting skills came in useful when he and younger brother Jack walked the dangerous streets. 'When I saw trouble I would tell Jack to go another way and I would carry on walking towards the skollies [hooligans]. When they came for me I would run. At first I wouldn't run flat out so they would think they could catch me, then I would speed up. I knew I could get away.'

Herman and Barbara married young. He was 22, she was 21 when they exchanged vows at the New Apostolic church in Mowbray, Cape Town, where Barbara still worships. Within a year, Barbara gave up her job in a clothing factory to give birth to the couple's first child. The young pair were living in one of the three bedrooms in the Crayenstein family home in Bonteheuwel.

A son was born at 4.30am on 23 February 1974 and almost immediately announced himself as someone special. The obstetrician at Cape Town's Somerset hospital tested the baby's grip on a finger and said to Barbara, prophetically, 'This child will grow up big and strong, look, he's very strong already.' Herman first saw him at 2pm, in official visiting hours, and he too was impressed by the infant's strength. 'Barbara's sister, Zaida, leant over. He grabbed her necklace and pulled it right off. There were beads everywhere.'

Barbara says, 'Herschelle was a beautiful baby with his father's broad shoulders.' He was named Herschelle Herman. The inspiration for the unusual first name was Herschel Road in the suburb of Claremont, for no other reason than Herman liked the name and it had the same three first letters as his own. Also, the son of one of the owners of the company Barbara worked for was Herschel. The 'le' was added to make the name distinctive.

Herman Gibbs was 23. Unlike his own father, he could look forward to playing games with his son. A champion sprinter, he had clocked 10,6 seconds for the 100 metres, played rugby for the City and Suburban club and soccer for Western Province Under 16. He had played first division baseball, turned out for his teachers training college at hockey and run in cross country races. 'Just about the only sport I didn't play, apart from a few social games, was cricket.'

An irony of the choice of Herschelle's name was that in apartheid South Africa the Gibbs family could not aspire to live in the road that had inspired it. They were coloured, of mixed race, according to definitions set out in the Population Registration Act. The Group Areas Act dictated that only white people could live in Claremont.

Especially when Herschelle was South Africa's only player of colour, it was often remarked that he didn't 'look' coloured, and his sister, Lucinda, is fair-haired. This is not surprising, considering the geneology on both sides of his family. Herman has traced the name Gibbs to 17 original families in South

Africa, 16 of which were of British origin and one French. He is descended from the French branch. He is unsure of the circumstances but says his grandfather arrived in South Africa having been a prisoner of war during the 1914-1918 conflict. 'I never knew my grandparents. I don't know who he married but apparently she had red hair.'

His father was married to a coloured woman and was compartmentalised under the Population Registration Act as coloured himself, although he was advised by his doctor that he could have been reclassified white. Herman's mother's maiden name was Hermans, which was the inspiration for his own name, and he believes there was some German blood in the Hermans family.

Barbara's paternal grandmother was white and ran a fish and chips shop in Sea Point. Her mother's father was of German and Chinese descent.

Herschelle is remarkably sanguine about apartheid and says race has never been a big issue for him. It was different in his parents' day, however. Legislation governed almost every aspect of people's lives, from where they could live, work, play and eat, to who they slept with and who they could marry. Separate park benches, train compartments, government offices and liquor shops were allocated for use by whites and 'non-whites'.

Barbara, the ninth of 10 children, was born and grew up in District Six, a multi-cultural suburb on the slopes of Devil's Peak, within walking distance of the centre of Cape Town. She has happy memories of a vibrant human melting pot that has been celebrated in song and commemorated with a museum. Her mother's sister lived across the road with her husband and son. Sundays were spent at home, playing games and cards. Her father loved sport, especially swimming and soccer, which he played on the beach with his sons and nephews when the family went camping at Ceres or Kommetjie over long weekends.

In one of the notable injustices of the apartheid era, District Six was declared a white area in 1966 and the residents were forcibly relocated across Cape Town to the Cape Flats. It was the first time Barbara became aware of the impact of apartheid. The Crayensteins were sent to Bonteheuwel and the children had to commute to their old school. This was hard on them, particularly the older ones. Barbara worked at her lessons and dreamed of going to a really good high school but it was typical of the apartheid era that she did not think beyond the best of the coloured schools, Harold Cressy or Trafalgar High.

Apartheid prevented whites and non-whites from competing on the same sports fields. Herman's athletics career, while he was a student teacher at Hewat College of Education, was under the auspices of the South African Council on Sport (Sacos), a 'non-racial' organisation vehemently opposed to any form of collaboration with apartheid structures. When a 'multi-national' meeting was announced for the Green Point Stadium in 1972, to be run on a new synthetic track, he was keen to participate but he was asked by Sacos, 'How can you even think of this?' In that year, he had clocked 10,6 on the cinder surface of the Green Point Track, across the road from the stadium. In a Sacos meeting on the 'tartan' track at the stadium he was given an official time of 10,6 again, but he is convinced he made better use of the faster surface. 'Two of the three stopwatches had me at 10,2 but the third said 10,6. Normally, if two times out of the three are the same they took those two times but the referee didn't believe it so they gave me 10,6.' The faster time was the qualifying standard for the 1972 Olympic Games in Munich. Even though South Africa was excluded from the Games because of apartheid, the achievement would have given him great satisfaction.

Denied the chance to test his speed against good opposition on the fast stadium surface, Gibbs became disenchanted with Sacos sport. He clandestinely trained with white athletes for the next year and a half and, with the advantage of good coaching, increased his knowledge of the sport. 'When I became a teacher and started coaching, I was an instant hit as a coach.'

Herschelle spent the first few months of his life in the room at the Crayenstein home before his parents moved to Lansdowne, then Salt River and finally to Elfindale, one of the 'better' coloured suburbs, which lay close to 'whites-only' Bergvliet, Plumstead and Wynberg. It was not far, either, from Newlands, where the home grounds of Western Province rugby and cricket are on either side of a suburban railway line. Barbara was pregnant with Lucinda, who was born two years after Herschelle. The Gibbs family moved into a flat overlooking the St Augustine's sports club, the first home they had owned. 'It was expensive but I wanted the kids to grow up in a good area,' says Herman.

It didn't take Herman long to realise that his son was notably more talented than the average youngster who attended Bridgetown High in nearby Athlone, where Herman was a physical education and sports teacher. When Herschelle was three, an anxious neighbour telephoned to report that the youngster, bare-footed, was drop-kicking a rugby ball off a tarred road. 'He couldn't believe it. He said Herschelle was getting the ball up in the air every time and hadn't once stubbed his toe into the tarmac.'

By the age of two, Herschelle could outrun his mother, who adds in her defence that she was heavily pregnant with Lucinda. 'Even at that early age, Herschelle was so good at running and kicking a ball around that he was in demand to play games with our neighbour's sons, who were then six and seven years old,' says Barbara.

By the time Herschelle was four he was starting to take a starring role in ball games, usually soccer or cricket, as groups of families went on Sunday picnics. It wasn't long before Lucinda was outshining the other neighbourhood boys as well. 'Herschelle was always number one, whether it was cricket or soccer, but Lucinda quickly became number two,' says Herman.

The flat was ideally situated for young Herschelle, who seethed with restless energy. 'I used to watch the games being played at St Augustine's from the flat and I'd join in whenever the young boys were playing soccer or cricket. I've never been one to sit still. I was always looking for things to do. The older boys would be surprised when I held my own against them.' Herman gave him every encouragement, buying his son rugby balls, soccer balls and cricket bats.

'I enjoyed what happened in class. Not the actual learning, I never was one to pay attention, but most of the teachers seemed to enjoy the sort of personality I had and seemed to have a soft spot for me.'

Herschelle enjoyed daredevil activities. There was a gravel road on a slope leading into St Augustine's and when Herschelle and his friends were old enough to ride bicycles they would 'ski' down the slopes, riding fast, then applying the brakes so the bikes would skid down.

With Herschelle and Lucinda safely ensconced in a healthy environment, education was the next big challenge. Government schools were strictly segregated, with the lion's share of funds allocated to schools for whites, which led to a disparity in the standard of education available to pupils of colour. Private schools were expensive but there were some who were prepared to defy the government by enrolling coloureds and blacks. St Joseph's, in the smart suburb of Rondebosch, was run by the Catholic Church and it was one such school. It meant a financial sacrifice for Herman and Barbara, but Herschelle was enrolled.

Herschelle

After his eventful first day of school in 1980, the young Herschelle was happy at St Joseph's. 'I enjoyed what happened in class. Not the actual learning, I never was one to pay attention, but most of the teachers seemed to enjoy the sort of personality I had and seemed to have a soft spot for me.' Which was just as well, because right from the start his school marks were poor. What he really enjoyed were the hours after class, when he could get out onto the sports field, either to take part in organised activities or to play in pick-up games of touch rugby.

There wasn't much sport for the smallest boys in the school, so he would watch the older pupils practising and playing. During his first year at school, Herman was approached by a sports teacher when he went to fetch his son. 'He told me that Herschelle had been hanging around behind the goalposts, watching the Under 16 boys practising rugby. When the ball rolled to him, Herschelle casually drop-kicked it through the poles. Everyone was so amazed at what the little guy could do that they asked him to do it again – and he did.'

> He was eight when he played for St Joseph's Under 10s. By his recollection he scored 74 not out against Rondebosch Prep School in his first match ...

As winter became spring, the youngster took to watching the big boys practising in the cricket nets. He was given a chance to bowl and he sent down seamers and leg-breaks that frequently bamboozled boys much older than him. Fortunately, perhaps, for the egos of the seniors, they did not offer him a chance to bat.

By the end of that first year Herschelle was offered a bursary. Lucinda, though, was soon to start school and Herman found that a coloured teacher's salary did not support a daughter at Springfield Convent, another private school, as well as meeting the costs for Herschelle that were not covered by the bursary. He stopped playing sport himself and, in addition to teaching, he went back to freelance photography, taking pictures at weddings and social events. He also worked in a liquor store and ran a sectional title managership, which included tasks such as reading meters.

Although no longer actively playing, Herman maintained his interest in sport. During the winter he coached soccer at the Yorkshire club, where Herschelle, as a six-year-old, played for the Under 10 team, and when Herschelle was 10, he managed the Young Cavaliers Under 13 cricket team for which the boy was playing.

Soccer was the first sport that Herschelle played on an organised basis and the first in which his unusual ability came to the fore. In the early days, he enjoyed it more than cricket or rugby.

Cricket came next. He was eight when he played for St Joseph's Under 10s. By his recollection he scored 74 not out against Rondebosch Prep School in his first match, although neither he nor Herman is certain about the exact score. Then came rugby at the same age, as scrumhalf for the Under 10s.

Herman wanted to make the most of his son's talent. The late Stuart Leary, the former Kent professional cricketer and English First Division soccer player, ran coaching clinics during the school holidays, using St Joseph's as a base. Approached by Herman, Leary was initially wary of allowing a puny eight-year-old to take part in what were relatively advanced courses aimed at 11- or 12-year-olds. Then Herman received a call from Leary asking him to take Herschelle to the nets one Sunday morning. Herman believes this was after Leary had been told by the late Noel Kirsten, the former Border wicketkeeper, Newlands groundsman and father of four cricketing sons, that he should take a look at Gibbs. Leary arrived with a bag of balls, Herschelle with his cricket bat. Afterwards, Leary was emotional. 'He had tears in his eyes,' says Herman. 'He said he couldn't believe a youngster could play so many shots.' Herschelle was invited to join the coaching clinics.

Herschelle says Leary was his first major influence. Leary, who had coached Western Province, died in 1988 but Hylton Ackerman, the former Western Province captain and coach, remembers Leary's excitement at discovering a cricketing gem. 'He would come and tell me, "I've coached this little youngster, his name is Herschelle Gibbs, and he's got fantastic talent. The trouble is, he's better at soccer, and other people tell me he's better still at rugby!"'

Noel Kirsten told his son, Peter, then one of South Africa's foremost batsmen, 'I've seen a youngster who plays just like you. You've got to go and watch him.' Peter did and Herschelle scored 165 not out off just 20 overs for St Joseph's Under 10s against Golden Grove Primary School. He followed up by taking six for 12 off seven overs.

Kirsten knew he had seen an exceptional young player. Asked to categorise the similarities which his father had noticed, he said, 'Hands and feet. He's got magnificent hands, with strong wrists. He's quick on his feet and times the ball superbly.'

Gibbs idolised Peter Kirsten. According to Herman, when he realised his hero was at the ground, he deliberately aimed to hit boundaries to where Kirsten was standing. Although Kirsten never coached Gibbs, he would see the eager youngster at Newlands, sitting in the scholars' enclosure, near the players' area. Kirsten liked to prepare for batting away from his provincial team-mates and young Gibbs would volunteer to help him with throwdowns on the outfield. Kirsten was flattered that a young player admired him to such a degree. 'I suppose it's the Newlands tradition. When I was a boy I would go and watch the Eddie Barlows and Graeme Pollocks, hoping that one day I would be out there playing in the middle like them. I'd like to think that right now there's some kid with talent who goes along to watch Herschelle Gibbs.'

Being a small school, St Joseph's played mainly against some of the lesser schools in the cricketing firmament. Centuries became so commonplace for Gibbs that the school abandoned a tradition of awarding a trophy made out of stumps which they presented to boys who made hundreds. In an Under 12 match against St Agnes, Gibbs pummelled an outclassed attack, hitting a double century in a 25-overs-a-side game at St Joseph's. Herman was umpiring. 'It's a small field and they ended up with all their fielders on the boundary. Still they couldn't stop him hitting fours and sixes.'

St Joseph's played their matches on Wednesday afternoons. At the weekends Herschelle played for Young Cavaliers. He also occasionally turned out for Avendale, the Athlone-based club that was a pioneering force in early attempts to achieve racial integration in cricket. Bob Woolmer, the former England player who was to become South African team coach, was coaching Avendale when he first saw Gibbs as an 11-year-old.

'In those pre-unity days, coaching in the black areas was pretty limited,' says Woolmer. 'We started a junior cricket scheme with about 15 boys and soon we had to turn boys away because hundreds came. Herman brought Herschelle one day and from the moment I threw the first ball to him I realised he had natural ability that was just phenomenal. I've seen very few children with such ability. He had this wonderful coordination. His ability to pick length off front and back foot was better than some 25-year-olds. Even at that age, he was obviously a mile better than anyone else. I think I told people then that this boy would play for South Africa.'

From Bonteheuwel to Bishops

Playing for Young Cavaliers enabled Herschelle to perform in front of the provincial Under 13 selectors. He took three wickets in the first three overs of a match against Bishops, one of the strongest schools. Herman, the manager, had him taken off. 'I knew some selectors were around and I wanted Bishops to set a target so Herschelle could show them he could bat.' Bishops made 164 and Herschelle hit 16 fours in an innings of 76. It won him an invitation to play in the B team in the final provincial trial at the Groote Schuur Oval. He was 11 and still tiny compared to most boys in the Under 13 age group.

He wasn't asked to bowl as the A team scored around 160 in the trial, and he was down at number seven in the batting order. One selector had already told Herman that Herschelle was too small and too young but that he would get another chance the following year. The B team crashed to 13 for five. Stuart Leary, who was watching, told Herschelle it was the best thing that could have happened to him. 'Stay until the end of the day and they must select you,' he said. There was no chance of a result. Herschelle calmly batted out the rest of the match, scoring 42, and Leary was proved right.

The smallest and youngest member of the side was the most consistent batsman for Western Province at the national Under 13 week in Paarl. He batted at number five and scored 208 runs in five matches with a highest score of 69 and a lowest of 24. His average was 52. Only team-mate Mark Bredell, his tally bolstered by a century, scored more runs. His skipper was HD Ackerman, who went on to become a Test player and a successful Western Province captain. One of young Ackerman's gambits in Paarl was to turn to Herschelle to bowl some leg-breaks when Boland were providing resistance. He took two quick wickets.

'Even then, as a spindly, thin little guy he was really talented,' says Ackerman. He also stood out from the other players because he had a sponsored bat. One evening the youngsters were invited to a barbecue and Herschelle was thrown into a swimming pool. 'We didn't know he couldn't swim. He sank to the bottom and sat there for a while until Mark Bredell dived in and pulled him out.' It wasn't quite true that he couldn't swim but, unlike every other activity he tried, swimming was a weakness. He could barely get from one end of a pool to the other and had to beg not to be forced to enter school galas.

His sense of humour soon asserted itself at the junior week. Lunches were served at a school hostel where it was a tradition that grace was said before meals. The captains had to take it in turns to perform the duty but Herschelle volunteered to take over from Ackerman. The youngster bounded to the front of the room. 'Gereed? Vreet!' Loosely translated from Afrikaans, it means, 'Ready? Eat!', though *vreet* is a vulgar term. It didn't amuse some of the teachers but his team-mates found it hilarious.

It was not only at cricket that the youngster excelled. He was the school's outstanding rugby player and he would play rugby for the school on Saturday morning and soccer for the Yorkshire club in the afternoon. He was selected for the Western Province Under 13 soccer team as a creative midfield player and was the leading scorer in an inter-provincial week in Pretoria, netting eight goals in 15 matches.

With his son's star on the rise, Herman Gibbs started receiving overtures from Diocesan College, a renowned Cape educational institution, more commonly known as Bishops. The school was founded in 1849 by the first Anglican bishop of Cape Town. An expensive private school, it was the *alma mater* of some of South Africa's most prominent men. Leaders of industry have studied in the old brick classrooms and some of the country's outstanding sportsmen have played on the spacious grounds in Rondebosch.

For teacher Herman, the fees at Bishops were simply unaffordable but the school was as keen to accommodate Herschelle as Herman was for him to be there. He was offered a bursary, only to become the subject of a tug of war. St Joseph's wanted him to complete his Standard Six year with them but Bishops had already accepted him. The headmaster of St Joseph's telephoned his Bishops counterpart and Herman in turn was told that Bishops could not be seen to be 'buying' sportsmen. As Herschelle had not written an entrance exam he would have to wait until the following year. Another problem was that a new bursary committee decided that the maximum subsidy that could be offered to the Gibbs family was 50 percent. 'I thought that was it,' said Herman. In the end, though, a way was found through the red tape and Herschelle became a Bishops boy, with Herman having to pay a token R200 a month.

Herschelle Gibbs would be one of two especially notable products of Bishops during the next five years. While Gibbs set records on the sports fields, another youngster, his senior by a year, would walk off with most of the academic prizes. Mark Shuttleworth, Bishops head boy in 1991, would become a renowned Internet entrepreneur and the first South African to travel into space.

CHAPTER **TWO**

Centuries, broken windows and records

It didn't take long for Herschelle Gibbs to start making the sort of impact at Bishops that would make him one of the most talked-about sportsmen to enter the white-pillared gates of the College. The first century recorded in the Diocesan College magazine against his name was 139 for the Under 14A team against another great Cape Town educational institution, SACS, the South African College Schools, during the final term of the 1987 school year. A report on the team noted there had been an improvement in the standard of fielding, 'mainly due to Herchel Gibbs behind the stumps'. Future editions of the publication would get the spelling right as his name became one of the more significant in Bishops sporting annals.

Melvyn Wallis-Brown, who coached the Under 14 team, knew of Gibbs by reputation and the new boy at the school more than lived up to expectations. 'I had coached cricket for 25 to 30 years and had never encountered such talent. He kept wicket or he bowled amazing leg-spinners and fielded at cover point. Even at Under 14 level, he pulled off a couple of run-outs in almost every match, he was so accurate and quick, with a flat throw.' His multitude of talents in the field were matched by his batting skills. The Under 14s played on Bishops' smallish Sahara field. Plate glass classroom windows were always in danger, while Gibbs upset the owners of neighbouring houses by hitting balls out of the ground and into their gardens. 'We had to keep a supply of spare balls because sometimes the neighbours refused to return them.'

Adrian Kuiper, vice-captain of the first South African World Cup team in 1992, was also coached by Wallis-Brown at Bishops. Kuiper became a star for Western Province, especially in one-day games, and was a legendary hitter who made a 49-ball century for the Springboks against Mike Gatting's rebel English team in Bloemfontein in 1989/90.

'Adrian was a wonderful striker of the ball but Herschelle had greater talent,' says Wallis-Brown. 'Adrian had all the shots but Herschelle had a more delicate touch. He could work the ball around and manufacture shots that were astounding in a boy that age.'

Wallis-Brown was disappointed when the young prodigy started experimenting with fast bowling in his Under 15 year. 'To this day I think he could bowl world-class leg-spinners. He had a good googly. Shane Warne has taken the world by storm over the last decade. In a Test match, if the opposition is batting last and the pitch is wearing, to have a leg-spinner is a huge plus.' Wallis-Brown passed on his advice but the intimidatory attractions of bowling fast were too strong. 'Unfortunately he persisted, although he was never going to be a good quick bowler. He didn't have the physique for it.'

Gibbs had been taught to bowl leg-spin by Stuart Leary when the precociously talented youngster was attending cricket clinics at the Vineyard ground in Newlands with older boys. Tossing the ball up and making it turn from leg was a sensible option for someone who couldn't expect to bowl fast like some of the bigger youngsters.

As a high school boy, though, the desire to bowl fast, 'or what I thought was a reasonable pace', outweighed the attractions of dabbling with the subtleties of spin. Although he was able to make the ball swing, he realised when he became a senior cricketer that his bowling had its limitations, mainly because he could not bowl fast enough to trouble good batsmen. He decided to concentrate on batting.

Not yet 14, he played for the Under 15A team in 1988 and started 1989 in the Second XI, before scores of 104 not out against SACS and 66 against

Wynberg Boys' High earned him promotion to the first team. Initially, he was not one of the stars. He earned favourable notice, however, for his fielding, and although his highest score was a modest 55, his ability was recognised by the Western Province Nuffield selectors. He was invited to the trials and despite not doing particularly well, the 15-year-old was one of four Bishops boys in the provincial team for the 1989 inter-provincial Nuffield Week in Johannesburg. 'They must have thought this little guy could play a bit,' he says. The Bishops teachers were less inclined to make awards on potential, awarding him only school half-colours for the year.

He contributed no outstanding performances in that week, and his abiding memory was of an innings he did not have to play. 'Our last game was against Eastern Province. Brett Schultz was scaring everyone and I was next in to bat. I was very happy the game ended before I had to face him.'

Gibbs, though, was an exceptional cricket talent and 1990 was the year in which he blossomed. Still on his school holidays, he made his Western Province Premier League debut for the Avendale club against Techs-Mutual and made 104 not out after his side had been 41 for four. At 15, he was claimed to be the youngest century-maker in the history of the senior league. He followed up by making 90 against Green Point.

Back at Bishops, he was a senior player in an inexperienced team, batting at number three, although he was floated in the order at times if an early wicket fell. He became such an important player to the team cause that other players happily moved up the order to protect their best batsman, according to Grant Norton, coach of the First XI. There were two centuries in the first term, 125 against Kearsney College at the St Alban's Festival in Pretoria and 123 against neighbours and rivals Rondebosch Boys' High. There was also an early indication of a liking for a suitable stage when he made an unbeaten 97 off 97 balls, also against Rondebosch, in a day-night challenge match at Newlands. 'It was a faultless display,' remembers Norton. 'Peter Kirsten was there as a guest and it was almost as though Herschelle wanted to put on a special performance for him.'

Norton noted in the Diocesan College magazine, 'Gibbs is technically very correct and times the ball beautifully.' Norton added that he was also a useful change bowler, 'who swings the ball sharply into the right-hand batsman'. Looking back, Norton chuckles at his star player's bowling success, sharing Wallis-Brown's opinion of his lack of genuine prowess. 'He wasn't a particularly good bowler. His reputation helped him get wickets. Opposition players knew it was Herschelle Gibbs bowling to them and gave him more respect than he deserved.'

One occasion, though, when a lack of reputation helped was when he played in a private schools week in Pretoria against St Stithian's, the strong school from just north of Johannesburg. Norton remembers, 'They had a very strong batting line-up, with three or four Transvaal Nuffield players. In the first over, one of their players pushed the ball wide of cover and set off for a run. Herschelle picked up in a flash and hit the middle stump. The poor batsman was a picture of disbelief. They fell apart. They had seen something special.'

He also had a way with words. Wallis-Brown recalls, 'He was a great "chirper" but in a humorous, not an unkind way. One of his comments had me in stitches when I was umpiring a first team game. Our opening bowler was pretty sharp and after the second ball, Herschelle said, "Drop it short, we want to have spare ribs for supper."'

> 'One of Gibbs's comments had me in stitches when I was umpiring a first team game. Our opening bowler was pretty sharp and after the second ball, Herschelle said, "Drop it short, we want to have spare ribs for supper."'

After a winter starring for the Under 16A rugby team, his performances for the cricket team in the final term were nothing short of phenomenal. He finished the year with 1 674 runs at an average of 76,09, more than double the number of runs made by the next highest scorer. Five more centuries flowed off his bat: 159 not out against Queens College and 100 not out against Graeme College in successive innings at the Cape Schools Week in Queenstown, then two more back-to-back hundreds, 105 against Westville High from Natal and 122 not out against Westerford High, before he capped the school year with 108 against Milnerton High.

His bowling figures were remarkable, too, with 49 wickets at an average of 13,18. No-one else took more than 29 wickets. In one match, against arch-rivals St Andrew's College, Bishops were bowled out for 98. Having contributed 34 runs with the bat, Gibbs went on to take six for 17 as St Andrew's tumbled to 58 all out.

A litany of sporting achievements was relayed to newspaper readers on a regular basis, notably those of the *Cape Times*, where Herman Gibbs was editing a weekly section on junior sport. Bishops teachers were both embarrassed and concerned by the amount of publicity the school and their star sportsman received. 'There were a lot of articles about Herschelle. There definitely seemed to be a bias towards him and Bishops. I think it put too much pressure on him,' says Norton.

'His father pushed him all the time,' agrees Wallis-Brown. 'Every time you opened the *Cape Times* on a Monday morning there would be a picture of Herschelle. The kid was embarrassed too, he's a sensitive lad.'

Herschelle admits he wasn't keen on his father writing about him. 'But I never told him that. It was his job and it was quite a good supplement. I got the occasional chirp about being in the paper but nothing too bad.' One of the features of the supplement was a regular sponsored Junior Sports Achievers' award, which culminated in an annual award. Herman, as editor, was one of the judges and Herschelle, undoubtedly deservedly, was the first winner.

Herman, who became a full-time journalist in 1987 after 17 years as a teacher, says the focus on his son was based on news value. 'Also, the people on the newspapers kept asking me what Herschelle was doing, so there was interest in him.'

Herman is unapologetic for what he describes as protecting his son's interests. 'The school was mainly interested in what was good for Bishops, whereas my concern was what was good for Herschelle. For instance, when he got into the first team they were keen on turning him into a wicketkeeper, because they had a tradition of producing SA Schools wicketkeepers. I didn't think that was right.' He also sought out sponsorships for Herschelle, whose photograph soon appeared in various Cape Town newspapers showing him receiving free equipment for cricket and soccer.

Being selected for the 1990 Western Province Nuffield XI was no more than a formality, as was the award of full school colours, but before the Nuffield Week there was another game to be played. The Western Province senior selectors, chaired by the late Gavin Pfuhl, had kept their eye on the phenomenon from Bishops and decided it was time to blood him in first-class cricket. After playing for a Western Province Invitation XI against South African Universities B and scoring a confident 37, he was selected for

Western Province B, who played against Transvaal B at Newlands from 10 to 12 December. The match was part of the South African Cricket Union's Bowl competition which, even though it was essentially a second XI competition, had first-class status.

The debutant, aged 16 years and 270 days, did not have long to wait before making his mark. He batted at number four and was at the crease before lunch after the first two Western Province wickets fell for 82. The *South African Cricket Annual* described his 77 as 'brilliant'. He hit two sixes and 10 fours in a 129-ball innings. He and future Test batsman, John Commins, who made an unbeaten century, put on 121 in 94 minutes for the fourth wicket.

At the time, Commins was 25 and determined to advance his career. 'Herschelle and I were vying for a place in the A side. He obviously had huge talent but I had played a lot of B cricket and I had a bit more experience. I still think it is a good thing for young players to spend some time in the B team. I remember Gavin Pfuhl telling me, "Until you make a B Section hundred you're not going to play for the A side."'

Gibbs, meanwhile, was worrying about the opposition. 'The big thing for me was how I was going to handle the quick bowlers.' The fastest bowler in the Transvaal side was Graham Stevenson and he was out of the attack by the time the debutant went in. Gibbs did face Stevenson later, when he was armed with the second new ball, but soon afterwards he was caught, ironically by Stevenson, off an attempted pull against Chris Lister-James.

The Cape Town press, always on the lookout for a local hero, recorded the occasion with suitable fanfare. 'Gibbs arrives,' proclaimed the main sports page headline in the *Cape Times* the next morning, with a second heading adding, 'Sixteen-year-old Bishops prodigy confirms his rich potential.' It was still the main sports story in the afternoon newspaper, the *Cape Argus*, which headlined its article, 'Cracking debut for Herschelle.'

By the weekend, the inevitable comparison was being made. 'The next Pollock? No, the name is GIBBS', was the headline in the Saturday edition of the *Cape Argus*. Writer Deon Viljoen hailed the youngster's 'effortless, stylish, controlled' strokeplay and the way Gibbs had used his feet to break the rhythm of Danie du Toit, an experienced left-arm seam bowler, and left-arm spinner Corrie Jordaan, who was at the start of a decade-long career.

In his first interview as an 'adult' sporting celebrity, young Herschelle told Viljoen, 'I was nervous out there. There was a lot of chirping but I soon settled down.'

Viljoen then raised what for young cricketers has become the dreaded comparison with Graeme Pollock, South Africa's greatest batsman and the benchmark against which so many young players are measured. The response from Gibbs was firm: 'I don't want to be compared with the Pollocks and Kirstens of this world, simply because I'm not as good as them. I want to be known as Herschelle Gibbs, period.'

Gibbs went on to say that he planned to make cricket his career. 'I've decided to quit soccer to concentrate on rugby and cricket. I would like to first gain Western Province Craven Week colours before giving up rugby as well.' Asked why cricket was top of his list, he revealed the impish sense of humour that would become a trademark. 'Because cricket does not require so much effort; I'm a bit lazy, you know.'

Daryll Cullinan, then playing for Western Province, contributed sensible advice in the same article. Cullinan's own early career was blighted by his scoring of a maiden first-class century when he was just 34 days older than Gibbs had been on his debut. Cullinan's feat, for Border against Natal B six years previously, beat by 31 days the record set by Pollock as the youngest century-maker in South African first-class cricket. 'The biggest favour you can do Herschelle is to let him develop at his own pace,' said Cullinan. 'Talking from experience, I can tell you he does not need the hype. Being labelled as the next Pollock was certainly detrimental to my early career. Herschelle has enough talent to make a name for himself but we should let him do it his way.'

In the second innings of his debut match, Gibbs was out for eight in an attempt to score quick runs.

Five days later, the new star of provincial cricket was back among his peers in the Nuffield Week in Cape Town. It was to be a week of disappointment. His only two innings of any distinction were 39 against Country Districts and 38 against Transvaal. Having gone into the tournament as a headline attraction in his own city, he failed to win selection for the SA Schools team.

His poor form during Nuffield Week notwithstanding, Pfuhl and the Western Province selectors decided the young prodigy was ready to take an even bigger step upwards. Gibbs had been practising with the senior Western

Centuries, broken windows and records

Province squad while the selectors, Pfuhl, former off-spinner Richard Morris, manager Robin Jackman and coach Hylton Ackerman, held a meeting to decide on a team to play against Northern Transvaal in a Castle Cup match at Newlands, starting on 26 December.

'It wasn't a very long debate,' recalls Jackman. 'Hylton's knowledge of the game is unsurpassed in my opinion and he told us, "This kid can play. He can play off the front and back foot and on both sides of the wicket." The rest of us said, "If you think so, Hylton, he'll play."'

Gibbs recalls the moment when he heard he had been picked. 'We were in front of the old members' pavilion when suddenly they said, "This is the team," and they read my name out.' It was stunning news, not least, Gibbs remembers, for senior players who had been left out of the side. 'I phoned my dad and he couldn't believe it and then it was in the papers and on the eight o'clock news on television and I was thinking, "What the hell's going on?" I got the kit and I realised this was the real thing. It was completely mind-boggling. I can't remember how I slept the night before but come the day I was so nervous I couldn't feel my legs walking out on to the field.'

Although he has subsequently tamed some of the world's fastest bowlers as an opening batsman, the schoolboy of 1990 had serious doubts about his ability to face fast bowlers.

Although he has subsequently tamed some of the world's fastest bowlers as an opening batsman, the schoolboy of 1990 had serious doubts about his ability to face fast bowlers. The Northerns pace attack consisted of the late Tertius Bosch, Fanie de Villiers and Steve Elworthy, who all went on to play Test cricket. Bosch and De Villiers reduced Western Province to 16 for three before Gary Kirsten and Brian McMillan led a revival. It was 126 for four when Gibbs went out to bat. One of his abiding memories of the B game was the amount of verbal abuse directed at him by the fielding side. He was able to get used to it fairly quickly but it was nonetheless discomfitting when Bosch announced, 'I'm going to kill you.' His first runs were off a thick edge to third man against Bosch and his mind was still in a whirl when, after scoring nine, he hit a short ball from Willie Morris, a left-arm spinner, down square leg's throat. What made it worse was that it was the last ball before lunch. He scored 14 in the second innings before again falling to Morris.

25

He stayed in the side for an even bigger occasion, the New Year clash against Transvaal at Newlands, the nearest thing to Test cricket there was in South Africa at the time. The rivalry between the two powerful provinces had been particularly intense during the years of isolation, with some titanic battles between sides packed with players of international quality. Eddie Barlow, Hylton Ackerman, Peter Kirsten, Allan Lamb, Garth le Roux, Stephen Jefferies and Denys Hobson were some of the stars for Western Province, while Transvaal had boasted players such as Graeme Pollock, Jimmy Cook, Henry Fotheringham, Kevin McKenzie, Clive Rice, Alan Kourie, Rupert Hanley, Alvin Kallicharran and Sylvester Clarke.

For the 1990/91 clash, both teams were below their previous heights but it still shaped up as a fiercely competitive match. Spectators packed into Newlands, which, prior to an extensive revamp during the 1990s, was arguably the most attractive major cricket ground in the world. The Oaks, with its rustic wooden benches under old oak trees, was a wonderful place from which to watch a game, with Table Mountain providing a majestic backdrop to the action in the middle. However congenial the atmosphere at Newlands may have been, though, the pitch was no place for children against a team led by Clive Rice, the last remaining stalwart of the 'Mean Machine', which had dominated provincial cricket during the 1980s.

Transvaal's bowling attack was spearheaded by two young fast bowlers, Richard Snell and Steven Jack, who would both play Test cricket, and Rice himself. Western Province were in a strong position after centuries by Kenny Jackson and Brian McMillan when Gibbs went out to bat at number six. The player who had made batting look so easy against so many bowlers was, possibly for the first time in his career, out of his depth as Rice applied the pressure. Rice himself led the intimidation, peppering the slightly-built newcomer with a succession of bouncers. There were no balls to hit and there was just a single run to his name when Gibbs edged Stefan Jacobs, a useful medium-pacer, to Rice at slip. The second innings was not a great deal better, with Gibbs making seven before falling to a legside stumping off Jacobs. 'It was obviously planned, they pushed one down leg. I tried to flick it away and lost my balance. It's something I wouldn't have done a few years down the line.'

Gibbs was caught behind for a duck off the lively Chris van Noordwyk in the return match against Northerns at Centurion before making an important

35 in the second innings when his side were in trouble, an innings which he says helped settle his own doubts about whether he belonged in such exalted company. In retrospect, he is not sure whether playing such high-standard cricket was good for him. 'I was very comfortable in the B Section even though the standard was high, but the A Section was a completely different thing. There was TV and the newspapers and I was playing with the real players. A lot of it had to do with nerves, being out of my league.'

The innings against Northerns impressed Robin Jackman, the Western Province manager. 'We had lost a few wickets and Tertius Bosch was bowling really quickly. Herschelle batted for an hour and a half or more. What was good was how he left the ball so well. It was a real struggle but he hung in there. It showed he could play at that level and he learnt that at a young age.'

Eric Simons, one of the senior Western Province players, had the perplexing experience of sharing a room with a hyper-active youngster who by his own admission didn't show proper respect for the sleeping habits of the more mature player. 'It was an eye-opener for Eric. When I think about it, it was absolutely shocking. I've never slept a lot. I used to wake up at five, half past five in the morning and turn on the television, which was disrespectful to Eric.' Simons was tolerant, though, and Gibbs recalls, 'We shared a lot of milkshakes together. He was known as the milkshake man.' It would not for long be a milkshake bar to which the young Gibbs would head as a first choice for libation. 'That was before I discovered Jack Daniels.'

He had, however, already made acquaintance with the attractions of the opposite sex. 'I met a little boeremeisie [Afrikaans girl] and I brought her into the changeroom to sit with the guys. I don't know what made me do it. Obviously, the scent of the female gender was getting to me at an early age, after being around the older guys.' It was hardly conventional behaviour but most of his team-mates accepted the intrusion into what was normally a male, team-only sanctuary with amusement.

Back at school, such was Gibbs's stature in the Bishops cricket team that he was made captain of the First XI in 1991, although he did not relish a formal leadership role. After the giddy heights of 1990, his performances in the first term were less spectacular but he was still in a class of his own, scoring 510 runs at 56,67, with five fifties but no centuries. He was given time off school to play twice more for Western Province B, scoring three half-centuries in four innings, including two in a drawn Bowl final against Border in East London. He was also let off school early to play for the senior Western Province team in the Benson & Hedges day-night competition against the Impalas, a composite team picked from the country's smaller provinces, at Newlands. He did not get a chance to bat as his team coasted to a nine-wicket win.

In his summary for the school magazine, Norton was critical of the Bishops batting in the first term but singled out his captain and star. 'He batted with enormous responsibility and maturity and we missed him sorely when he was playing for Western Province B . . . what a pleasure and a thrill it is to watch the way he goes about the business of making runs.'

As the days grew shorter, cricket made way for rugby and Herschelle Gibbs graduated to the Bishops First XV. For the next few months he would concentrate on honing his rugby talent.

For the administrators of the summer game, however, significant events were under way which would have a major impact on the young Gibbs and, indeed, future generations of cricketers.

While Gibbs was scoring so many runs during 1990, the game at national level was going through a crisis. South Africa had been excluded from international cricket since 1970 because of the policies of the apartheid government. It was apartheid which drove Basil d'Oliveira to make a career for himself in England and it would have prevented Herschelle Gibbs from playing on the same fields as white cricketers if he had been born a generation earlier.

After decades of division, cricket administrators sat down together in 1991 and the United Cricket Board of South Africa was formed in June. The new body was admitted to the International Cricket Council 11 days later. At a stroke, 21 years of isolation had come to an end. An era of rebel tours was over. Official international cricket was around the corner.

Thus, when Herschelle Gibbs prepared for the 1991/92 season, it was to play cricket in an altogether different environment, one in which the sky, in the form of Test and one-day international cricket, was the limit.

CHAPTER **THREE**

More than just cricket

There is a videotape that should be seen by anyone who enjoys creative rugby. Sold for the princely sum of R20, it is the story of the Bishops rugby team in 1992. If it was a Hollywood production, the billboards would proclaim, 'Starring Herschelle Gibbs,' even though some future famous rugby names, including three who went on to be Springboks, were also in the cast.

A favourite staple of bar-room sporting discussions starts with, 'If only', and there are many rugby folk who say, 'If only Herschelle Gibbs had carried on playing rugby.'

Among them is Naas Botha, the great Springbok flyhalf of the 1980s and early 1990s. 'Rugby lost out when Herschelle decided to play cricket. He had brilliant hands, his kicking was brilliant, he had whatever you expected from a flyhalf.'

Botha was among the spectators when Gibbs reached what was probably the peak of his short rugby career, the 1992 Craven Week for schoolboy provincial teams at Loftus Versfeld in Pretoria, the ground where Botha was idolised when he played for Northern Transvaal and the Springboks.

In his newspaper column at the time, Botha wrote that Gibbs was 'the outstanding player of the week and the best young flyhalf I have seen'. Botha

29

sought out the youngster, joining him at a practice where they spent some time chatting about flyhalf play. Herschelle told the *Cape Times*, 'It was a great privilege to practise with Naas and he gave me some good tips.'

He also told the newspaper he had received scholarship offers from several universities but admitted he was not academically inclined and would not be going to university. 'I mean to make a living with sport . . . and to be rich, very rich.'

Rugby folk still talk of the two tries that Gibbs scored for Western Province in the Craven Week final against Free State. The first came from a set piece about 30 metres out. The second was when he ran back to collect a missed kick for touch, deep in his own half. He took the ball over his head, running towards his own try line, and then ran through virtually the entire Free State team.

What the admiring spectators did not know was that he shouldn't have been playing at all. He had first attracted attention when he engineered a defeat of Northern Transvaal, the host province, earlier in the week. During the Northerns match he was concussed but, with whispered prompts from his Bishops captain and centre, Hilton Houghton, he was able to convince a doctor that his brain was functioning normally.

Northern Transvaal officials were so impressed with his play that they flew the Gibbs family to Pretoria in an unsuccessful attempt to persuade the young prodigy to play rugby for the then-mighty Blue Bulls.

Basil Bey, a noted rugby coach, who taught and coached rugby at Bishops from 1971 to 1998, says, 'Herschelle was the best flyhalf we produced in my time. I never coached him, he was too good to coach. All I had to do was find a pattern that suited his game.'

Under Bey, Bishops were renowned for their running rugby. 'Herschelle never dropped the ball and he could kick it a mile, although he preferred to use his backs. He had wonderful backs outside him but they were wonderful because he put them away. He made other players good. He would pass and appear outside the fellow he had passed to without seeming to have run particularly fast. He could read a game as few others could.'

Although he is right-handed, he took place-kicks and dropped goals with his left foot. 'I was naturally right-footed but I knew I had to develop my left foot. When I was about 13 or 14, I would kick from the try line near the corner flag and aim to get the ball to go through the posts, swinging it in from one side with my left foot and from the other with my right foot. After a while I could kick better with my left foot.'

Selborne Boome, a Springbok lock and flank, played at number eight in the 1992 Bishops team. Dave von Hoesslin, who also became a Springbok, was the scrumhalf. The school video provides ample proof of the importance of a quality axis in the positions eight, nine and 10. Not that the spectators who thronged to the grounds where Bishops played were given any assistance in identifying the players. Bishops have long resisted pressure to put numbers on the backs of their players. 'It's part of our culture, our tradition. We believe it's a team game,' said Bey.

Boome said on a television programme some years ago that Gibbs was the best rugby player he had played with or against. Interviewed for this book, he said he stood by that opinion. 'He was unbelievable. He was the brains behind the team. Basil didn't have to tell him what to do. He just went and did it. He was so quick and he had the ability to read play and put other people into space.'

Gibbs was a prodigious kicker, even at Under 14 level. 'With Peter Kirsten having been his hero, he had heard how Peter could kick a drop goal from halfway when he was Under 14. We were at a practice when Basil Bey was watching from behind the poles, so our coach said, "Show Mr Bey what you can do," and he dropped one over from the halfway line,' said Boome.

On another occasion, when Bishops were playing in a high schools festival at St John's in Johannesburg, Bey suggested that if the team were awarded an early penalty in their own half, Gibbs should have a go at a place kick because the ball travelled a long way at altitude. The chance duly arrived. There was derision from the crowd when the flyhalf indicated he wanted to go for the posts from his own 10-metre line but he silenced the sceptics by sending the ball soaring over the crossbar.

The inter-school rivalry among the leading schools was intense. He destroyed Wynberg Boys' High, for whom Jacques Kallis would shine at flyhalf the following year, scoring the first 25 points, including a try when he followed up a huge up and under from his own 22, catching it and going on to score. One of the toughest games each year was against Paarl Gymnasium, an Afrikaans school with a proud rugby tradition. Their flyhalf was another schoolboy star, Louis Koen, yet another Western Province youngster who went on to play for South Africa. Gibbs had one of his most dominant games and Bishops built up a winning lead within the first 20 minutes.

Future Springbok centre Robbie Fleck, a year behind Gibbs and an occasional first team player in 1992, remembers a try in the win over Paarl Gym. 'He decided to run around their flyhalf, both centres and their wing, and went all the way to score under the posts.'

'I had some of my best games as a centre when Herschelle was my flyhalf,' says Fleck. 'He was probably the best rugby player I've played with. He was streets ahead of everyone else. He had such a quick rugby brain. His passing was outstanding and he could pass both ways, which even a lot of senior players can't do properly. I think he was better at rugby than he was at cricket.'

The two biggest matches each year were against neighbouring Rondebosch Boys' High and St Andrew's College from Grahamstown. 'Whatever else happens, if you beat those two you've had a good year,' says Bey, who remembers how Gibbs landed a crucial kick in windy conditions to seal a tense 19-16 win in Grahamstown in his first year in the first team. 'Afterwards I found him leaning in a corner of the dressing room. He was crying. I asked him why and he said it was because he was so happy that we had managed to win.'

To Bey, that incident indicated Gibbs's commitment to the team. 'He saw himself as a team player and despite his exceptional ability he never became swollen-headed.'

'Never at Bishops have we had such crowds to watch the First XV,' reported the Bishops magazine, which hailed 'the exhilarating panache and joy of the First XV game'.

The Western Province Craven Week team was particularly strong. Gibbs was picked at flyhalf and Louis Koen played alongside him at centre. Schoolmate Dave von Hoesslin was the scrumhalf and future Springbok captain Corné Krige was the eighthman. Also in the team was Percy Montgomery, from SACS, who played at fullback.

Montgomery, who would play in 50 Tests for the Springboks, said it was better playing with Gibbs than against him. 'He had such a good boot. When

SACS played Bishops he used to move me around quite a bit.' Speed was a major asset. 'His pace helped him get out of trouble so quickly.'

Montgomery and Gibbs were selected for the South African Schools team that played in a curtain-raiser to a Test between South Africa and Australia at Newlands. 'I have never experienced anything like the roar we got when we came out of the tunnel at Newlands. There is no feeling in the world that can match that, not even going out to bat in a Test match,' says Gibbs. It was memorable, too, because a hailstorm broke over the ground while the match was on.

Such was Gibbs's form that there were suggestions he should be selected that season for a struggling Western Province senior provincial team. It didn't happen but he was signed up for two years by the provincial union at R1 000 a month. 'Rugby was still a so-called amateur game. It wasn't much less than the senior players were getting,' said Herman. 'They basically wanted to make sure he didn't sign for Northern Transvaal.'

He joined the Western Province training squad before the start of the 1993 season but turned down a chance to go with the provincial side on a pre-season tour of Australia because it clashed with cricket.

In the meantime, there was the thrill of being invited to join the famous New Zealand All Blacks, who were in South Africa to play the first big post-isolation Test, in August 1992. Journalist Dan Retief remembers how the All Blacks wanted to make a public relations gesture. They asked their South African hosts to identify a suitably talented black rugby player to join them for a few days of training. 'When they saw Herschelle, they were disappointed because they thought he was too pale.' His rugby talent soon won them over, however. 'He dropped a goal from halfway and they said, "We want him."'

It was an enjoyable experience. He shared a room with his favourite player, Va'aiga Tuigamala, who was a forerunner of Jonah Lomu, a powerful wing who could crash through defences using brute strength. 'I'd like to play in a game with him,' Gibbs quipped to a journalist, 'he is so big and strong that I'd feel safe.'

In his first year out of school he joined the Villager club, where Basil Bey was coaching, and played for their Under 21 team. He was picked for the adult Western Province B team but his father persuaded him to withdraw and to continue playing with the Under 21s. The decision caused debate for several days in Cape Town newspapers, with Mark Keohane pointing out in the *Cape Argus* that several world stars had played full international rugby as teenagers.

In 1994 he played for Western Province Under 21 but his season ended early when the cruciate ligaments of his left knee were damaged while playing against Border Under 21 in East London. It proved to be the end of his rugby career. He and Herman had both already indicated that his future was in cricket and the injury had too many uncomfortable similarities to that suffered by Peter Kirsten, who had been a talented flyhalf as well as a gifted cricketer. At 19 he played for a South African Barbarians side against the indomitable British Lions side of 1974 and came within a whisker of inspiring them to a famous victory. He played for Western Province in the same season but his career was ended by a clumsy tackle that wrecked a knee.

Gibbs had barely turned 20 when he stopped playing rugby. Looking back, he has no regrets. 'Club rugby was a lot harder than playing at school. I didn't feel that comfortable. I was still quite tiny, even though I had started going to gym.'

Selborne Boome acknowledges there is an adjustment between schoolboy and senior rugby but believes Gibbs could have coped had he had the desire. 'I think by then his focus wasn't there. If he really wanted to put his mind to it, he could have been amazing. I have heard comments that defensively he was a bit light but that's absolute rubbish. He was quite aggressive on the field when he wanted to be. He'd have smoked guys.'

Naas Botha agrees that Gibbs could have made an impact at senior level. 'There was a time when we wanted our flyhalves all to be 90kg and play like forwards but now suddenly we're back to skill. Herschelle could definitely have succeeded.'

Basil Bey has no doubts at all. 'He would have been another Mark Ella.' He says Gibbs had all the attributes to have put his individual stamp on international games in the same way as Ella, a great Australian stand-off.

He may have no regrets about rugby but does feel he stopped playing soccer too early. 'Soccer was a breeze for me. At an early age I enjoyed soccer more than cricket or rugby.'

Soccer gave him his first experience of the political divide which existed in South African sport. Under the 'double standards' policy of the South African Council on Sport (Sacos), he was not allowed to play Sacos soccer at the William Herbert grounds in Wynberg. The youngster, then aged nine or 10, was labelled a collaborator with the apartheid system because he attended a 'white' private school. He had to leave the Yorkshire club and played for Rygersdal, based near his school. Rygersdal played under the Western Province Football Association, whose players were mainly white but which embraced the 'normal' sport which Sacos claimed could not be played in an 'abnormal' society.

Soccer had no place, other than as a curiosity, at most 'white' schools. Gibbs continued to play club soccer in his junior years at high school, turning out for Bishops on Saturday mornings before going on to play soccer for the Rygersdal club in the afternoons. When Cape Town Spurs played against glamour teams like the Soweto-based giants, Kaizer Chiefs and Orlando Pirates, he would be invited to play in curtain-raisers. Herman says he was a natural showman who enjoyed displaying his repertoire of skills in front of an audience. Not surprisingly, his favourite team was Kaizer Chiefs, whose side included some of the most flamboyant players in the South African game.

He played for Western Province as a left midfield player in the national Under 16 tournament in Cape Town in 1990 and, despite being hampered by an injury which restricted him to playing mainly as a second-half substitute, he was selected for the South African Under 16 team. One of the other players in the side was Mark Fish, from Pretoria, who went on to become a star for Bafana Bafana, the South African national side, and played professional football in Italy's Serie A and England's Premier League.

Gibbs gave up soccer when he started playing for the Bishops First XV the following year. 'That is something I regret. I would like to have seen how far I could go, maybe to have tried out for a big English club.'

Speed has been one of the notable attributes in all his sports. He inherited his father's ability as a sprinter but did not have the time or inclination to pursue an athletics career. However, he participated in the annual sports day at Bishops, and won the 100 metres sprint every year. In Standard Nine he won the sprint in 11 seconds and in his final year at school he was clocked at 10,9. It was a school record and has remained unchallenged.

As Herman points out, it was a remarkable time, considering it was set on a grass track and he did not use starting blocks. Gert le Roux, editor of the *South African Athletics Annual*, agrees, although he provides some realistic perspective. 'A hand-timed 10,9 would probably be around 11,15 if it was timed electronically. That is still a very good time on a grass track by someone who didn't train specifically for athletics.' Le Roux reckons that, given his Bishops time, Gibbs could, with a modicum of training, have been among South Africa's leading junior athletes, 'good enough to get into the semi-finals, if not the final, of the junior championships'. The winning time at the national Under 19 championships that year, staged in Cape Town on a synthetic track, was an electronically-timed 10,73 by Glen Elferink.

Tests conducted by a physiologist, Thierry Tison, confirmed what to most casual observers was obvious: Gibbs had exceptional physical attributes. In an interview in the *Cape Argus*, Tison said he had conducted numerous tests on Gibbs and found him to have a phenomenal 'explosive burst'.

One test was a leap from a standing-still position. 'At his peak and after years of muscle conditioning, it's estimated Carl Lewis jumps between 3,5 and four metres. Gibbs, without any sprint training and coaching came close to three metres ... this puts him in the elite field.'

Sister Lucinda also inherited strong sporting genes, becoming a junior tennis star. As a young child she joined in the games of soccer and cricket with the boys but, as she now says, 'As a girl it's not like you can play rugby or soccer or cricket. You can make a career out of tennis, but the other sports for girls are pretty minor.'

She started playing tennissette at Springfield Convent and graduated to tennis at Bergvliet Primary when she was 11. There were several junior provincial players at the school and she improved rapidly. Within a year she was invited to join an elite squad coached by former Davis Cup player Leon Norgarb. At 13 she was chosen by the South African Tennis Union as one of four girls to spend two months at an academy in Texas, training and playing in tournaments. She was a good enough player to win some international satellite tournaments and to be in South Africa's Federation Cup team before she turned to full-time coaching.

Lucinda makes an interesting observation. 'When we were young, Herschelle and I were not aware there was anything special about being able to play ball games so easily. It was only later that we realised that not everyone had the same amount of talent.'

In both their cases, sporting ability would provide a basis for their livelihood. For Herschelle, though, there had to be a choice. He would only be able to star in one sport.

CHAPTER **FOUR**

Tough going – and a tour

The schooldays of Herschelle Gibbs were a kaleidoscope of achievements in a variety of sports. Events were happening in cricket, however, which would endorse his decision to make a career in the summer sport. Less than a year after South Africa's return to the international fold, he would be making his first overseas cricket tour.

In November 1991, a South African team captained by Clive Rice played, at short notice, three one-day matches in India. Rice was 42 years old when he led his players onto the vast expanse of Eden Gardens in Calcutta. It was a crowning moment for the last man still playing first-class cricket who had been selected for the previous 'official' South African team. As a promising young all-rounder in 1971/72 he had been picked for a tour of Australia that did not take place because of South Africa's political polecat status.

If, for Rice, the tour of India was the last leg of a long cricketing journey, for youngsters back in South Africa it was a tantalising glimpse of a new world. Among the many who turned on their television sets in the early hours of a Sunday morning, 10 November 1991, was Herschelle Gibbs, little knowing that Eden Gardens was to provide a seminal moment in his own career, just over five years later. Three Western Province team-mates were in

Tough going – and a tour

the touring squad, Adrian Kuiper, Brian McMillan and Craig Matthews. So was his boyhood hero and mentor, Peter Kirsten.

'I was still very young and not really concerned about taking it to the next stage. I was still trying to find my feet at provincial level. But watching the games was phenomenal. Playing with those guys and then seeing them play for South Africa overseas, it changes the whole mindset. You start to think, maybe one day you too could be there.'

The Bishops season was already well under way and three centuries had flowed from the Gibbs bat. Watching the South Africans in faraway Calcutta provided endorsement of a difficult decision he had been forced to make. The Bishops rugby team were about to depart on a tour of Britain and Ireland but the team's star flyhalf decided to stay in Cape Town to pursue his cricket career. Tempting as the rugby tour was, it would have clashed with his cricket and he had already put on record his choice of cricket above rugby as a long-term sporting option. There was one more century, his 11th for the First XI, before the term ended.

The school year over, he prepared for his third Nuffield Schools Week, but first there was another opportunity to play among adults, for Western Province B against Transvaal B. He made a career-best 81 at the Wanderers No 1 Oval, across the road from the Wanderers Stadium.

Then it was off to nearby Potchefstroom for the Nuffield Week where, finally, he shone among his schoolboy peers, scoring 80 not out, 47, 60 and 92 in his first four innings to win selection for the South African Schools XI. His manager was Keith Richardson, now the headmaster of Wynberg Boys' High. Their relationship was not always smooth. Herschelle had gone to Bloemfontein with the senior Western Province side for a night game in which he had been 12th man. The side had won and some of the older players had plied their young 'mascot' with more strong drink than was wise or indeed legal, as he had yet to turn 18. The Nuffield team were playing a warm-up match at Newlands the next day and the normally livewire Gibbs was in no condition to play. 'He just stood at cover and allowed the ball to pass him left and right,' recalls Richardson. 'I got steadily more irritated. For the other boys Nuffield was something they really aspired to but it was old hat to him, he had played amongst the men. I remember standing at the top of the old members' pavilion, clapping my hands and shouting, "Herschelle, off the field please." I said, "You can pack your bags and go because you're too big for us mere mortal schoolboys here."'

There was to be an even more spectacular run-in at the next Nuffield Week, yet Richardson remembers Herschelle with fondness. 'We had a good relationship. He bears no malice and he apologised for his behaviour.' Gibbs himself doesn't recall the Newlands incident, although he has clear memories of what happened in Stellenbosch a year later.

The Week traditionally ends with a match between the schoolboys and the host provincial senior team. The 1992 side had the comparatively rare pleasure of outplaying the men, beating Western Transvaal by five wickets, mainly due to a dashing 77 by the left-handed Anthony Pollock, son of the great Graeme. For once, Gibbs was content to play a supporting role, scoring 25 in a third-wicket stand of 84 with Pollock. The team was captained by Nicky Bojé of Free State. A young Shaun Pollock, still well short of his full height, was another future full international.

There was a three-match tour for the SA Schools team in the Western Cape and Gibbs made a half-century against a Western Province Colts XI. Then it was back to the Western Province B team. Once more a century beckoned as Herschelle reached 90 against Eastern Province B. Old divisions had finally been healed as cricket unity took proper root in the Western Cape and the Western Province team included Hassan Pangarker, Faiek Davids and Vincent Barnes, all former SA Cricket Board players. Much was expected of Davids, who was acclaimed as the Board equivalent of Adrian Kuiper, the big-hitting Western Province star. On this occasion, Davids lived up to his reputation, hammering 146 as he and Gibbs put on 202 for the fourth wicket.

Barnes, who was about to turn 32, had set one bowling record after another in Board three-day cricket. Unity in cricket may have come a season or two late for him as a player but he became a respected coach for Western Province and was put in charge of the South Africa A team in 2002/03.

Gibbs had to wait until February before he made another first-class appearance for the Western Province senior side, by which time a nation's attention was focused on the imminent debut of South Africa in the World Cup. Adrian Kuiper, Brian McMillan and Meyrick Pringle from Western Province were part of the history-making squad in Australia and New Zealand.

Tough going – and a tour

Batting at number four, Gibbs made 15 and 41 against Eastern Province in Port Elizabeth. He also held a sensational catch in the deep, running some 40 to 50 metres before diving to catch Rudi Bryson, an effort that would earn him a prize for the best televised catch of the season. He made top score of 44 against Free State at Newlands and 23 in the second innings.

Schoolwork came a poor third to playing first-class cricket and watching the World Cup. Bishops gave him time off to play provincial games, but he also skipped classes to watch the matches from Australasia. 'Every time there was a game, I'd sneak away to one of the boarding houses and try to watch some cricket. It was a magnificent experience.' Peter Kirsten, his hero, was South Africa's player of the tournament and there was no way that lessons were going to interfere.

> **Schoolwork came a poor third to playing first-class cricket and watching the World Cup. Bishops gave him time off to play provincial games, but he also skipped classes to watch the matches from Australasia.**

Gibbs played regularly for Western Province in the second half of the season in the Benson & Hedges floodlit competition. Although the World Cup stars were available for the final, he was selected for the showpiece match, against Eastern Province at the Wanderers Stadium, which in those days was the automatic venue for the deciding match. With cricket fever at a peak just four days after an emotional welcome home for the World Cup squad, who reached the semi-finals before going out in controversial fashion against England in Sydney, it was a spectacular end to the domestic season. Gibbs did not bat as Terence Lazard and World Cup vice-captain Adrian Kuiper hit unbeaten centuries in a 45-over total of 244 for two. It was not enough, however. South African captain Kepler Wessels hit the third century of the match and shared a stand of 140 with Mark Rushmere, another World Cup player, as Eastern Province won by six wickets.

While the World Cup was being played, South Africa were invited to send a team to the West Indies to play three one-day internationals and the country's first Test under the new united board. Part of the deal was that an Under 19 'development' side would tour alongside the senior national team. The 15-player squad was captained by Dale Benkenstein of Natal. Herschelle Gibbs was a natural selection for a side that included five white youngsters and 10 players of colour in what officials hoped would be a foretaste of South Africa's cricket future. The side was managed by Jackie McGlew, a distinguished former Test captain, while Conrad Hunte, the former West Indies vice-captain, accompanied the team as National Development Coach. Three days after the night series final, Herschelle Gibbs was checking in at Jan Smuts airport to fly alongside some of his boyhood heroes on a South African Airways flight that, to the irritation of other passengers, was diverted to Kingston, Jamaica, adding some six hours to the scheduled journey to New York.

The tour was no more than partially successful in achieving the long-term goal of preparing youngsters for the highest honours, as only Benkenstein and Gibbs went on to win full international colours. Lulama Masikazana served briefly as Eastern Province's first-choice wicketkeeper and Cedric English turned out regularly for Griqualand West.

The West Indian adventure was as exciting as any involving the emerging South African team. This time, instead of watching on television, Herschelle Gibbs was part of another new chapter in his country's cricketing saga. South Africans had previously been barred from most of the West Indian nations, with Jamaica particularly vociferous in their criticism of the apartheid regime. Thus, when the tourists touched down in Kingston, Ali Bacher was able to claim, for the umpteenth time that season, another 'historic day' for South African cricket.

While the senior national team prepared for the first one-day international at Sabina Park, the youngsters were in action a day earlier against a Jamaica Youth team at Chedwin Park. Herschelle Gibbs wrote for himself a minor footnote in the history book by becoming the first South African player to make a half-century in the Caribbean. The Jamaicans, though, thoroughly outgunned the tourists. Apart from struggling to come to terms with local conditions, it was an eye-opener for the South Africans to see the rudimentary state of facilities in the West Indies. Under-privileged South Africans were not the only cricketers having to make do with inadequate nets, fields and pitches. The pitches, however, were rock-hard, quick and bouncy, much more so than when Gibbs toured with the full national side nine years later. 'We couldn't even wear spikes when we batted. Our rubber soles made the squeaky noise you get on a squash court.'

The Under 19 players, many on their first trip outside South Africa, learnt more than just cricket. CLR James, the great West Indian writer and historian once asked, 'What do they know of cricket who only cricket know?' It was an appropriate question from a man of the Caribbean. Hotel guests in nearby rooms in the pink-walled Wyndham hotel in New Kingston were kept awake by a rowdy party one evening before the next leg of the journey to Trinidad. It was apparent that some local knowledge was being acquired that had nothing to do with bat and ball. They were a mischievous bunch. Sweet-smiling Xhosa lads greeted the stewardesses on a British West Indian Airways flight with what the charmed ladies assumed was a friendly greeting. But those who understood the language knew they were saying something altogether less flattering. The youngsters had less to smile about soon after take-off when the aircraft banked to the right and lost height. There was, the pilot announced, a technical problem and the flight returned to the airport.

Several hours later, nervous South African and West Indian cricketers re-boarded the same aircraft for what, mercifully, was an uneventful flight to Port-of-Spain. The young South Africans played at Queen's Royal College, the island's famed educational institution whose past scholars included CLR James. There, not much more than a big six-hit away from the Queen's Park Oval Test ground, and in an atmosphere not dissimilar to Bishops, with grand old colonial buildings framing the ground, the South Africans easily beat a Secondary Schools XI in a one-day match. They encountered stiffer opposition against a Trinidad Youth XI in a two-day match at the ground of St Mary's College, Port-of-Spain's other famous school, and had the worst of a draw.

'It was exciting, being around the national team and staying in the same hotels as them but Mr McGlew had a hard time keeping us all under control.' Young Gibbs acknowledges that 'the rum was an eye-opener' and he sampled it in places like the Pelican club, within walking distance of the Hilton hotel in Port-of-Spain, where live calypso music was as hot as the sultry Caribbean nights.

Fortunately, the rum was not too big a factor in Gibbs's performances, and the Under 19 team's star fielder found himself called up to do duty as 12th man for the national side in the second of back-to-back one-day internationals at the Queen's Park Oval. Injuries had laid low several players, including Jonty Rhodes. Gibbs was pulled out of the junior team's practice to don the national kit and field during a comprehensive victory by the West Indies, for whom a youthful Brian Lara, whose name appeared on the Queen's Park club notice board as a junior player of the year, was in scintillating form. During a drinks break, Western Province team-mate Meyrick Pringle squashed a banana down the front of Gibbs's shirt. For a talented young player, there was a growing sense of excitement that he too could become an international cricketer.

The third leg of the historic tour was in Barbados, where Kepler Wessels's national team, having been well and truly beaten in the one-day internationals, played the West Indies in a Test. The Under 19s drew two matches against a Barbados Youth squad and easily beat a Conrad Hunte XI. With their own playing commitments completed, the youngsters, like the rest of the small South African contingent who followed the tour, settled down to watch the final day's play of the Test at the Kensington Oval in a state of near-euphoric expectation. South Africa needed just 79 runs to win, with eight wickets standing, and seemed on the verge of an astonishing triumph at a ground where the West Indies had not been beaten for 57 years and where they had won their previous 10 Tests.

Exhausted by a non-stop round of partying in the final days and nights of what for many would be a once-in-a-lifetime tour, the Under 19 players opted to watch on television. 'We had been going out quite a lot, with some of the senior guys too.' In St Lawrence Gap, an area of bars and restaurants, they had bumped into some of the Test bowlers, who clearly felt they had done their bit and didn't expect to be called into action as batsmen.

Two men who had definitely not pounded the pavements of St Lawrence Gap were South Africa's most experienced batsmen, Wessels and Peter Kirsten, who resumed batting on the fateful final morning. They were up against Courtney Walsh and Curtly Ambrose, two great West Indian fast bowlers. The bounce on a dry pitch was becoming increasingly uneven, although it seemed inconceivable that South Africa could lose. Wessels went early but in his hotel room Gibbs applauded as Kirsten, playing in his first Test at the age of 36, reached his half-century, giving an indication of what might have been had he not played most of his career during the years of isolation. Runs, though, were proving almost impossible to find as Walsh and Ambrose bowled unchanged for almost two hours. There were no loose deliveries or no-balls to relieve the pressure. Eventually, Kirsten was bowled by Walsh off an inside edge as he tried to break the shackles and South Africa crumbled to defeat as eight wickets fell for 26 runs. Little was the youthful Gibbs to know that seven seasons later he would be opening the batting for South Africa

Tough going – and a tour

against the same two bowlers, on a brute of a pitch at the start of what would prove to be the most important phase of his career.

For the time being, though, he had been given a graphic illustration of the demands of Test cricket. There was much to think about as a subdued group of South Africans whiled away the rest of a long day, waiting for another diverted South African Airways flight to pick them up from Barbados's Grantley Adams airport that evening.

The 1992/93 season was something of a letdown for Gibbs, although it started with a highlight when he was invited to play for Nicky Oppenheimer's XI against the Indians in the first match on South African soil against an officially sanctioned team for more than 22 years. It was also the start of what has become a tradition in South African cricket. Oppenheimer is heir to a mining fortune and, like his father and grandfather before him, chairman of the De Beers diamond company. After the success of the India game he has regularly hosted the first match played by touring teams, with the proceeds going to cricket development, in much the same way as the Duke of Norfolk hosted touring teams to England at his ground at Arundel Castle.

'The NFO XI has always been a strange combination of old traditions and modern methods,' wrote Oppenheimer, whose initials are NFO, in a foreword to a history of the team. 'For example, the players are expected to turn out in long-sleeved shirts, and old-fashioned long-sleeved shirts at that! The game is always played with deadly seriousness, no quarter is either expected or given. It is this combination of determination and tradition which, I believe, gives the side its special character.' Oppenheimer aims for a mix of past and present national players and promising youngsters. Bishops was represented in all three categories in the form of Vintcent van der Bijl, the venerable former fast bowler, Adrian Kuiper and Gibbs.

Scampering about the field in his long-sleeved shirt, Gibbs had a close-up view as Sachin Tendulkar, only 10 months his senior but already an established international star, made an immaculate, unbeaten century. 'Up until that stage I didn't really know who he was,' Gibbs admits. 'Obviously after that I learnt a lot more about him.' The NFO XI were soundly beaten, but not before Gibbs top-scored with 36 and shared a 66-run third-wicket stand with Kuiper. 'They didn't have anybody quick and so I felt comfortable.'

His last Nuffield Week was in Stellenbosch and it proved eventful on and off the field. Celebrating the new age of South African cricket, it included teams from England and India and was followed by a quadrangular tournament that also featured Zimbabwe. Gibbs started the Week in fine form by making an unbeaten 53 in a drawn match against Eastern Province before, for the first but not the last time, he hit the front pages of the newspapers for an off-the-the-field escapade.

With no play on the Sunday of the tournament, the boys were given a late night 'pass' on Saturday. They could return to the hostel at which they were staying by 11.30pm instead of the usual time of 10pm. Five boys failed to make the curfew, Gibbs being the last in at 2.30am. A wedding party had been in progress at the Stellenbosch town hall, where he was recognised and invited in. Earlier he was in a bar where he met a pretty 13-year-old, Liesl Fuller. It was to prove a significant and ultimately costly meeting.

Team manager Keith Richardson expelled him from the team. 'I sent him home,' he said. The Nuffield organisers, however, felt the action was too harsh. A disciplinary hearing was held and Gibbs, along with the other four boys, was banned for one match. He sat out the next game and then made an unbeaten half-century against Transvaal. The Transvaal bowlers had an early taste of the problems bowlers throughout the world would face in future years as Jacques Kallis, who had just turned 17, made 92 not out and Gibbs 62 not out in a total of 221 for one. Gibbs was duly picked for South African Schools. Kallis, from Richardson's Wynberg Boys' High, had to wait another year.

Gibbs returned to familiar territory in the international tournament, with the matches against Zimbabwe Schools and England Under 18 played at Bishops. He made 41 against Zimbabwe and a match-winning 72 not out against the English boys, whose side included future international players Marcus Trescothick and Vikram Solanki. He was out for 20 in a three-wicket defeat against the Indians at Plumstead in a match in which future Northerns and South Africa A captain Gerald Dros made a century.

The final at Newlands was hard-fought and controversial, with Gibbs playing a central role. He made 60 and shared a partnership of 123 with Dale Benkenstein, the captain. In a tense run chase, an Indian batsman refused to walk when he hit a waist-high full toss to a fielder, reckoning the delivery should have been called a no-ball, and then continued to protest after he was given out. The South African wicketkeeper, Lulama Masikazana, started walking off the field soon afterwards when a player was given not out despite a thick edge to the keeper but his protest ended when he realised his teammates were not following him. With three needed to win off the last over and with the last Indian pair at the wicket, Gibbs sprinted to save what seemed a certain boundary to third man, thus saving two runs. With the scores tied, Cedric English bowled the last batsman and South Africa won the tournament because they had lost fewer wickets.

Richardson still feels the breach of trust was sufficient for Gibbs to have been expelled from the Nuffield Week, which would almost certainly have kept him out of the international tournament. 'He really does not think before he acts and his subsequent acts of ill-discipline, right up to the West Indian tour, show that he always learns the hard way.'

Richardson hastens to add, though, that he also saw Herschelle's good side. 'He bears no grudges and he's prepared to take the rap when he's done wrong. He had an attractive personality and was comfortable in the company of adults.' Richardson revealed a surprising aspect of his character. 'He was absolutely fastidious about his kit and his personal neatness. The average boy, when he goes away for a week, will go into his room, tip his bag open and that's how it will stay unless someone makes a plan. Not Herschelle. He would have his toothbrush, his toothpaste and his hairbrush immaculately lined up and his bag would be packed with precision. There were a lot of appealing aspects to his character.'

'He bears no grudges and he's prepared to take the rap when he's done wrong. He had an attractive personality and was comfortable in the company of adults.'

One characteristic noted by all the teachers who spoke about Gibbs is his lack of arrogance. His teachers at Bishops said he was kind to younger boys, who hero-worshipped him because of his sporting ability, and Richardson saw how the public responded to him, particularly in Stellenbosch, where there is a large coloured community. 'One night we all went out for supper and we couldn't get through the meal. The word had spread, not only through the restaurant but into the street. People kept coming to him, wanting his autograph, even if they only had a paper serviette to hand.' On another occasion a car swerved in front of the mini-bus in which they were travelling. 'We had to stop. The man jumped out of his vehicle and said he wanted Herschelle's autograph.' Girls idolised him as well and would go to matches to watch him play.

For a while, though, there was not much for his burgeoning group of supporters to cheer. The rest of his season lacked both drama and significant performances.

The United Cricket Board had decided it could no longer justify granting first-class status to B team provincial cricket and instead instituted a short-lived President's Cup Under 24 competition, which was not classified as first-class. Gibbs played in two three-day matches and three one-day games. His highest score was 35. He played in 11 limited overs matches for Western Province but his highest score was 22 and he was dropped towards the end of the night series.

The only first-class match he played was at the end of the season when he played for a below-strength Western Province team against Yorkshire, who were preparing for the English county season. He made 34 and 26.

The transition from schoolboy to young adult was not easy and his performances reflected a loss of focus, which came as no surprise to Keith Richardson. 'There needs to be some research done into how much this early adulation, this early fame, this early pushing, affects a boy. It actually took him a long time to break into the South African cricket side.'

Despite his modest accomplishments the previous season, Gibbs went on Western Province's pre-season tour of Zimbabwe in 1993/94 but without doing enough to win a place in the province's Castle Cup side. The Bowl had been brought back after a one-season absence, however, and it gave Gibbs the chance to register a maiden first-class century, an unbeaten 152 for Western Province B against Eastern Province B at the Goodwood Stadium, a venue seldom used for major matches. It was a fine effort, showing character and application as Gibbs faced 320 balls in a patient innings to save his side from defeat after they had been forced to follow on.

With the national side on tour in Australia, his century won him a return to the senior Western Province team for four successive matches during December and January. There were no fireworks, though, his highest score being 43 against the touring England A side.

His fielding was a factor in keeping him in the Western Province one-day side for most of the season. He had yet to master the art of scoring in limited overs games but he made his first half-century in the short version of the game when he steered the team to a win over Northern Transvaal in a low-scoring match at Newlands. By the end of the season, though, he was dropped for the deciding leg of a semi-final against Free State after playing in the first two, shared games.

The return of the national team players meant there were no further first-class matches for Gibbs in the Western Province team but there was another taste of international cricket when he received an invitation from Nicky Oppenheimer to play in the first match of the tour by Australia in February. Before rain brought an early end to the game, he made 31 not out. He didn't face Shane Warne but had his first experience of Aussie 'sledging' from off-spinner Tim May. 'He kept telling me, "You're so incompetent." I asked one of the senior guys what the word meant because at that stage I didn't know.'

He completed the first-class season playing for the B side in the Bowl final against Transvaal B at the Wanderers, making 57 not out in the second innings and helping the side earn a draw and share the title after they had trailed in the first innings.

He had recently turned 20 and in five seasons had gone forward without making giant strides. After 20 first-class matches his career average was 33,27. It was not bad for a youngster but hardly special.

CHAPTER **FIVE**

Too much, too soon?

The career graph of Herschelle Gibbs shows that, after making his first-class debut at the age of 16, it took him fully six years to establish himself in first-class cricket. The inevitable question must be: was he pushed too much, too soon?

Duncan Fletcher, the former Zimbabwe captain and future England coach, took over as Western Province cricket manager in 1993/94. One of the first players to benefit from Fletcher's man-management skills was Gibbs.

Fletcher has no doubt that premature demands on an exceptional talent did not help. 'He started out too early. He is not the first young player to find himself in a trough having been pushed too soon. The younger you are, the longer it takes to get out of it. When I got involved he was trying to find himself. He was confused. He was obviously talented and I didn't have to teach him anything in terms of technique. But he didn't know whether to trust his normal game or to play more cautiously, which led to him curbing himself too much.' According to Fletcher, Ashwell Prince, who played for South Africa in the home Tests against Australia in 2001/02, had a similar start to Gibbs, with unrealistic early expectations followed by a period of stagnation before his career took off again.

Gibbs is brutally honest about the early years. 'Nerves were a factor for the first four or five years of my provincial career. I still felt overawed by the occasion. There I was playing with Kuips [Adrian Kuiper] and company when just a few years before I had been a little boy watching them at Newlands. I did a lot better in the B Section. I felt more relaxed and comfortable in the B side.' Fast bowling was still a significant concern when he took the step up to the senior team. So was the intensity of the cricket and the public attention.

The selectors who set Herschelle on the way at first-class level remain convinced that they did the right thing.

Western Province selector Richard Morris says the era in which he and his fellow selectors played had influenced them to give youth its head. 'We had played with the likes of Graeme Pollock, Barry Richards and Ali Bacher, who had all started out very early. We felt Herschelle had the ability. He struggled for a few years and I believe his father played a part in that. But I always believed he would come good. It has taken longer than I expected but he is now in a class with the very best.'

Hylton Ackerman defends the early selection in pure cricket terms. 'Herschelle always had so much talent. The game was so easy for him he got bored. He is the closest I have seen to the great Barry Richards, who would hit one ball through the covers and think to himself that was too easy, so he would hit the next one over midwicket. Normal cricketers can't do that. Herschelle was doing it as a boy.'

Ackerman says the Western Province selection panel that year was as good as any he served on, and he believes they made the right decision. Ackerman of all people knew about the challenges of being a schoolboy prodigy. A left-handed batsman, he played for South African Schools at 14, made his first-class debut at 16 and hit a century for Border against the MCC at 17.

'One reason why he got my vote was that I had played when I was 16 and I thought if I could have done it and felt pretty comfortable, Herschelle Gibbs should have the opportunity. I had the feeling that this was a talent such as I hadn't seen since I played with the great Graeme Pollock, Barry Richards and Mike Procter,' said Ackerman.

Ackerman believes Gibbs has always had a superior 'cricket brain' and cites a match when Western Province encountered North West, who included an unorthdox seam bowler in David Pryke, who bowled off the wrong foot. 'In that side were people like Haynes, Eric Simons, Kallis and HD [Ackerman], and they were all getting cramped up by Pryke. Herschelle worked out quicker than anyone how to play him, where to hit it. A lot of people blamed us for picking him too early but he needed a challenge which he wasn't getting by making hundreds against Under 17 players.'

Changing social mores may have distracted the young Gibbs. 'When I was picked for Border as a 16-year-old,' says Ackerman, 'I wasn't allowed to stay in the hotel with the men. I was given a Coke at the end of the day and then I had to go home.' Given that Herschelle admits to having fallen easily into the drinking habits of adults, Ackerman wonders, although without great conviction, whether Gibbs too should have been sent home to bed after a day's play. More pertinent, he believes, is the difficulty Gibbs had in understanding how to harness his talent. 'When he was told that runs had to be scored quickly, he didn't realise that with his talent he just had to stay there and they would come without him having to force it.'

'I'm still convinced it was the right decision to pick him,' says Robin Jackman. 'I'd like to think that exposure at an early age stood him in good stead, maybe not in the first few years but certainly he is reaping the benefits now.' Jackman points out that many young players have a difficult time after making their initial mark. 'Players talk and work out how to bowl to the newcomers, so they have to make adjustments. There are also off-field factors, such as girlfriends and parental influence.'

Bishops coach Grant Norton had no objection to the principle of being picked for provincial cricket at 16. 'If you're good enough, you're old enough,' was his view, but he notes that the young star took time to adjust to each new higher level he reached. 'Even in school cricket it took him some time to find his feet in the first team. Then it took him a few years to be a consistent performer for Western Province and later to establish himself in international cricket.' These stutters in his career, Norton feels, may have been the result of a basic insecurity. 'He lacked confidence sometimes and didn't fully back himself.'

Norton's colleague, Melvyn Wallis-Brown, was consulted by the late Kevin Commins, father of John, who was managing director of Western Province cricket. 'I begged them not to pick him. Emotionally, I didn't think it would be good for him at such a young age.' Commins placated the teacher by assuring him that the youngster would share a room with Richie Ryall, the long-serving Western Province wicketkeeper, an Old Diocesan, who would be a good influence. In the end, on his first away trip, to Pretoria for the Northerns game, he shared a room with Eric Simons, a highly respected senior player who played for South Africa in one-day internationals and would become South African coach in 2002. Even so, Wallis-Brown believes to this day that the experience nearly ruined Gibbs's career.

If the selectors were criticised for pushing Herschelle too fast, his father castigated them for being too cautious. In a 1990 interview with the *Rapport* newspaper, before Herschelle's debut for the B side, Herman Gibbs was harshly critical of Western Province for holding his son back. 'The Western Province selectors are ultra-conservative,' he complained. 'They keep their young players too long on the shelf.' Gibbs senior told Province manager Jackman and coach Ackerman that he was fed up with the situation. He cited the way Pakistan regularly threw teenagers into Test combat and quoted the rapid rise of the Indian prodigy, Sachin Tendulkar, who was playing Test cricket at 16 and made his first Test century at 17.

Looking back, Herman says, 'Being picked for Western Province at that time was not a problem. It was unfortunate for Herschelle that there was a weak set-up in Western Province. Robin Jackman was at the end of his career as manager and the team was going through a slump. They weren't really equipped to receive a talented youngster. Jealousy also seemed to be a factor. Herschelle had a bat sponsorship and most of the senior players didn't. I don't think they wanted him to feel at home.' Nonetheless, when Herschelle went out socially with the team one night before a game and didn't get home until the early hours, Herman viewed it as evidence of lax discipline among the players.

Brian McMillan, South Africa's leading all-rounder in the immediate post-isolation years, partially endorses Herman's comments about the lack of welcome in the Western Province dressing room. 'It's a natural thing. If you are a batsman, you are not going to be so keen to be friendly with a youngster who might take your place.'

Typically, Herman has no hesitation in criticising the people in charge. 'When I took Herschelle to his first Province practice I was very disappointed. I was a physical education specialist and could see they didn't know what they were doing when they exercised before a practice, so I told Robin and Lawrence Seeff, who led the training, that it was a waste of time.'

Teachers and cricket officials complain that Gibbs senior was an interfering parent. While giving him credit for making the sacrifices which enabled Herschelle to go to private schools and get the best opportunities to develop his sporting talent, there is a distinct feeling that Herman's influence was not helpful once his son had stepped over the threshold into adult sport.

Herschelle says, however, that his father didn't interfere with the way he played, although he did try to convince his son to put more effort into his schoolwork. 'But I think he eventually saw the light and realised it wasn't going to happen.' Father and son had occasional long discussions about sport, but for the rest Herman left Herschelle to work out his own approach and take advice from qualified coaches. 'I was lucky enough to fall into the right hands, from the days when I was at Stuart Leary's clinics.'

Herschelle acknowledges that a teenage romance complicated his life. One evening during the rugby season the then 17-year-old went to the cinema with four school friends, all of whom had 'interests' at St Cyprian's, a private girls school. Herschelle was instantly attracted to Gwyneth Roberts, who was dating a friend of his. A braai [barbecue] at the friend's home after the movie gave Herschelle and Gwyneth a chance to get to know each other a little better. 'I fell in love, heavily,' he admits.

It was the start of a relationship that continued for six years. Herman Gibbs was opposed to the match. 'The way I saw it, she was from an affluent family who didn't understand how important it was for his sporting career that he stayed focused and got home at a certain time.' As with many a young couple, love found a way. Her parents liked Herschelle but, unbeknown to them, he had to lie to see her. 'I'm not proud of it but I used to tell my parents I was going to a friend's house after school when actually I was being picked up by her parents.'

It was particularly awkward when Herschelle went with Gwyneth to her matric farewell dance. By then Herman had bowed to the reality of the relationship but arranged to pick up his son at 12.30am. 'After-parties' are regarded by matriculants as an essential element of the big night out, with festivities going on at a different venue after the end of the dance. When Herschelle told Gwyneth he was being fetched early, she was, according to him, so upset that he felt he couldn't let her down. He hid in a toilet while Herman searched in vain for him, then went on to the party. It still rankles Herman. 'They may have thought going on to a party was a normal thing but I didn't think it was right. To me Herschelle was special and his sport came first.'

Whether or not the romance had a serious effect on his sporting progress, Herschelle is not sure. He admits that he was thinking about Gwyneth while he was on the cricket or rugby field. 'Her mom had a blue Renault and I'd be looking out for it while I was playing, until I saw they had arrived.'

> Cricket people were starting to wonder whether yet another bright young talent was going to flicker without ever bursting into full flame.

Cricket people were starting to wonder whether yet another bright young talent was going to flicker without ever bursting into full flame. Duncan Fletcher believed in him, however, and the recruitment of Desmond Haynes, the great West Indian opening batsman, was also to have a positive effect on Gibbs's approach to batting.

'Duncan believed in discipline and that how you handled your life was how you should handle your cricket,' says Gibbs. 'He didn't make batting complicated. He was probably my first major influence in senior cricket.' Western Province had four talented youngsters in Gibbs, Jacques Kallis, HD Ackerman and Sven Koenig. Fletcher was keen that they should share a house and learn to take responsibility for themselves and each other. The plan didn't come together, however, and the house that had been earmarked for them was eventually occupied by Haynes, the star overseas recruit.

Gibbs, for so long the prodigy, was suddenly fourth in line of Fletcher's young batsmen. Kallis, less than a month after his 19th birthday, was picked for the first match of the 1994/95 season, as were Ackerman and Koenig, both 21. All three played in every one of the province's Castle Cup matches. Gibbs, 20, started the season in the B team.

Once again, run-scoring proved easy at the lower level. A century against Griqualand West, which followed two half-centuries in the previous two matches, earned him promotion to the senior side. At last came the breakthrough he had been waiting for as he hit his maiden Castle Cup century, 102 against Boland at Newlands, against an attack which included

Charl Willoughby, Henry Williams and Claude Henderson, all of whom went on to play for South Africa, and Kevin Curran, the Zimbabwe all-rounder. It was an innings that gave him considerable satisfaction. 'It was the first match played on a part of the square that had been relaid and it was really quick. I remember my hundred included 20 fours.' A check of the record books reveals that his memory was spot on.

He stayed in the side for the rest of the season but there was only one other significant innings in six matches, a fighting top-score 79 against Northern Transvaal, for whom Fanie de Villiers bowled superbly. Koenig, Ackerman and Kallis all finished above him in the Western Province averages, and Ackerman and Kallis were picked for the South African Under 24 team which toured Sri Lanka in the off-season. Gibbs was not.

If his first-class season in 1994/95 was unexceptional, his performances in the Benson & Hedges limited overs series were downright disappointing. He played only four times in Western Province's campaign, scoring a total of 77 runs. His career average after 20 one-day innings was a modest 15,88.

Fletcher did not lose faith, however. When a journalist wanted to interview Kallis and Ackerman, the two players he perceived as being Western Province's stand-out youngsters, Fletcher insisted, 'We've got four outstanding batsmen.' Fletcher had his way, and Gibbs and Koenig were part of the interview, while the photograph published in the *Sunday Times* included all four players.

Haynes was an ideal role model for Gibbs, combining West Indian flair with discipline and powers of concentration. As Gibbs says, 'You had to respect his record. He was a guy who averaged over 40 in Test cricket and at that time he was still the leading run-scorer in one-day internationals.' Haynes did not have to say much to get his message through. 'I'm not one to go out and ask people to tell me how to bat,' says Gibbs. 'I've never wanted to make batting complicated. Just observing Dessie and the way he went about his practices and the sort of shots he played, I took a lot of notice. I never really had a one-on-one with Dessie, or Duncan for that matter; I just used to listen and observe and key points would stick in my mind.'

Michael Owen-Smith, who was reporting on Western Province cricket, says, 'Duncan could only coach up to the point where the players crossed the white line and went on to the field. That was where Desmond was able to have such a huge influence. He was batting with the young players in the middle.

He was particularly good for Herschelle because he encouraged him to play shots like the square cut for six when there was a short boundary, or the lofted drive over cover.'

Nonetheless, Fletcher played an important role off the field. 'Herschelle was a sensitive person who had some hard times,' said Fletcher. 'Part of my man-management role was to help other people understand him. Off the field he could be excitable, like a jack-in-the-box. Some in the team thought it was arrogance, when a lot of the time he was trying to hide his nervousness. We often had quite emotional chats and at times I used to think I was being like a father figure.'

By contrast, Fletcher was able to guide Jacques Kallis to cricket maturity at a measured pace. Says Gibbs: 'I was amazed just how easily Jacques fitted in when he came on the scene. I think they probably pushed him at the right time, whereas for me the first four years or so were completely different.'

For Fletcher, it was no lucky accident. Recognising that he had another exceptional talent in his squad, Fletcher kept the pressure off Kallis by batting him at number six in the first-class games. He was floated in the day-night series and Fletcher protected him, even when Western Province were on top. In a floodlit match against Northern Transvaal, Desmond Haynes made a fine century and, with about five overs to go, Fletcher moved Kallis down the order, reasoning that he did not want to rush the young player into changing the rhythm of his developing game by being expected to play an unnatural, over-attacking innings.

Kallis's success created an opportunity for Gibbs to take over from his younger provincial team-mate, who was playing club cricket for Netherfield in the Northern Lancashire league. When Kallis left for Sri Lanka, Gibbs went to Lancashire where he made some runs and had some fun.

The 1995/96 season was to prove crucial. It started with Western Province going on a pre-season tour of Australia for matches in Queensland and New South Wales. Kallis entrenched his position as the best of the young guns when he made a maiden first-class century against Queensland at the Gabba in Brisbane. It was a big one, too, 186 not out. Gibbs, who had made 76 not out against a Queensland Country team, did not play, although he did get a chance in the second first-class match, against New South Wales at Sydney's Hurstville Oval, making 17 and 15.

57

Gibbs was still on Nicky Oppenheimer's guest list but failed to score against Mike Atherton's England tourists. He also admits to abusing the magnate's hospitality, which may be why he was not invited again. 'When you play for him, everything is taken care of, your accommodation, room service, telephone calls, the lot. Gwyneth was in the United States and I spent R3 000 on a phone call.'

He was not picked for Western Province's early Castle Cup matches. Once again it was Kallis who was dominating the headlines. He followed his innings against Queensland by making 146 against Transvaal at Newlands, just 12 days after his 20th birthday, and it was no surprise when he was called up to play for South Africa A against England in Kimberley. Also selected for the A side, after a sensational Castle Cup debut against Northern Transvaal, in which he took eight wickets and bamboozled experienced batsmen with his peculiar action, likened to 'a frog in a blender' by journalist Andy Capostagno, was 18-year-old Paul Adams. Both shone against England. Kallis made a calm, elegant 93 while Adams caused consternation among the tourists, taking nine wickets in the match. Bolder national selectors might have picked both for the first Test the following week, especially with the surprise element of Adams being so new. Neither was chosen, though both made their debuts later in the series.

Herschelle Gibbs seemed to be sinking in the backwaters of provincial cricket. He was not even batting well for the Western Province B side, averaging under 30 in four matches without making a fifty. The Test series, though, created openings in the senior provincial team and in his second match back he made 112 against Boland, showing patience on a slow pitch in Paarl.

Then came a turning point, perhaps the most important of his career. Coach Fletcher was supervising a middle practice and marvelled, not for the first time, at the array of strokes unleashed by Gibbs, particularly at the way he was hitting perfectly controlled lofted drives. How was this wonderful talent to find full expression in matches that mattered? Suddenly, the answer seemed obvious. 'Why don't you open in the one-day games?' he suggested. 'Bat just the way you are now.'

The batsman who had made only one fifty in 20 previous one-day innings, batting in a variety of positions in the middle order, had been given the clearly defined role he needed to play successfully in limited overs cricket. He seized the opportunity. Having been omitted for Western Province's first five Benson & Hedges Series matches, he started his new role against Border at Newlands, going in first with Desmond Haynes. He blazed his way to 45 off 44 balls, dominating an opening stand of 61. Haynes went on to make a century. In his next four innings, Gibbs made 57 off 67 balls, 73 not out off 85 balls and 89 not out off 104 balls, in each case improving on his previous career-best. In the fifth innings of this remarkable sequence he made his first senior limited overs century, 101 off 128 balls against Natal at Newlands, before the runs dried up in the two legs of a semi-final against Free State. He was out for 10, then run-out for nought, as Western Province's campaign was brought to a halt.

Province did, however, win the Castle Cup for the first time since Gibbs had played a minor role in his debut season in 1990/91. Now, he opened in the match against Border, making five and 27. It was the match in which the title was secured, and it was the only time he opened in first-class cricket before he was picked in that role at Test level.

> Suddenly, the answer seemed obvious. 'Why don't you open in the one-day games?' he suggested. 'Bat just the way you are now.'

Having seen more recent recruits to the Western Province ranks overtake him for national team, South Africa A and South Africa Under 24 honours, Gibbs was picked for the South Africa A team which toured England during the South African winter of 1996. The itinerary consisted primarily of first-class matches but Gibbs's one-day form in the second half of the season was an important factor in his selection. Joining him on the flight to London were five Western Province team-mates: John Commins, who was captain, Jacques Kallis and Paul Adams, both already with Test experience, HD Ackerman and Sven Koenig. Duncan Fletcher was the coach.

Although he was one of the most experienced players in the A team, with 38 first-class matches and 2 113 runs to his credit, an average of 33,53 did not suggest him as one of the likely stars. It was, though, to be a breakthrough tour. 'If there was anything that turned it around for me, it was that tour,' he recalls.

Fletcher remembers Gibbs playing some outstanding innings, while Commins says Gibbs was an ideal man to have in a touring team. 'There are certain people in life you laugh with and there are others you laugh at. Herschelle is one of those you laugh with. We enjoyed Herschelle and his humour and you need that sort of person in a team. Every successful side I have been involved with has had someone who can turn a serious moment into something light-hearted.'

The travels around the counties started quietly enough with innings of 28 against Yorkshire and 27 not out against Derbyshire. In the second innings of the Derbyshire match he was moved from number six to number three and made a splendid 68 off 78 balls. He stayed at number three for most of the rest of the tour and the runs flowed. Against a useful MCC team at the attractive Shenley ground in Hertfordshire, South Africa were forced to follow on despite 57 by Gibbs. The main destroyer was the lively Nigel Francis, from Trinidad and Tobago, one of the tall fast bowlers who had made an impression on a younger Gibbs on the 1992 tour of the West Indies. With more experience of playing against good fast bowling now under his belt, Gibbs defied Francis and the rest of an international roll call of bowlers, which included Paul Strang of Zimbabwe, Robert Croft of England and Tony Dodemaide, the former Australian all-rounder. He made a career-best 183 off 294 balls with 25 fours and five sixes as the match was safely drawn.

He went on to make 55 against Gloucestershire and had successive innings of 95 and 85 against Nottinghamshire at Trent Bridge, and 58 and 178 against Surrey at the Oval. Although both the latter counties fielded weak teams, *Wisden* described the century at the Oval as 'electrifying'. It included 19 fours and eight sixes and was made off 209 balls.

'The thing about a tour like that is that you are playing virtually every day, so once you hit form you just keep going,' says Commins. 'We didn't play against the best bowlers so most of the batsmen did well on that tour. One thing you know with Herschelle is that you are always going to get 100 percent, whether he's batting or in the field.'

Commins and Duncan Fletcher spoke to each other about their star performer. 'Duncan told me one day he had never come across anyone he had thrown to in the nets who hit the ball like Herschelle. He said the ball came back at him so quickly he actually felt uncomfortable. He said, "We've got a genius here." I'll never forget that because Duncan was not the sort of person to throw compliments around.'

Now that Commins has stopped playing, he only watches cricket occasionally but he tells how he and Mark Rushmere, another former international player, were having a braai when Commins's five-year-old son told him Herschelle was batting. 'We both put down our beers and went to watch television. I said to Mark, "What are we doing here?" and Mark said, "We're not watching cricket, we're watching Herschelle." I'm not knocking the other players but I've seen them play and I know what they're going to do. Herschelle's an entertainer.'

When he returned home from England in mid-August 1996, Gibbs had comfortably topped the tour batting averages with 867 runs at 66,69. He topped the bowling averages, too, albeit with only three wickets, which included two for 14 against Somerset as the swing bowling of his schooldays was brought into sporadic action. Suddenly, the name of Herschelle Gibbs was one that the national selectors would have to consider seriously, not for subsidiary teams but for full national honours.

He did not have long to wait. Within weeks, he was named in the South African squad for a quadrangular one-day tournament in Nairobi to mark the centenary of the Kenya Cricket Association. 'We had a long discussion about whether to pick him,' recalls national team coach Bob Woolmer. 'He was obviously a raw talent but because of his reputation and his irresponsibility we probably didn't select him for South Africa early enough. We knew he had the ability to play but he didn't perform solidly enough. The pressure to pick players of colour was beginning to build up and he was the obvious choice, so we wanted him to do well.'

Also called up after a successful A tour was Natal's off-spinning all-rounder Derek Crookes. 'We had a training camp in Johannesburg before the squad was picked. I can't actually remember who told me I was going to Kenya,' said Gibbs. All that mattered was that he was now an international cricketer.

His career was about to take a major step forward. His personal life, though, was on the verge of a crisis.

CHAPTER **SIX**

Unexpected fatherhood

Herschelle Gibbs's eye for the girls has sometimes landed him in hot water, but his relationship with Liesl Fuller had particularly painful consequences.

He met the attractive schoolgirl when he was breaking his curfew during the 1992 Nuffield Week in Stellenbosch. She was 13, and they kept in touch. When he was in Johannesburg with the Western Province team in February 1996, to play two Benson & Hedges Series matches, against Western Transvaal and Transvaal, he telephoned her and she joined him at his Sandton hotel.

Although she was still at school, she stayed over. Liesl told her story to *You* magazine in June 2000. 'I'm not the kind of person who sleeps around and at that stage I wasn't using any contraceptive,' she said. 'But then Valentine's Day arrived and one thing led to another. It was the only time Herschelle and I made love.'

That is a detail Gibbs disputes. 'I used to see her from time to time. It wasn't the first time I slept with her.'

Gibbs was in the middle of a spell of excellent form. He made 73 not out and 89 not out in the two matches and he had enjoyed what he regarded as a pleasant off-the-field diversion with a willing partner. Still a few days short of his 22nd birthday, he went back to Cape Town in good spirits.

Unexpected fatherhood

Liesl claimed she did not realise she was pregnant until five months later. She said that as soon as pregnancy was confirmed, she telephoned Herschelle. 'He was furious. He wanted to know how it could take me five months to find out I was pregnant.'

Gibbs was still living with his parents. His cricket career was taking off and he had a close relationship with Gwyneth Roberts. He said Liesl was crying when she telephoned and he was anxious and confused. 'I didn't want anyone to find out so I kept it to myself.'

Rashad Fuller was born on 1 November 1996, while Gibbs was on tour in India. Liesl's account portrays him as an uncaring father who wanted nothing to do with the child. 'Herschelle was playing cricket overseas and didn't even know his child had been born. He never phoned to find out how the baby and I were.'

Two months later she arranged to meet him in Cape Town. He told her he didn't want to see the child, nor did he look at pictures she took to the meeting. He agreed without argument to pay maintenance. 'Her dad drew up this contract for huge amounts of money. I was a youngster and I didn't know much about these things. I didn't consult anyone, I just wanted to keep it under wraps, so I went ahead and agreed.'

Gibbs went to Johannesburg in February 1997 to sign the agreement. Liesl met him outside his hotel with the child. She told *You* magazine, 'Herschelle didn't once look at Rashad sitting in his baby seat in the back of the car. At one stage Rashad started crying bitterly and I asked Herschelle if he could do something. He refused. I told him I was driving on the highway and couldn't comfort the child. Without looking back he put his hand out and rocked the baby seat a few times.'

Gibbs still hadn't told his parents and they only found out when the lawyers in Johannesburg sent him a copy of the agreement. 'I was still living at home and the envelope was addressed to Mr H Gibbs, so they naturally assumed it was for my dad. That's how they found out.'

Liesl, whose surname had changed to Naidoo as a result of a brief marriage, acknowledged that Herschelle had never shirked his responsibility to pay maintenance. She did not tell the magazine the terms of the settlement, which included a 15 percent annual escalation on an already generous monthly amount. He committed to paying maintenance until Rashad reached the age of 21. He also agreed to pay 'all reasonable education requirements', defined as including primary, secondary and tertiary education.

It was a major financial obligation for a young man, who at that stage had no guarantee that he would become a regular international cricketer earning good money. What was 'reasonable' in terms of education was specified as being at the sole discretion of Liesl. She put down a marker in this regard by applying for Rashad to be enrolled at one of Johannesburg's more expensive private preparatory schools.

The magazine article painted a heart-rending portrait of a young boy who knew who his father was but only ever saw him when he watched him playing cricket on television.

Gibbs admits that initially he felt anger and frustration that she had allowed the pregnancy to happen and had gone through with it. 'For the first few years of his life I wasn't supportive.'

Time has healed the wounds and he says that over the past three years he has had regular contact with Rashad and sees him when he visits Johannesburg. 'We have a lot of fun together and we're forming a nice bond.' Rashad spends time with his father at his hotel and has started to go to games with him as well. They speak to each other regularly on the telephone.

Herschelle and Liesl have reached an amicable agreement to modify the terms of the maintenance settlement.

Herschelle is not the first member of the family to have become a parent ahead of schedule. His mother, Barbara, had a child before she met Herman. The son, Clinton, was brought up by Barbara's mother in Bonteheuwel but he and Herschelle have always got on well. 'I love him to pieces. When he was growing up, my mom used to visit my grandmother every Saturday and we had a great time together.'

Clinton is three years older than Herschelle and is married with two daughters. He is the service manager of a motor dealership in Bellville and Herschelle is in regular contact with the family.

Above: The Gibbs family celebrates Herschelle's selection for South Africa in 1996. From left, mother Barbara, sister Lucinda, Herschelle and father Herman.

Right: Best friends. Herschelle and the family dog, Tasha, outside the Gibbs flat in Elfindale.

Pictures courtesy Gibbs family

A young star of the soccer field, crowd favourite Herschelle is carried off the field by referee Elton Hendricks after shining for the Yorkshire Under 10 team in a curtain-raiser to a big game at Athlone Stadium.

Picture courtesy Gibbs family

Above: Playing in his first representative cricket week, 11-year-old Herschelle at the crease for Western Province Under 13. 'Even then, as a spindly, thin little guy he was really talented,' says his captain, HD Ackerman.

Left: Sprint star Herman Gibbs, aged about 20, gets ready to run another fast 100 metres at the Green Point Track.

Pictures courtesy Gibbs family

Above: The South African Schools team picked after the Coca-Cola Week in Potchefstroom in 1991. Herschelle is second from left in the front row. Others who went on to play Test cricket were Shaun Pollock and Nicky Bojé (Full team: back row, left to right, D Watson, R Maier, S Pollock, J Ehrke, L Masikazana, S Koenig, M Mfobo; front row, left to right, Mr PG Hamilton, organising secretary, H Gibbs, A Pollock, vice-captain, N Bojé, captain, V Vermeulen, G Miller, Mr D Wilkinson, manager.)

Picture courtesy Gibbs family

Right: Herschelle, aged 16, shows a sound defensive technique as he makes his Castle Cup debut against Northern Transvaal at Newlands in December 1990.

© *Cape Argus/Trace Images*

Herschelle the rugby star. Kicking for Bishops (left) and doing the same for Western Province Schools (above).

Anne Laing

Top: Quick off the mark. Herschelle clocked 10,9 seconds for the 100 metres at the Bishops sports day in his final year at school, running on a grass track without starting blocks.
Picture courtesy Gibbs family

Above inset: Playing for Western Province in a Benson & Hedges Series semi-final at Newlands in 1993/94, Herschelle looks back anxiously after getting an inside edge to a ball from Free State's Corrie van Zyl, who went on to become South Africa's assistant coach.
Anne Laing

Right: Getting ready for action. Jacques Kallis, Alan Dawson, Herschelle and HD Ackerman at pre-season training in the mid 1990s.
Picture courtesy Gibbs family

Above: Herschelle, one day short of his 18th birthday, hits out for Western Province against Free State at Newlands in February 1992. He made top score of 44.
Anne Laing

Left: From his early days, Herschelle was renowned as an outstanding fielder. Here he takes a sliding catch while playing for the Bishops First XI.
Anne Laing

All-round sportsman. Herschelle, aged 18, after he was selected for the South African Schools rugby team, completing a hat-trick of national junior honours in soccer, cricket and rugby.
Anne Laing

CHAPTER **SEVEN**

A step onto the world stage

His personal life may have become complicated but the closing months of 1996 took Herschelle Gibbs onto the world cricket stage. He made his one-day international debut in Kenya and within months became a Test player in India. It was in India, too, that the seeds were sown which would lead to one of cricket's most notorious episodes.

The South African players who went to Kenya at the start of the 1996/97 season were determined to re-assert themselves. The side contained the bulk of the squad that had played in the World Cup in Pakistan earlier in the year, sweeping through the round robin phase before crashing out in the quarter-finals to a Brian Lara-inspired West Indies side.

Kenya offered a chance to show what might have been. Sri Lanka had gone on to win the World Cup and they were playing in Nairobi, along with Pakistan and Kenya.

Gibbs was still only 22 but felt at home in the company of the national team players, most of whom he had played with and against often enough. Although he was in the squad there were no guarantees that he would get on the field. He watched from the sidelines as Daryl Cullinan and Jonty Rhodes both hit centuries in a high-scoring win over Pakistan and sat out again as

Sri Lanka's slow bowlers strangled the South African strokeplayers on a poor pitch at the Nairobi Sports Club, the more modest of the two venues used for the tournament. The defeat made the remaining round robin match, against Kenya, a must-win affair.

Cullinan had fallen ill and Gibbs knew there was a chance he might play. Cullinan, who was sharing a room with the newcomer, was given until virtually the last moment to recover. It was only after the team's elaborate pre-match exercise routine that Gibbs was told he was playing. After the tension and drama of his Western Province debut, his international debut was almost an anti-climax. It was a relatively low-key game against opposition that wasn't as strong as many provincial teams and although the ground was packed with home supporters, it was a small club venue. 'I wasn't very nervous. I actually felt quite comfortable when I went out to bat, probably because I had been playing first-class cricket for such a long time.' He batted confidently to make 17 off 22 balls before he was stumped off Maurice Odumbe, the Kenyan captain and off-spinner. South Africa made 305 before Allan Donald ripped through the Kenyan batting and they won by a record margin of 202 runs.

Gibbs has two off-field memories of Nairobi. One was that for the first time on a tour he experienced 'the runs' as a result of an upset stomach. The other was sharing a room with Cullinan, not the most socially tolerant member of the side. Gibbs believes it was one of the penalties of being the new boy in the team. 'It was a very interesting experience, not that enjoyable, but interesting. I got to know Daryll very quickly and learned how to stay on his good side.' He was alone in the room when Cullinan's wife, Virginia, telephoned. He promised to pass on the message and did so. 'She had sounded a bit upset and I knew it was difficult to get through to the hotel from South Africa. I gave him the message and I almost thought he had forgotten, so I asked him, "Are you going to phone your wife?" He said to me, "What the f*** has it got to do with you?" I was quite stunned but then I found out that was a usual sort of thing for him.'

Pakistan thrashed Sri Lanka to qualify for the final, with Shahid Afridi, another newcomer to international cricket, said to be 16 years old, hitting a sensational century off 37 balls. Cullinan was fit again, so Gibbs did not play in the final, in which South Africa gained an efficient seven-wicket win, with

Gary Kirsten making an unbeaten century after good bowling and fielding had restricted Pakistan to 203 all out.

A significant difference for the young cricketer was the vastly enhanced earning power of international cricketers. 'I was still living with my parents and all of a sudden I was earning a proper living. Coming from the background I did, the money was a big thing. For the first time I had my own pocket money.' The increased income continued to flow when he was retained in South Africa's squad for a tour of India, the first full-scale visit to the country. The itinerary included three Tests but the first challenge was the Titan Cup, a triangular one-day tournament involving India, Australia and South Africa. The selectors retained the squad that had won in Kenya for the one-day matches in India.

Once again, Gibbs had to wait his turn as the South Africans rolled into action, winning their first four matches, two each against India and Australia. Assured of a place in the final, South Africa gave Gibbs and Lance Klusener a chance against India at Rajkot. Regular opening batsman Andrew Hudson was unwell, so Gibbs went in first with Western Province team-mate Gary Kirsten after India had been bowled out for 185. A sparkling innings of 35 off 49 balls, during an opening stand of 62, set South Africa on the way to a fifth successive win. Hudson returned for the next match and Gibbs was again a spectator. Klusener played and made 88 not out off 98 balls, batting at number three.

Looking back, Gibbs says that first tour was the most difficult he experienced. The one-day matches were crammed in at two-day intervals and travel plans did not always make sense. It was especially hard when teams played back-to-back matches. Even the shortest journey in India was a time-consuming business because of heavy traffic and long waits at airports. On several occasions, teams would arrive in a new town without enough time for so much as a fielding practice at the ground where the next day's match would be played. Although hotels in the main cities were among the best in the world, the standard of accommodation in smaller centres was variable. South Africa were sent to some of the backwaters of Indian cricket, including Indore, Rajkot and Guahati. 'There were some places you couldn't sleep, the beds were dirty, there weren't even carpets on the floors. Guahati was probably the worst place I've been to.' Journalists on the trip had their problems, too, with telephone calls particularly troublesome from remote locations.

For a young man on his first major tour, however, travel and accommodation problems were a minor distraction. 'I've never been one to complain about touring. I don't need much to keep me happy and wherever I go I find something to do. Even on that trip, I would say I enjoyed every minute of it.' Particularly fascinating were the crowds who thronged around the team wherever they went – at the hotels, at practices that were frequently chaotic in the outlying venues because of a lack of proper security and at the grounds. In one small hotel, with the players wanting to escape a crush of well-wishers, they had to wait their turn to use a single tiny lift, which could only accommodate four burly South Africans at a time. 'There we were with all our luggage, wanting to get to our rooms. The lift was so small but this Indian guy insisted he had to stay in to operate it.' Brian McMillan, a giant by comparison with most Indians, took direct action. 'He just lifted the guy up and put him outside, saying, "There's no room for you."'

> 'I've never been one to complain about touring. I don't need much to keep me happy and wherever I go I find something to do.'

Occasionally, the overwhelming attention became too much. Paddy Upton, the team's fitness specialist, dispersed one crowd outside a hotel by tossing some of the huge firecrackers so beloved of Indian fans at matches. 'Even then they didn't get cross. They just laughed and enjoyed it. Basically, I found the Indian people very friendly, always wanting to help.'

Like many sportsmen, Gibbs was conservative in his eating habits. 'At that stage I wasn't a big lover of Indian food, so I lost a lot of weight.'

Tempers were put to the test. For the first time, Gibbs became aware that Hansie Cronjé could lose his in quite spectacular fashion. 'It was on one of our bus trips during the one-day series. We seemed to have been sent to all the remote places in India and Hansie was fed up. He really lost it with Robbie Muzzell [the tour manager]. I had never seen that side of Hansie before.'

Although originally picked only for the one-day series, in which he had played one game, a selection meeting back in South Africa brought good news. Whereas they had reserved the option of choosing different players for the first-class and Test matches, the selectors decided to stick with those who had done so well in the triangular tournament. The only change to the squad was the addition of Paul Adams, who had been unavailable for the one-day games due to injury.

South Africa went into the Titan Cup final against India at the Wankhede Stadium in Mumbai with every reason to be optimistic. Gary Kirsten and Daryll Cullinan were the two leading batsmen in the tournament, while Allan Donald had been by far the best bowler. The toss proved crucial, however, with Sachin Tendulkar calling correctly and batting first on a pitch which deteriorated markedly during the course of the match. India won by 35 runs, with Anil Kumble, the brisk-paced Indian leg-spinner, almost unplayable as he took four for 26. The result brought back unhappy memories of the World Cup. As *Wisden* noted, South Africa had won 11 out of 13 matches in Pakistan and India during 1996 and yet had failed to win a trophy. Headlines in some South African newspapers, which labelled the team 'chokers', did nothing to promote good cheer in the camp.

But there was no time to dwell on the setback. There were two first-class matches before the first Test and it was crucial that South Africa made the most of them. With playing programmes distorted by the World Cup, South Africa had played 29 one-day internationals during the year but many of the players had not played in a first-class match since the final Test against England in January. It was now November. The first warm-up game against Karnataka in the coastal city of Kochi was not ideal preparation. Although South Africa won comfortably, batting conditions were not easy and no South African batsman could make a half-century. Gibbs was out for 14 and five.

After the privations of travel and poor practice facilities, Baroda was a pleasure, with the well-appointed Indo Petrochemicals Company ground, on the premises of the company, providing good pitches both in the middle and in the nets. The match pitch provided more bounce than is usual in India and Fanie de Villiers led a rout of a reasonably strong Board President's XI, who were bowled out for 179. The touring batsmen continued to struggle to adapt to the change from one-day cricket to the longer version of the game. The exception was Herschelle Gibbs. While the other batsmen became tied down by the Indian spinners, the left-armer, Venkatapathy Raju, and the leg-spinner, Narendra Hirwani, Gibbs used his feet well and mixed patience with some delightful strokes as he made top score of 74 in a total of 206. De Villiers, Klusener and Brian McMillan skittled the Board team in the second innings and South Africa needed only 70 to secure a 10-wicket win.

The first Test was at the Sardar Patel Stadium in Ahmedabad, only some 120 kilometres from Baroda but a three-hour journey by bus on a traffic-clogged, single-lane road. If Baroda had been a pleasant surprise, Ahmedabad was a disappointment in almost every aspect. It was a grimy, sprawling and polluted city and the team hotel was some distance from the ground and not nearly as comfortable as a newer, more conveniently situated establishment used by the television commentators. The stadium itself was a huge, unattractive concrete edifice on the outskirts of the city. The surrounding area was bare and grassless. Clouds of dust rose from the parking area as cars and buses streamed to the game. The pitch was brown and bare, the outfield patchy. The dressing rooms and the media facilities were among the worst the author has seen in the course of reporting on matches at more than 50 Test venues around the world. The players were housed in a dark and dingy room underneath the main grandstand. Once again, Bob Woolmer, the South African coach, had cause to complain at the granting of Test status to venues with inadequate practice facilities. John Reid, the International Cricket Council's match referee, said he would submit a highly critical report on the ground to the ICC. If any action was taken it was not made public.

Given his showing in Baroda, Gibbs must have come close to selection for the Test team, but having elected to go in with two spin bowlers in Pat Symcox and the newly-arrived Adams, South Africa needed the all-round skills of Brian McMillan to back up the pace of Donald and De Villiers, leaving only five specialist batting places. These went, not surprisingly, to Hudson, Kirsten, Cullinan, Cronjé and Rhodes. India won an important toss and went on to win a low-scoring game on a poor pitch. Dubious umpiring, which included two shocking lbw decisions in the first innings by the Indian official, SK Bansal, added to South Africa's woes. Daryll Cullinan was given out when he stretched his front pad so far down the pitch to the left-arm spinner Sunil Joshi that he almost lost his balance, while Hansie Cronjé was far outside the line of leg stump when he was struck by a sharply spinning leg-break from Hirwani. Despite only needing 170 to win in the final innings, South Africa never looked like achieving the target. Javagal Srinath, the Indian fast bowler, three times took two wickets with successive balls in an innings which included six ducks.

The nightmare of Ahmedabad was quickly forgotten as the touring party moved across the width of India to Calcutta, one of the most vibrant cricket cities in the world. The players' wives and girlfriends joined them in the opulent, colonial-style Oberoi Grand hotel. Across the Maidan, a huge area of parkland and a myriad cricket fields, was the majestic Eden Gardens, where the second Test would be played. Jonty Rhodes had returned home because of a hamstring injury, so Gibbs had even more reason to enjoy Calcutta. Before the players attended a sponsors' cocktail party at the hotel where the Indian team were staying, Gibbs and Lance Klusener were told they would be winning their first Test caps the next day. Klusener, surprisingly, was included ahead of Fanie de Villiers.

In Ahmedabad, almost everything had gone wrong for South Africa. In Calcutta, almost everything went right. Hansie Cronjé won the toss and the team sat back and enjoyed a double century opening partnership between Andrew Hudson and Gary Kirsten, who both made hundreds. Gibbs was batting at number three. The openers scored at virtually four runs an over before Kirsten was bowled by Srinath immediately after tea. Gibbs had been nervous but by the time it was his turn to bat he felt relaxed enough to savour the atmosphere in a stadium which throbbed with the hubbub of 60 000 spectators who at last had something to cheer about. 'It was a great feeling. I enjoyed it as I walked out.' He enjoyed his innings, too, driving Srinath through the covers for four and sweeping both spinners, Kumble and Hirwani, to the boundary.

Hudson edged an attempted square cut against Prasad into his stumps after making 146 but runs continued to be scored quickly as Gibbs was joined by Cullinan. The second new ball was punished by Cullinan, who took over the dominant role in the partnership. By close of play, South Africa were 339 for two. Gibbs was on 28 off 85 balls. As they cooled off in the dressing room, Cullinan suggested his partner could go on to make a fifty on debut. 'I was feeling very content, not excited, just content. Later on at the hotel, when I met up with Gwyneth, I felt pretty pleased.'

The next morning was a different matter. Test cricket in India is played in the winter months to avoid the extreme summer heat and the downside is that play has to start early to maximise the hours of daylight. Early morning moisture and the breeze off the Hooghly river has undone many a batsman.

Armed with a ball only 10 overs old, Srinath and Prasad bowled splendidly and neither Gibbs nor Cullinan could take control. Gibbs was dropped off Srinath by Sanjay Manjrekar, a substitute fielder, at second slip, in the second over of the day with his score on 30. At one stage there were four successive maidens. After adding only three runs off 27 balls since the start of play, Gibbs played across a ball from Prasad and was lbw for 31. 'The ball swung a bit more and I was stuck on the crease.' The rest of the batting was whittled away as South Africa were bowled out for 428.

What India did not realise was that although South Africa may have lost Rhodes, they had gained another remarkable fielder. Nayan Mongia, the wicketkeeper who was doubling as an opening batsman, was the first to learn the folly of taking a risky single as Gibbs swooped from cover and threw down the stumps at the bowler's end. Sunil Joshi became a second victim when he was sent back by Srinath after Gibbs again moved at lightning speed to pick up at cover before lobbing back to Allan Donald, the bowler. Anil Kumble, the last man out, completed a trio of run-out victims when he tried a risky second run to Gibbs, fielding on the cover boundary. The player carries a permanent reminder of that moment. In sliding to pick up the ball, he jammed the little finger of his left hand into the turf, dislocating it badly. He had X-rays but was determined to carry on playing. He still cannot straighten the finger fully and it is swollen and misshapen compared to the corresponding digit on his right hand.

South Africa led by 99 runs on the first innings, despite a sensational innings by Mohammad Azharuddin, who blazed his way to a hundred off 74 balls. Lance Klusener had a rude introduction to Test cricket, conceding 75 runs off 14 overs, including five successive boundaries by the rampant Azharuddin.

South Africa put themselves into an indomitable position as Gary Kirsten helped himself to his second century of the match, with Daryll Cullinan also making a hundred. Gibbs made just nine before being caught at short leg off Srinath. Donald could not bowl in India's second innings because of the left heel injury that was to plague him through the later years of his career, but Klusener, in a remarkable turnaround, took eight for 64. South Africa gained a crushing 329-run win. No wicket was more satisfying than that of

Azharuddin, who played another attacking innings, hitting 52 before edging Klusener to the safe hands of McMillan at second slip.

The match remains a highlight of Gibbs's career. Having played at most of the great venues of the world, he says the nearest comparison to Eden Gardens is the Melbourne Cricket Ground. Eden Gardens, though, is noisier and more vibrant. 'You get this huge cheer every time they hit a four and then complete silence when you hit a four. The people live for their cricket. They get so excited when anything happens.' There was never any feeling of hostility towards the South Africans and after the match Cronjé led his men on a lap of honour around the ground as a tribute to the spectators, who reciprocated with warm applause for the players who had vanquished their heroes. One small, sour note for Gibbs was that he had his first run-in with an ICC match referee. John Reid fined him 15 percent of his match fee for the illegal display of advertisements on cricket gear, a manufacturer's logo being visible on his armguard. India's VVS Laxman was fined for the same offence because of an emblem on his pads.

Between the second and third Tests, South Africa played India A in a three-day match at Nagpur, the central Indian city that was to become an unfortunate landmark in Herschelle Gibbs's career. His first visit to the Vidarbha Cricket Association Stadium will be remembered for all the right reasons. Opening the batting with Cronjé, he took full advantage of a good pitch and fast outfield to make the first double century of his career, exactly 200 not out, and treated a modest attack with something approaching contempt. He had a chance in the second innings to become the second player in cricket history, after Arthur Fagg of Kent in 1938, to score two double centuries in a match. He reached 171 before he skied the part-time bowler WV Raman to long-off. He was only the second South African to score a double century and a century in a first-class match, joining Adam Bacher, shortly to become a Test player, who had punished the Griqualand West attack in similar fashion while playing for Transvaal three weekends previously.

'His batting at Nagpur was some of the finest I have seen,' said Woolmer. Had his reservations about Gibbs's irresponsibility been put to rest? 'Not really. He still had a rather casual attitude. Although he was obviously very pleased to play, there was no discernible difference in Herschelle Gibbs. He was brought into line on many occasions by people in the team and he gradually started to learn, although he would still play an indiscriminate shot.'

The South Africans, and Gibbs in particular, had every reason to be in good spirits as they set off for Kanpur for the Test series decider. Although Donald had returned home for treatment, leaving the bowling attack weakened, the batsmen were in splendid form. Kirsten, Hudson and Cullinan had made hundreds in Calcutta while Gibbs, McMillan and Klusener had enjoyed the ideal batting conditions in Nagpur. The team, it seemed, was on a roll which could take them to a rare series triumph in India, a feat not achieved by any of the 10 previous touring sides to the country. They were to learn, however, that nothing is simple in India.

It is not especially germane to what happened in Kanpur but the journey from Nagpur was a microcosm of the difficulties of travelling around India. When the itinerary was announced, there seemed some logic to having successive games in Nagpur and Kanpur. Although they are 600 kilometres apart, they are in the same central region of a vast country. The snag was that there were no direct flights. After the match against India A, the tourists had to take a night flight to Mumbai and stay overnight at a government-run hotel at Mumbai airport. The hotel has a thriving trade because many flights have Mumbai as a hub but few have same-day connections. The only similarity between the luxury Oberoi and Taj Group hotels and Mumbai's airport hotel is in the price charged to a captive clientele.

After a late-night check-in and an early-morning check-out, there was a flight to Lucknow, via Varanasi, followed by a two-hour road trip to Kanpur. Any potential joy at the eventual arrival was immediately dissipated by the realisation that this was the worst kind of polluted industrial city. The hotel, in a busy street, was besieged by eager fans kept at bay by security men and police though somehow no journey in a lift seemed to be possible without the company of at least one autograph hunter. Both teams stayed in the same hotel though on separate floors. Security guards kept the passages leading to players' rooms free of intruders.

Nor was a first sight of Green Park, the city's Test ground, any more encouraging, even though the name has a promising ring and it ranks as one of India's most important venues. It first staged a Test match in 1952 and only four other Indian grounds have staged more Tests. It turned out, though, to be a shabby place, with haphazard concrete stands and rusty fencing. The pitch horrified Bob Woolmer, who could not hide his distress as he inspected an under-prepared, cracked and grassless surface. It was in complete contrast to the excellent pitches on which South Africa had prospered in their two previous matches.

There were allegations of skullduggery, with a claim that Madan Lal, the Indian coach, had made a special trip to Kanpur after the Calcutta Test to ensure that conditions suited his team. Lal strenuously denied any suggestion of impropriety. Another surprise was the weather. A cold wind blew off the Himalayas.

A critical toss went India's way and South Africa could be well-pleased after bowling them out for 237, with Paul Adams picking up six for 55. Run-scoring was difficult and it took the great Tendulkar 173 balls to score 61. If South Africa were to win the series, it was essential to build a big total while the pitch was still in reasonable condition. This did not materialise. Gibbs laboured to 17 off 67 balls before being bowled when he tried to cut a delivery that spun back sharply from Ashish Kapoor, an off-spinner whose selection had been a surprise after the pummelling he had taken while playing for India A in Nagpur. Trailing by 60, South Africa's fate was sealed when Azharuddin played another remarkable innings. Batting at number six, he made a glorious, unbeaten 163, with the combination of nimble footwork, powerful wrists and a marvellous eye ensuring that he took full toll on any delivery not pitched in exactly the right place.

The third day closed with Azharuddin on 88 not out and India 330 ahead. That evening, there was a curious meeting at the Landmark hotel, which only became public knowledge when Hansie Cronjé gave his evidence to the King Commission in Cape Town in 2000. Azharuddin invited the South African captain to meet a man he described as a friend, Mukesh 'MK' Gupta, who was staying in the same hotel. According to Cronjé, Azharuddin left him alone with the new acquaintance in Gupta's room. After telling Cronjé that he was a jeweller who wanted to organise contacts with the De Beers organisation in South Africa, he got down to the nub of his real business in Kanpur, which was that he had a great deal of money riding on an Indian victory. In Cronjé's words, 'He wanted to be sure that India would win. He would like to know if I would be interested in making sure that no miracles took place when we went out to bat for the second time.' He urged the captain to speak to his players to ensure they would give their wickets away. Reasoning that this was 'money for jam', Cronjé accepted about $30 000 in cash.

It was an eventful evening. A few hundred metres away, in another Kanpur hotel, a remarkable triumph of ingenuity was reaching fruition. Gawie Swart, an engineer for the radio services of the South African Broadcasting Corporation, had organised a South African braai, so that the touring media could entertain the players. This was a nice idea but a lesser man than Swart would have been daunted by what to most mortals would have seemed insurmountable obstacles. The concept of a braai was unknown in India, while beef, an essential element of the traditional South African boerewors sausage, did not feature on Indian menus for the good reason that cattle are sacred. The more difficult the task, the more it seemed to serve as a challenge to a man legendary for his ability to arrange live broadcasting facilities from remote soccer fields throughout Africa. Swart was joined by his wife, Carin, and he prevailed upon her to pack a minimal amount of clothing and fill her suitcases with vacuum-packed beef, supplied by a generous South African butcher. Swart's enthusiasm rubbed off on the hotel staff, who enlisted a civil engineer to build a braai from a steel drum, according to Swart's specifications, and he was able to source bags of charcoal for the function, held on the flat roof of the building. Hansie Cronjé, now some $30 000 richer, smiled broadly for the cameras as he tucked into one of 48 substantial portions of boerewors brought to India by Carin Swart.

Hansie Cronjé, now some $30 000 richer, smiled broadly for the cameras as he tucked into one of 48 substantial portions of boerewors...

Cronjé was able to justify his acceptance of a bribe from Gupta on the grounds that the match was as good as lost anyway and that he would not have to involve any of his team-mates. This was a realistic assessment but on the night there was a surprising amount of optimism among the South African players, who felt a quick wrap-up of the Indian innings next morning would leave them with an achievable target.

There were no breakthroughs on the fourth morning, until Azharuddin and Dravid had added another 87 runs. De Villiers and Klusener bowled three overs each before the bowling was left to Adams, the off-spinner Pat Symcox and Cronjé himself. Whether Cronjé's bowling strategy was devised with half a mind on ensuring that there was no Indian collapse to jeopardise Mukesh Gupta's bet only the captain himself could know. In fairness, there was nothing in the pitch for the fast bowlers and the spinners were as likely as anyone to take wickets, as Adams had shown in the first innings.

A target of 461 was not remotely likely to be reached, especially after Kirsten, Gibbs and Cullinan were out by the time the total reached 29. Gibbs made five before being bowled by Prasad, pushing forward defensively and the ball beating the outside edge of his bat. India won by 280 runs and South Africa suffered their first series defeat since losing the one-off match in the West Indies five seasons before.

The team had been away for almost two months. The journey home was about to begin. First, though, there was an unwanted task. Tacked onto the end of the itinerary was a 'Mohinder Amarnath benefit game' at the Wankhede Stadium in Mumbai.

CHAPTER **EIGHT**

The meeting in Mumbai

The South Africans did not want to play in the Mohinder Amarnath benefit match on the last night of a demanding tour. It would have been bad enough if it was a not-too-serious benefit knock-about for a 1983 Indian World Cup hero they neither knew nor knew much about. It was unacceptable to them to learn that it had been classified as a full-scale international.

Hansie Cronjé was furious. A proud record would be at stake in an unnecessary game and injuries and illness had taken a heavy toll. For Cronjé personally, it meant the milestones of his 100th one-day international and his 50th as captain would take place at the Wankhede Stadium in Mumbai and not, as he had hoped, in Bloemfontein, when India made a return tour later in the season. It would be difficult to find 11 fit players to take the field and motivation was always likely to be a problem. To make matters worse, the match was staged on a Saturday night and the flight home was early on Sunday morning.

One of the minor mysteries for the author was why there appeared to be such confusion about the status of the game. Before flying out to report on the Test series, more than a month earlier, I had checked with the United Cricket Board and it had been confirmed that it would be an official international. It seemed to be rather late to be making a fuss on the eve of the match.

The meeting in Mumbai

Bob Woolmer explained, however, that the team management had been trying to get the decision reversed but were told that Indian strongman Jagmohan Dalmiya would not compromise. Sponsorship had been arranged and television rights had been sold. It would remain official. Better communication between officialdom and the team could have taken some of the heat out of the issue.

It was against this background of resentment, Cronjé said, that he received a telephone call from his new friend, MK Gupta. According to Cronjé's statement to the King Commission in June 2000, 'MK asked me to speak to the players about throwing the game, which I agreed to do. By that stage we were exhausted, it was the end of a long and arduous tour and a number of key players were suffering from injuries. MK asked me to convey an offer of $200 000 to the team to throw the match.'

In newspaper reports and at the King Commission, there were different accounts of the number of meetings held. It is also not clear when the approach was made to Cronjé.

Derek Crookes told the Commission that Cronjé had approached him after the Kanpur Test. Crookes said that before the first of two team meetings to discuss the issue, Cronjé had spoken to him on a flight to Mumbai on the day before the game. 'Hansie sat behind me on the plane and said he needed to speak to me and Andrew Hudson [Crookes's room-mate]. He said the team had been asked to throw a game.' Crookes said his reaction was one of disbelief. 'I asked him whether he was joking but he said I should think about it.' Crookes had the impression that Cronjé had already spoken to other players.

The flight to Mumbai was on 13 December, the day before the Amarnath match. Cronjé admitted to meeting Gupta and receiving money from him on the night of 10 December, after the third day's play of the Test in Kanpur. Yet he claimed that the approach about the Mumbai game was made by telephone.

In Mumbai, it seems there was an initial discussion between Cronjé and some senior players. David Richardson, then the team wicketkeeper and now general manager of cricket affairs at the International Cricket Council, told the King Commission that as he recalled it, the captain first spoke to some of the senior players, informing them he had received an offer to influence the result. Richardson could not remember the amount of money offered. 'I do remember thinking though, immediately, that if you divide it by 15, it's not

79

going to be that much money.' The players apparently did not tell Cronjé that the very idea of accepting such an offer was repugnant. Their reaction, said Richardson, was, 'We've got to have a team meeting.'

Brian McMillan was one of the players first spoken to by Cronjé. 'He asked us whether we would be interested in making some extra money. Our attitude was that if the money was right we should open it up to the whole team to discuss.'

According to Cronjé, a meeting of the full team was held the evening before the game, though some accounts have this crucial event in South African cricket history taking place the next morning. Cronjé said, 'I conveyed the offer to the team, which rejected it. I recall, in particular, that Andrew Hudson, Daryll Cullinan and Derek Crookes spoke out strongly against it. It was agreed that the decision had to be unanimous or not at all.'

What exactly was the offer? According to Gibbs, it was not just a simple matter of losing the match and collecting the money. The deal that Cronjé proposed was a detailed one, virtually a script for the match. 'He told us, these were the conditions, that after this over we would have to lose this amount of wickets and at that over we would have to have a certain amount of runs. Our batting innings was all planned. I didn't actually look at it myself but I knew that if we batted second it could easily be done because we knew the wicket would deteriorate.'

Gary Kirsten confirmed Gibbs's version. 'We had to fulfil different stipulations throughout the match. Someone had to get out in the first eight overs, then someone had to score so many runs and so on.' Unlike Gibbs, he did not think it would be easy to follow orders. 'It was very complicated and would have been extremely difficult to execute. I've found with batting it's easy to get out when you're not trying to get out but extremely difficult when you are trying to get out without making it too obvious.'

McMillan recalls what he describes as 'parameters' that were spelt out by the captain. 'There had to be x amount of runs, x amount of wickets falling. If we had gone with it, we could have done that.'

Crookes said he was part of a meeting which might not have included all the players. Cronjé again told those present to 'think about it'. At another meeting on the morning of the match, Cronjé said, 'We are either all in or all out.' Crookes said he and Hudson were the first to stand up against the offer, 'because it was immoral, the wrong thing to do and it could jeopardise our futures'. They were supported by Cullinan and Richardson.

In his testimony, Gibbs said there was one meeting but was not sure when it was, and thought the amount offered was $250 000. He stayed quiet. 'Being only my second tour I thought I'd leave it up to the senior players to have a discussion, and if we were individually asked our opinions, I can't remember what my opinion was or if I did give an opinion, but I was happy to go along with the general consensus.'

Two years later, Gibbs remembers it this way: 'Two guys said no. Hansie went around the room and asked everyone's opinion.' As a new player, Gibbs said he would go along with 'whatever the guys decided, anything goes'. A strong view in the team appeared to be, 'It's good money, everything is against us anyway, let's take it.' He was disappointed when Hudson and Crookes opposed the move. 'I looked at the two guys and thought, "Oh shit, everyone else is saying yes, why are you saying no?"'

Richardson said he offered a summary after listening to his team-mates, 'almost taking the responsibility of giving advice as to what I thought the team should do, that I was an attorney and if I, for instance, got caught or it came out, it would jeopardise my practice, and it was summarised as something that we just mustn't get involved in, no matter how much or how tempting the offer might be'.

The meeting, of players only, with no members of the management team present, lasted about 40 minutes, according to Gibbs.

Gary Kirsten is relieved that the team turned down the offer. 'It was amazing. We were a squeaky clean team at the time in terms of the things that had come out and been publicised about what was going on in the game. What it taught me was how easily someone could get hooked into something without knowing the consequences and then they would be hooked into it so deeply. That's exactly what happened to Hansie. I'm just so glad there was a team decision not to get involved. It wasn't that everyone agreed straight away. Some guys were buying into it, thinking, "It's the end of a long tour, a waste-of-time game, let's make some extra cash on the side." We were never going to win the game anyway, with all the injuries and everything. It was tempting but it was lovely to be part of a team decision where we said, "Hold on, this is crazy."'

Cronjé warned the players to keep the meeting a secret. If they accepted the promised money they should tell no-one outside the team, including their wives. This dismayed Crookes, who was already opposed to accepting the offer on moral grounds. 'I had just got married and wasn't prepared to hide anything from my wife,' he said.

Cullinan made the surprising claim in his evidence that he thought Cronjé's conveying of an offer to the team to lose in Mumbai was a 'stroke of genius', an opinion which he had not expressed in his written statement. 'It was his way of testing the team. We left the meeting better for it, united that we were against match-fixing.'

It was not yet the end of the matter. There was another meeting on the day of the game, said Cronjé, 'at which it was confirmed that the offer was rejected'.

Richardson felt the fact that the meeting excluded the team management and had not been reported to them, arose from an 'us and them' situation with the manager, Robbie Muzzell, seen by the players as 'a bit of a board member . . . he was regarded as them rather than us'. Richardson said the UCB needed to appoint to management positions men who had the respect and trust of the players and who had 'their ears to the ground'.

Bob Woolmer, the coach, heard there was going to be a team meeting on the morning of the match. 'I asked Hansie if he wanted me there and he said, "No, we're going to discuss a variety of issues." Apparently someone said at the meeting, "If we're going to take this money, the coach needs to be in on it as well." I then got a phone call in my room from Hansie. I still didn't know what the meeting was about. I thought maybe they wanted to get rid of me as coach.'

Like several of the team, Woolmer was feeling ill. 'I went down in pyjamas and track suit top. It was about 11am. I was told about it. From what I can remember, I said, "Listen guys, it's very tempting and with the condition of the team as it is we're probably going to lose this game anyway. People are injured, we don't want to play and we're not in the right frame of mind. It's money for old rope. But what you don't want to do is get involved in this. If I were you I'd stay really clear." Hudson, Crookes and company were absolutely anti anyway. I was in there for about 20 minutes and they said no. I walked out.'

At lunch-time Woolmer sat with Cronjé at the hotel having a sandwich. 'I said, "It is unbelievable that this is happening in cricket." He said, "Wouldn't it be nice if we had two million rand? We could buy a house at Fancourt and we could all go down and play golf and get the team together." We were joking, it was rather like saying, "If I win the lottery, this is what I'm going to do."'

Pat Symcox added a fascinating detail when he told the King Commission that after the meeting that rejected the offer, which he said happened the previous evening, he was among a small group of senior players who stayed in the room. 'We laughed and joked about it and then someone said, "Why don't we try and see if we can get any more out of them? Let's see how far they'll go." Which at the time wasn't a bad thing, you know? So Hansie picked up the phone, phoned, put down the phone and said, "We've got another $100 000." Phew, just like that. And then suddenly there are only four of you. You know, the cut's a big difference then, all of a sudden. Anyway, we laughed, and then eventually it was Hansie that actually said, "Guys, I'm not comfortable – if the whole team aren't involved and other guys aren't here, there's no ways we can actually get involved in this." And we left it at that. Finished a beer and walked out.'

Cronjé confirmed that he made the call referred to by Symcox but said that Gupta refused to increase his offer by $100 000, although he was prepared to go up by $50 000 to $250 000.

Thus was the South African team first presented with a proposal to sell themselves to a corrupt gambler. In the end the players took the moral decision but it was clearly a close-run thing.

Hansie Cronjé's powerful grip on the team had been strengthened. He was the man calling the shots and he had shown that if he so decreed, decisions could be made without the involvement of management or officialdom. He was the boss. He also knew that several of his players could be tempted. They already shared a guilty secret.

The detail about the 'script' for the game is significant. In his statement to the King Commission in June 2000, which varied considerably from his initial confession, Cronjé continued to claim he had never 'thrown or fixed a match'. This may be so but it is known that the bets placed on cricket are many and varied, ranging from who will bat first, who will open the batting or bowling, to what the score will be and how many wickets will have fallen by a certain number of overs.

Several of these aspects are capable of manipulation by a captain, without necessarily jeopardising the outcome or involving other players.

Given the build-up to the game, South Africa were hardly likely to mount a serious challenge. Richardson and Klusener could not play because of illness and De Villiers went onto the field despite having a high temperature. It was a woefully unbalanced team. De Villiers was able to labour through five overs and the bulk of the bowling was done by four spinners, Symcox, Bojé, Crookes and Adams. Kirsten kept wicket. Paddy Upton, the team's fitness specialist and a former first-class cricketer, was the emergency fielder. It was a miserable night all round for the South Africans.

With a pitch similar in character to that on which they had lost the Titan Cup final, South Africa's only slight chance was to win the toss and bat first before the surface deteriorated. Tendulkar won the toss, however, and though he was dropped early on by Gibbs and stand-in wicketkeeper Kirsten, he went on to make a century. The match was interrupted by crowd trouble after Azharuddin was given out, and Cronjé led his team off the field, threatening not to return. When the match resumed, South Africa were trounced by 74 runs. Gibbs made 31.

Two years later, Cronjé was interviewed by the *Sunday Times* on the subject of match-fixing. It was at the time that the Australian players, Mark Waugh and Shane Warne, had been exposed for taking money from a bookmaker several years earlier and Judge Malik Qayyum's report into cricket match-fixing in Pakistan was said to be imminent.

Had the South African players been approached by any shady characters? Under the heading, 'Proud SA cricketers hit match-fixers for six,' published on 20 December 1998, Cronjé told how the South African team had 'laughed off' an offer to 'make a lot of money'. The revelations in 2000 made it obvious that neither the offer nor the way it was conveyed was a joke.

In the article, Cronjé told how he had received a telephone call in his hotel room before the Amarnath benefit match. Cronjé said he told the caller he was not interested. 'To be honest, I'm not sure whether he was a bookmaker or just a member of the public. We didn't get to the point of discussing any details.' He said he raised the issue at a team meeting. 'We basically laughed it off but we did agree as a team that we would never be open to any such offers. One of the things that makes me proud to play for South Africa is the team spirit and the knowledge that every member of the side will always try his best to win for his country.'

Although the story was displayed prominently, it was not followed up by any officials, or by other journalists. It was just another story. No-one believed that South African players would give even a fleeting thought to allowing themselves to be corrupted. At the very least, the UCB should have demanded to know why the phone call to their captain had not been reported immediately to the team management and through them to the board and to the International Cricket Council.

Amarnath reputedly made $75 000 from his benefit match. Two years later, Cronjé said the former player had yet to thank the South African team for their part in easing his retirement years. Amarnath, it seems, was the only real winner on a sad occasion for cricket.

For an impressionable Herschelle Gibbs, a seed had been sown. His revered captain thought there was nothing wrong with accepting 'easy' money. The same captain would corrupt his young player three years later.

CHAPTER **NINE**

Back to earth

After a fair amount of success in India, Herschelle Gibbs had reason to look forward to advancing his career when the international programme continued at home in South Africa. He was to learn quickly that nothing could be taken for granted at the top level in cricket.

Twelve days after their unsatisfactory outing in Mumbai, South Africa and India were back in action against each other in the first Test of a return series on a 'green mamba' of a fast bowler's pitch at Kingsmead in Durban. It was always likely to be an unequal struggle. If the South Africans had experienced difficulty in coping with conditions in Ahmedabad and Kanpur, the Indians were out of their depth on a fast, grassy surface. In addition, their only warm-up game had been in Port Elizabeth, where a high-scoring draw on a benign pitch offered no realistic simulation of what they would face in the Test.

Adam Bacher won his first Test cap and batted at three, while Gibbs was given the number six slot in a team that contained an extra batsman and no spin bowler. Jonty Rhodes was fit again but was not picked. Conditions were seam-friendly and South Africa struggled to 235 all out, with Andrew Hudson making a splendid 80 on his home ground. Gibbs was out for nought, caught behind when he flashed at a ball from David Johnson. He made 25 in the second innings before being given out lbw to a ball from Srinath that cut back. But with Allan Donald back for South Africa, India were bowled out for 100 and 66, the second innings total being the lowest made by any side against South Africa.

Bacher, who had made a promising debut, scoring 25 and 55, was retained for the second Test at Newlands. With Paul Adams recalled to add a spinning option to the side, there was no room for Gibbs, who was named 12th man, and his dream of playing for his country on his home ground had to be put on hold. South Africa won a wonderfully entertaining match, which included centuries by Gary Kirsten, Brian McMillan and Lance Klusener for South Africa and Sachin Tendulkar and Mohammad Azharuddin for India. The same team did duty in the drawn third Test, while Gibbs returned to the Western Province team, making 49 against Griqualand West.

Gibbs was not picked for a triangular one-day series against India and Zimbabwe. His quest to regain his place was not helped when he was caught behind second ball for nought off Salil Ankola when he played for South Africa A against the Indians in Pietermaritzburg. A long international season was not over, however, because the mighty Australians were about to arrive in South Africa. A second innings century for Western Province against Transvaal at the Wanderers came as the triangular series was reaching its final phase, and a week before he was to come up against the Australians.

If luck had not exactly been going his way since the false dawn of Calcutta, Gibbs was fortunate that the opening first-class fixture of the Australian tour was a three-day match against Western Province at Newlands. Somewhat bizarrely, the hours of play were pushed back to suit television, with play starting at 11.30am and due to finish at 7pm. Western Province had an all-seam attack and with no penalties for slow over-rates, cricket went on until almost 8pm on the first day as the Australians put in some solid batting practice.

John Commins, the Western Province captain, declared with his side 178 runs behind in a successful attempt to set up a good finish. Australian captain Mark Taylor reciprocated and set a target of 354 in 81 overs. Gibbs, out for 28 in the first innings, was in his element. He hit a thrilling 80 off 92 balls as Western Province fell 32 runs short in an exciting match. The Australian attack lacked the big guns of Glenn McGrath and Shane Warne but Gibbs had given the selectors a timely reminder that he was a batsman of quality.

Rhodes was picked ahead of Gibbs for the first Test at the Wanderers, in which South Africa suffered a humiliating innings defeat, set up by a record fifth-wicket stand of 385 between Steve Waugh and Greg Blewett. He was back in the side in place of Rhodes for the second Test in Port Elizabeth, however, after hitting a magnificent 163 not out off 226 balls against Natal. In that match he had gone from 47 to 163 before lunch on the second day and shared a third-wicket stand of 257 with Jacques Kallis, who had shown his ability to play at Test level with a determined top-score 39 in the second-innings rout at the Wanderers.

The Port Elizabeth pitch was nothing like the one the Indians had played on less than three months previously. It was under-prepared and grassy. The breeze was blowing from the east, off the sea, which locals believe helps seam and swing bowling because it carries enough moisture to keep the pitch fresh. Australia sent South Africa in and barely an hour later Gibbs was going out to bat with the side in dire straits at 22 for four. Glenn McGrath and Jason Gillespie had two wickets each, and Gillespie had not conceded a run in six overs.

Daryll Cullinan and Gibbs set about rebuilding the innings, making 34 and 31 respectively. Even so, South Africa were 95 for six when Gibbs, on the back foot, played down the wrong line and was bowled by Gillespie. Some lower order resistance by McMillan and Richardson enabled South Africa to reach 209. Astonishingly, Australia crashed to 108 all out in reply. Shaun Pollock, in a splendid opening spell, dismissed both Australian openers, Mark Taylor and Matthew Elliott, but then was ruled out of bowling for the rest of the match because of a hamstring injury. The rest of the bowlers proved equal to the challenge, however, as Australia suffered a rare collapse.

When Gary Kirsten and Adam Bacher took South Africa to 83 for no wicket at the close on the third day, it seemed that once again South Africa's resilience had won the day. Crushed in the first Test, surely they would be triumphant in the second. They were 184 runs ahead in a low-scoring match with all their second innings wickets standing.

Not for the first time, the obituaries for Australia proved premature. They came out for a fateful Sunday morning focused and determined. Only four runs were scored in 5,3 overs before Kirsten was bowled by a ball from Gillespie that cut back and kept low. The runs were eked out painfully slowly. The pressure told on Bacher, who could contain himself no longer and, with his score on 49, called Kallis for a risky single that would have raised his half-century. Blewett made a direct hit from midwicket and Kallis was gone. Three balls later, Bacher compounded his error by hooking Gillespie to fine leg where McGrath held the catch. He was still on 49. When Cullinan also fell to Gillespie, Gibbs joined Cronjé but after a half-hour struggle he edged a drive against McGrath to second slip after scoring seven. South Africa crumbled to 168 all out, having added just 81 after the opening stand. Australia needed 270 to win, the largest total of the match, but Cronjé was right to be 'very disappointed' that the target had not been stretched to more than 350.

Bob Woolmer, the coach, was angry at the way the South African batsmen squandered a potential winning position. To him, Gibbs was one of the culprits. 'He played a loose drive and when I spoke to him about it afterwards his attitude was, "It was a half-volley so I went for it." It was a wide half-volley and it was one of those situations where you just have to bail out of a shot like that. We had just lost a few wickets and he needed to understand that situation. Hansie was in there holding the ship together and in Test matches you have to sell your wicket very dearly. Another 50 runs and we would probably have won.'

> Bob Woolmer, the coach, was angry at the way the South African batsmen squandered a potential winning position.

With South Africa defending fewer runs than they would have liked, the loss of Pollock was felt in an innings in which Donald bowled entirely without luck and could not take a wicket. Mark Waugh made one of the most significant centuries of his career and Australia won by two wickets, Ian Healy ending an afternoon of tension by hooking Hansie Cronjé for six.

At a team meeting after the second innings collapse, the six specialist batsmen stayed on for a lecture from Woolmer. The gist of his comments was the need to concentrate, to be patient and to eliminate risks, before he added, 'For heaven's sake, don't worry about your places in the side.' For Gibbs, the words were to prove ironic.

The series was lost. Once again Gibbs was one of the victims of the team's failure. He was in the squad for the final Test at Centurion but ended up 12th man as a reorganisation of the batting order saw Brian McMillan batting at number three with Jacques Kallis moved to number five, ahead of Cronjé. Lance Klusener returned to the side and so did Brett Schultz, the fiery left-arm fast bowler who Gibbs had been happy to avoid at his first Nuffield Week, but whose career had been blighted by injury. South Africa gained a consolation victory in the match.

Gibbs had now played in four Tests, but only one of them on a pitch which suited batsmen.

He was included in the squad for a seven-match limited overs series and played in six of the games, opening the batting on each occasion. He got off to some reasonable starts but his highest score was 33. In his first full international match at Newlands he made a streaky 28 off 33 balls. Twice he edged Paul Reiffel for four and although he hooked the same bowler for six, the shot was mistimed and flew high but just beyond the boundary. A sumptuous cover drive for four off Adam Dale was followed by a loose drive against an in-swinger from Gillespie and he was bowled.

It had been an eventful season but he had not done enough to make himself a fixture in the national side. After four Tests and nine one-day internationals he had yet to score more than 35. There was an outcry in the Cape Town newspapers at the end of the season when the selectors announced that he was not included in South Africa's team to tour Pakistan at the start of the 1997/98 season. In truth, he had not given the panel irrefutable evidence that he belonged at the highest level. He was naturally disappointed, though, and told the *Cape Argus*, 'It once again highlights the uncertainty all the players in the national team feel. No-one knows whether he will be in for the next match or the next tour. A player is never made to feel comfortable. In my own case, I did not know where I stood from match to match ... no-one communicates. If you get dropped, you read it in the newspapers or see it on television. There are no reasons given.' As an example, he said he had been told he would open the batting in the first five one-day matches, but after just one game he was left out. Although he did then open in the next five games, an element of trust and security had been destroyed.

Looking back, he stands by those comments but admits he had not done enough to take the decision out of the selectors' hands.

A long season reached an unnecessarily drawn-out conclusion when the Standard Bank final between Natal and Western Province was decided over three legs. Western Province won the first game in Cape Town but Natal won twice in Durban to take the title, with Gibbs ending his season on an undistinguished note with scores of 30, 40 and six.

While the national team were taking on Pakistan at the start of the 1997/98 season, Gibbs was in Kimberley with Western Province playing in the Standard Bank League. He scored just six runs, and the road ahead seemed ever steeper, ever longer. His summer burst into life two weeks later, though, when he made an impressive 110 against Free State in the day-night competition. He needed to make up some lost ground, too. Over in Pakistan, South Africa had already played two drawn Test matches and were about to go into the series decider in Faisalabad.

Two low-scoring games were followed by 94 against North West at Newlands, a spectacular innings in which Gibbs displayed his penchant for showmanship. North West had been bowled out for 145 and it would have been easy enough to take the runs as they came and ease to victory. Instead, Gibbs slammed his runs off 79 balls. With four needed to win and six short of his century, he was caught in the deep.

By then, South Africa were one match away from winning a quadrangular jubilee limited overs tournament in Pakistan to add to a remarkable Test series triumph. Gibbs was firing but so were the men in possession. When the team for Pakistan had been announced all those months ago, selection convenor Peter Pollock left open the possibility that there might be changes for the one-day games at the end of the tour. No call came to the Gibbs household.

The call that did come, though, was one that is the dream of so many young cricketers. The next tour was to Australia. His performances for Western Province had not gone unnoticed and Herschelle Gibbs was on his way to play against the best cricketers in the world.

He might have been in the squad but it was still going to be a struggle to win a place in the side for the Tests and the one-day internationals. Gibbs played in the pipe-opener against a Board Chairman's XI in the pleasantly rural setting of Lilac Hill, on the banks of the Swan river outside Perth. Batting at number six, he watched Daryll Cullinan lead a strong top-order performance. Quick runs were needed when he went to the crease with overs running out. He made just six. He didn't play in the first-class match against Western Australia, nor did he turn out against the Prime Minister's XI in Canberra. Nor, hardly surprisingly, was he in the side for the first two one-day internationals in the triangular series against Australia and New Zealand. He watched as Jacques Kallis was tried, unsuccessfully, as an opening batting partner for Gary Kirsten.

Two poor starts by the team, a loss against New Zealand and an injury to Cullinan brought Gibbs back into the side as an opener against Australia in front of 55 673 spectators at the Melbourne Cricket Ground. It seemed to be his fate, however, to be picked to play on pitches which did him no favours.

It had rained earlier in the day and conditions were awkward on a damp, bouncy surface. Kirsten was out for nought and Gibbs struggled to 15 off 33 balls before being run out, by a matter of centimetres, by a direct hit from Ian Harvey at mid-off. South Africa managed only 170 for eight in 50 overs but it was enough for a 45-run win. Yet another tricky surface, slow with uneven bounce, awaited the South Africans against New Zealand at Hobart, where Gibbs again lasted longer than Kirsten but could make only 12 before hitting a catch to mid-off. Once again South Africa won a low-scoring match, this time by a single run. Remarkably, South Africa had won three of their first four matches in the series but no batsman had made a half-century. 'We're still a bit in the sub-continent,' said Cronjé, referring to the vastly different conditions in which the runs had been piled up in Pakistan.

With the one-day series halfway through the round robin phase, it was back to first-class cricket, with two matches before the first Test. Gibbs didn't play in the first of these, against Tasmania in Devonport, but batted handsomely against Australia A in Brisbane, reaching 54 with a glorious six over extra cover off the unpredictable, slingy left-arm wrist spin of Michael Bevan. Doing the sensible thing and taking stock instead of going for another big hit, he played defensively at the next ball and edged it to slip. Bevan claimed his wicket for 22 in the second innings as the match meandered towards a draw.

There are few events in cricket quite as stirring as Boxing Day in Melbourne, traditionally the first day of a Test match, attended by vast numbers of the citizens of a sports-loving city. The players' wives, girlfriends and children had arrived, but there was little joy for Gibbs as he joined in the festive lunch which followed the team practice on Christmas morning. There was no place for him in the team and he, like 73 812 paying customers, watched from the sidelines as South Africa fought it out on the first day. The match ended in a draw, with Jacques Kallis laying definitive claim to the number three batting position with an heroic century on the last day. Kallis defied relentless pressure, particularly from home-town favourite Shane Warne, whose theatrical appeals ignited the fervour of the fans but did not sway the umpires.

One South African who did not succeed in Melbourne was Daryll Cullinan. He had failed on his previous tour in 1993/94 and became the subject of taunts from Warne, who claimed Cullinan was his 'bunny'. Cullinan was run out for five in the first innings but not before he had been jeered by the crowd and beaten by a sharply-turning leg-break from Warne, who did not hold back in expressing his low opinion about Cullinan's ability. In the second innings, Cullinan seemed mesmerised, going back in his crease when he should have gone forward, to be bowled by his nemesis for nought. The selectors decided Cullinan had had enough. He was left out of the side for the second Test in Sydney, which started two days later. Gibbs was back, batting at number five.

Sydney had been the scene of one of South Africa's greatest triumphs, the famous match in 1993/94 when Fanie de Villiers and Allan Donald bowled out Australia for 111 in the final innings to snatch an improbable five-run win. Warne had taken 11 wickets in that match and the pitch was again expected to favour him. The key was to win the toss and bat first while conditions were at their most favourable. Cronjé called correctly but the South African batsmen, who had struggled throughout the tour, were unable to impose themselves. They occupied the crease fairly successfully but scored too slowly as they eked out 287 in 124,1 overs.

For Gibbs, though, there was a crucial breakthrough as he made his first international half-century. By the standards of a drab day his was a fine innings that included some handsome strokes, although he admits, 'I never really felt settled. I was still very edgy and nervous.' Nevertheless, he outscored Cronjé, making 54 in a fourth-wicket stand of 97, the best of the innings, before he fell to Bevan for the third time in as many innings. Gibbs went to drive the left-armer but was well caught off an inside edge by the wicketkeeper, Ian Healy. 'I was in two minds. I wanted to hit over the in-field and then I pulled out of the shot. I should have gone through with it. By the time I realised it was his other one [the ball which spun in to the right-hander], it was too late,' he said.

It was Steve Waugh's 100th Test but it was twin brother Mark who made 100 runs. Steve, though, was not far behind, battling his way to 85 as Australia gained a crucial lead of 134. South Africa started their second innings midway through the fourth morning. Warne was always likely to be the main threat but McGrath and Reiffel dismissed South Africa's openers, Kirsten and Bacher, within the first five overs. Warne was on after 11 overs and in his second over had Cronjé caught at short leg. The floodlights were already on when Gibbs came out with Kallis after lunch but after being virtually strokeless for just over half an hour he fell to an outstanding reflex catch by Blewett at short leg off Warne.

It was a disastrous day for South Africa, 'carnage', according to Gibbs, with only Kallis and Symcox showing any real resistance. Rain stopped play for more than three hours and there was an eerie atmosphere when play resumed at 6.20pm, with only 1 000 diehard fans on hand to see Warne take his 300th Test wicket with a venomous delivery which bowled Kallis for 45. Australia claimed the extra half hour and rain was falling when, at 7.09pm, Allan Donald was caught behind off Reiffel with what surely would have been the last delivery before the umpires would have been obliged to call off play. Australia had won by an innings and 21 runs. 'We knew the pitch was going to turn and that it would help Warney,' says Gibbs, 'and we went into our shell too much.'

A return to the one-day series did not bring any joy to Gibbs, who failed twice in a double-header against New Zealand and Australia, scoring two in both games, batting in the middle order because Klusener had become yet another opening partner for Kirsten. How he would have loved to have played in these matches with the freedom he displayed when the tourists made a detour to Bowral, the New South Wales country town where Don Bradman grew up. The opposition were a Bradman XI, captained by Test skipper Mark Taylor, who was not in the Australian one-day squad.

Gibbs opened the batting and slammed 131 off 127 balls against some reasonable bowling, although it was hardly a high-pressure innings. Interviewed by journalists afterwards, Gibbs confessed he didn't know much about Bradman and hadn't visited the museum at the Bradman Oval dedicated to the man regarded as the best batsman of all time. 'It didn't really mean anything, it was just a game to me,' he said with typical honesty. Perhaps he sensed that wasn't quite what Australian journalists, expecting the obligatory homage to the Don, were seeking. 'It would be a great thing to meet him,' he added gallantly.

'Obviously you hear a lot about Bradman when you go to Australia,' he says. 'My hero was Peter Kirsten. I always spoke so highly of him. It was Peter this, Peter that. I didn't know much about Bradman, his stats or anything like that. When they asked questions about Bradman, I didn't know what to answer. Now I know that he scored two triple centuries in Tests and was the best batsman of all time. What was great for me then was to get a hundred and I was also pleased for Makhaya [Ntini] because he got Mark Taylor out.'

A return to the more serious business of the triangular series yielded just eight runs against New Zealand at Perth. With South Africa assured of playing in the final, Ntini and Mark Boucher made their one-day international debuts. 'Makhaya bowled really quickly,' remembers Gibbs. Ntini took two wickets, those of Stephen Fleming and Adam Parore, both through catches behind the wicket by Boucher, his provincial team-mate. Gibbs shone in the field, holding three catches and pulling off a run-out, but he wasn't in the side for the final round robin game against Australia, nor did he play in the three matches that made up the final. South Africa won the first leg of the final in Melbourne, their fifth successive win over the host nation, but lost the next two games as Sydney again proved a hoodoo ground.

Gibbs confessed he didn't know much about Bradman and hadn't visited the museum at the Bradman Oval dedicated to the man regarded as the best batsman of all time.

South Africa had to win the final Test at the Adelaide Oval to square the series. Gibbs retained his Test place and on a perfect pitch was part of the solid team batting performance the tourists had spent most of the tour seeking. He again did the hard work, setting himself up for a big score as he reached 37 and shared a stand of 109 with Cronjé. Mark Taylor had been casting about with some desperation for someone to break the partnership and it was Greg Blewett, bowling relatively innocuous seamers, who persuaded Gibbs to drive in the penultimate over of the first day, edging a ball well wide of off stump to wicketkeeper Healy. South Africa went on to score 517, with Brian McMillan's unbeaten 87 the highest score.

The third day was baking hot, with temperatures reaching 39 degrees Celsius, but Shaun Pollock bowled magnificently, taking seven for 87 as South Africa took a lead of 167, despite the absence of Allan Donald through a buttock muscle injury. In the second innings, Gary Kirsten made an unbeaten century, while Gibbs was the fourth of four men out cheaply in a chase for quick runs before a declaration, stumped for two off the leg-spinner, Stuart MacGill, playing in his first Test.

Australia lost two wickets before the close of play on the fourth day but Mark Waugh, whose century had clinched the previous season's series, saved the series at home with his fourth Test century against South Africa. He was lucky, though, being dropped four times, with Adam Bacher failing three times to hold on at short leg. The most crucial let-off of all, though, came six overs into the last 15 of the match, when Waugh was hit above the left elbow by Pollock. He stumbled away and shook his arm, his bat hitting the stumps. There was an impassioned appeal by the South Africans and the decision was referred to Steve Davis, the television umpire, who, together with anxious television viewers on both sides of the Indian Ocean, viewed the incident several times before ruling that Waugh was not out.

According to Law 35, a batsman is out if his wicket is broken 'as a result of any action taken by him in preparing to receive or in receiving a delivery or in setting off for his first run immediately after playing, or playing at the ball'. Thus, Waugh could only have been out if the shaking of his arm was a direct consequence of receiving the ball. It was a debatable point. Cronjé was bitterly disappointed and jabbed a hole in the door of the umpires' room as he left the field carrying one of the match stumps. 'He just lashed into it,' says Gibbs of the incident, which happened out of the public eye, with the umpires' room and the visitors' dressing room located in the same corridor in the members' pavilion. In an interview after the tour, Cronjé expressed contrition but said he had given the door a relatively light tap. 'He just about demolished the door,' is what Gibbs remembers.

To cap an unhappy end to the tour, Dave Richardson, the team's 38-year-old wicketkeeper, who had played in 42 of the country's 43 Tests since 1992, announced his immediate retirement. He had been struggling with a painful hip condition and the gruelling trip around Australia had made him realise he no longer relished the challenge of staying fit enough to take his place behind the stumps.

Feeling they were the victim of a 'home-town decision', some of the players made the most of one last, long night in Adelaide before returning home. The 'four rats', Gibbs, Boucher, Ntini and Paul Adams were put in charge of arranging a final party. The quartet had gained the collective nickname because of their nocturnal activities. With only Gibbs playing regularly, the four youngsters made the most of the opportunities for mischief off the field. 'That was probably my best tour as far as enjoyment is concerned,' he says. The final party was proclaimed a success by one of its organisers. 'It went on until about five minutes before we had to take the bus to the airport the next afternoon.'

A highlight in a match of triumph and disaster for Herschelle. He lifts his bat after reaching his century in the 1999 World Cup match against Australia at Headingley. Putting down a catch off Steve Waugh in the same match was one of the low points of his career.

Clive Mason/Getty Images/Touchline Photo

Above: In full flight. Herschelle in his first match for South Africa at his beloved Newlands, a one-day international against Australia in 1996/97. He goes on the drive against Paul Reiffel.
Anne Laing

Left: Teammates for South Africa, Paul Adams and Herschelle Gibbs in their national team blazers before the second Test against Australia in Port Elizabeth in 1996/97.
Anne Laing

Above: Celebration time after victory against the West Indies in 1998/99 as Herschelle takes a drenching from, among others, Gary Kirsten, Allan Donald and Hansie Cronjé, while Shaun Pollock moves to a drier spot.
Picture courtesy Gibbs family

Right: Protecting the shaved head. Mark Boucher fools around as the players get ready for a match during the World Cup in England in 1999.
Rian Botes

Above: Before the big game. Jonty Rhodes and Herschelle in pensive mood as they wait for their turn to bat in the nets in preparation for the World Cup semi-final against Australia at Edgbaston in 1999.
Duif du Toit/Touchline Photo

Right: Shane Warne tries to wage psychological warfare during Herschelle's World Cup century at Headingley in 1999. In the next match, the semi-final at Edgbaston, Warne produced what he described as one of the best balls of his career to bowl Herschelle at a crucial stage of the game.
Clive Mason/Getty Images/Touchline Photo

Left: Time for the truth. Herschelle in serious mood before giving his sensational evidence to the King Commission in 2000 about Hansie Cronjé's approach to him before a match in Nagpur.

Touchline Photo

Below: Former South African captain, Hansie Cronjé, here in conversation with Herschelle during a one-day international against the West Indies in Port Elizabeth in 1998/99, had a powerful influence over the players under his control.

Touchline Photo

Above: Practice, Caribbean style. Herschelle enjoys the sun at a net practice in Kingston, Jamaica, before the one-day series in the West Indies.
Rian Botes

Right: Partners. Gary Kirsten and Herschelle stay in character in a dressing room celebration picture after South Africa beat the West Indies in Port-of-Spain, Trinidad. As happens when they open the batting together, Gary is sound and sensible, Herschelle is more flamboyant.
Rian Botes

Above: The flying fielder. Herschelle is airborne as he makes a diving stop during the second Test against Sri Lanka at Centurion during the 2002/03 season.
Duif du Toit/Touchline Photo

Below: Congratulations and commiserations from the captain. With Shaun Pollock after making a dazzling 97 not out against Bangladesh in Benoni in 2002/03. A leg-side wide which went to the boundary robbed him of a fourth consecutive one-day international century.
Anne Laing

Another tough day on tour. Herschelle relaxes next to the swimming pool at the South African team's hotel in Kingston, Jamaica. Being in the West Indies, he reckons, is about as enjoyable as touring can get.

Rian Botes

There is seldom time to catch breath in modern international cricket. Two days after the long flight home from Australia, Gibbs was at Newlands, playing for Western Province against Eastern Province. In what was becoming a pattern, the step down from the pressures of international cricket coincided with a flowering of his gifts as Gibbs batted for six hours in the second innings to make 152. HD Ackerman, his old provincial Under 13 captain, was in prolific form and scored his third century in successive games. Together the long-time team-mates put on 184 for the third wicket.

The selectors, it seemed, were no longer impressed by big Gibbs centuries in provincial games. He was not picked for the first Test against Pakistan at the Wanderers, despite Hansie Cronjé having to end a sequence of 41 consecutive Test appearances in order to have knee surgery. Gary Kirsten captained South Africa for the first and only time. There was a late call for Gibbs, however, when McMillan was ruled out because of a strained ligament in his left foot.

The match was anything but memorable for Gibbs. He padded up to what umpire Cyril Mitchley saw as a straight ball from leg-spinner Mushtaq Ahmed and was lbw for four. 'It was actually a leg-break. You could see it on the replay. It would have missed off-stump,' reckons Gibbs. The rain-hit match will be remembered primarily for Pat Symcox's bludgeoned Test century, batting at number 10, and the delay of the start of the match by a day because of the alleged mugging of two Pakistan players, Saqlain Mushtaq and Mohammad Akram. It was initially reported that the two had been assaulted and robbed outside their luxury hotel in Sandton, but police and hotel security were not convinced, which cast serious doubt on the players' version of events. Lurid stories were whispered of an altercation at a house of ill repute. 'We heard they had been to this place, a strip joint or whatever. The guys apparently didn't want to pay and the bouncers laid into them.' The postponement, says Gibbs, confirmed a feeling among South African players that their board 'were sometimes too friendly to the touring teams'.

Yet again, Herschelle Gibbs was not on the list when the team for the next Test in Durban was announced. Instead, Ackerman won his first Test cap. The season's remaining four Tests, two each against Pakistan and two against Sri Lanka, went by without a game for Gibbs. He was in the squad for the triangular one-day series against the same two countries but played in only three matches, with a highest score of 33 in South Africa's only defeat of the series, against Sri Lanka in Port Elizabeth.

A five-Test tour of England in 1998 lay ahead but there was no place for Herschelle Gibbs. He was still only 24 but his international future was looking dubious. His average in seven Tests was 17,15 and in 17 one-day internationals it was 17,17. In all those matches, the 54 in Sydney was his only half-century.

Having both had hopes of touring England, Gibbs and Ackerman were the batsmen most instrumental in South Africa A, captained by Dale Benkenstein, winning a three-match four-day series against Sri Lanka A in Sri Lanka. In the only encounter to yield a result in a rain-hit series, Gibbs made 153 and Ackerman 102 in the second match at Kurunegala in the Sri Lankan interior. Their third-wicket partnership of 265 set up an innings win.

> 'We had to eat at the hotel, which wasn't great. It got so bad I used to count the croutons in the tomato soup which we ate every day.'

It was, according to Gibbs, an 'horrendous' tour. 'For the first two weeks it rained every day. There was absolutely nothing to do. We weren't staying in smart hotels. We didn't get our pocket money, which we were supposed to get from the Sri Lankan board, until we had been there for two-and-a-half weeks, so we couldn't go out and eat anywhere. We had to eat at the hotel, which wasn't great. It got so bad I used to count the croutons in the tomato soup which we ate every day.'

A side effect of boredom was excessive use of his cellphone. 'In five weeks I ran up a bill of R42 000.'

There was no play in a scheduled three-day warm-up game and only 37 overs were bowled in the first four-day international. The first day of another three-day match was washed out. It got to the stage where it was decided that if there was any more rain the tour would be ended early. 'That was the first day it didn't rain.'

Even when the rain wasn't falling, it was difficult to get on the field. There were showers during the Kurunegala match and the ground staff were reluctant to take off the covers when the sun came out again. 'There were some arguments that almost broke out into fights.' Skipper Benkenstein and coach Graham Ford had to use all their persuasive powers to get play under way again. Tempers flared on the field, too. While he and Ackerman were dominating the Sri Lankan bowlers, Gibbs was on the receiving end of a head-high 'beamer' from Chaminda Vaas, the left-arm pace bowler. When the wicketkeeper, Tillekeratne Dilshan, shouted 'Well bowled,' Gibbs reacted angrily. 'It was the only time I have really lost my cool on the cricket field. I turned round to the keeper and threatened to hit him with my bat.'

While batting, he felt a 'niggle' in his right knee. There was another four-day game and three one-day matches to be played but this was one time when his usual enthusiasm for playing had deserted him. Shane Jabaar, the team physiotherapist, 'came to the party' with a diagnosis which suggested rest. Gibbs was on the next flight home. 'That was magnificent!'

In England, meanwhile, the South African team were struggling. Having won the second Test, then getting to the brink of victory in the third, they lost two closely contested battles at Trent Bridge and Headingley to lose the series. A key factor was the poor form of Gerhardus Liebenberg, who opened the batting, and an injury to Adam Bacher, another opener. Woolmer admits that McMillan only got into the side because of a last-minute anxiety about the stability of the batting. As it happened, McMillan had a poor tour and was unwilling to move up the order. Either Gibbs or Ackerman could have made all the difference.

CHAPTER **TEN**

The big breakthrough

The 1998/99 season saw the political heat turned up on cricket over the number of black cricketers in the South African team. One of the consequences was that Gibbs was brought into the Test side as an opening batsman against the West Indies, and he would take this opportunity to establish himself in the national team during what would be a turbulent summer.

In Kuala Lumpur, Malaysia, there was heat of a different kind in the humid sweatbox that was South East Asia. For the first and only time, cricket was included in the Commonwealth Games, and Australia picked a full-strength team and made no secret of their expectation that they would take the gold medal. South Africa rested many of their experienced players following their tour of England and Shaun Pollock led a young side which included Gibbs.

The young cricketers entered enthusiastically into the spirit of the Games, socialising with athletes from other sports and other countries. There was a 24-hour dining facility and a bar and entertainment area where bands played live music. There was no real pressure on the South African team because the Australians were overwhelming favourites and several other countries had picked full-strength teams.

'We were very relaxed and we played some good cricket,' says Gibbs, whose socialising got him into a scrape one evening when a powerlifter from England accused him of flirting with his girlfriend. 'I had put away a few drinks and so had he. He called to me, "Hey you," and the next thing this big, powerful guy pushed me. It was quite late and the floor was a bit slippery, so I went sliding and knocked over a whole bunch of plastic chairs.' He turned to some fellow South Africans for support, 'but they were just laughing'.

With no serious damage done, he played in all five matches, opening in the first two and then dropping into the middle order, where he made his best score of the tournament, 54 against a Barbados team which had a strong bowling attack. In extreme heat, he suffered from cramp and dehydration, a problem which would recur in future years.

South Africa pulled off an unlikely win against Sri Lanka in a low-scoring semi-final, when last-wicket pair Nicky Bojé and Alan Dawson took them from 96 for nine to the winning target of 131 on a spinner's pitch. Pollock bowled magnificently in the final, taking four wickets and breaking the back of the Australian batting to set up a memorable victory for South Africa. During the Australian innings, Gibbs fumbled in the covers and Steve Waugh shouted to his batting partner, 'I think these guys are more nervous than we are.' Gibbs thought it was an unusual admission of vulnerability by the Australian captain.

There was an end-of-Games party for all the South African athletes. Gibbs and Mark Boucher took pleasure in showing off their gold medals to a cyclist who had made snide remarks about the amount of partying indulged in by the cricketers. 'How many gold medals did you win?' they asked him.

All the regular players were back for the first ICC Knockout tournament in Dhaka, Bangladesh, a month later. Jacques Kallis, man of the match in both the semi-final and the final, was named man of the series as South Africa took the title. He was established as one of the finest players in the world. Gibbs remained in the wings, making useful but not huge scores for Western Province at the start of the domestic programme.

The season was built around a five-Test tour by the West Indies, led by Brian Lara. By reaching the final in Dhaka, the once-mighty islanders had raised hopes that they might contribute to a memorable summer of cricket but a dispute over pay nearly scuppered the tour. Instead of flying from

Bangladesh to South Africa, the players went to London where they informed their board that they were not happy with the arrangements for the tour. Clive Lloyd, the revered former captain who had been appointed manager, only learnt of the rebellion during a stop-over in Bangkok.

Seven players, who had not been in Bangladesh, arrived in South Africa as scheduled, only to fly out again and join their team-mates in a hotel near London's Heathrow airport. The board fired Lara and his deputy, Carl Hooper. An appeal from Nelson Mandela, taken to London by Ali Bacher, was ignored. It took almost a week to sort out the mess, which ended with Lara and Hooper being reinstated and the team arriving six days late. There was a bizarre casualty on the flight out when Jimmy Adams suffered a cut finger tendon, apparently self-inflicted, while he was slicing through a bread roll. He went home.

Not surprisingly, the West Indies never reached their full potential. There was controversy on the South African side, too, with a storm of political criticism unleashed by Mvuso Mbebe, chief executive of the National Sports Council, when no black players were included in the team for the first Test at the Wanderers. Mbebe reminded Ali Bacher, his United Cricket Board counterpart, of a statement Bacher had made earlier in the year that it was no longer acceptable to field an all-white South African team. The selectors' view was that neither Makhaya Ntini nor Paul Adams, at least one of whom had played in each of the previous nine Test matches, were in good enough form to be picked. Herschelle Gibbs did not even rate a mention while the controversy was raging.

South Africa won the Test but there was no applause from the politicians. A planned visit by President Mandela to the Wanderers was cancelled, while Steve Tshwete, the Minister of Sport, said he could not support an all-white team. A transformation charter, which had been pieced together after a series of seminars around the country, was due to be announced when Mandela visited the Wanderers. It was eventually unveiled during the fourth Test in January. In the meantime, the UCB met to formulate a selection policy document which directed the selectors to pick at least one player of colour for all future international games. If there were compelling reasons why this directive could not be complied with, the selectors would have to get the approval of a special committee before announcing their side.

Ntini and Adams were again not selected for the second Test in Port Elizabeth. There was just one change. Herschelle Gibbs was picked as an opening batsman ahead of an out-of-form Adam Bacher. There was an element of expediency in the choice, as Gibbs's experience of opening the batting was limited almost entirely to one-day cricket. There was a genuine problem in filling the opening slot, though, with Bacher struggling and Andrew Hudson's international career having ended. Nor could there be any doubt about Gibbs's ability and, as Hansie Cronjé pointed out, he now had a chance to have an extended run in the Test team. Up to that point, he had appeared in only seven out of 24 Tests played by South Africa since his debut against India in Calcutta two years earlier. He had not been lucky with the games he had played in. Most had been on tricky pitches and he had been in a winning side only twice.

According to Woolmer, there were instructions to pick a player of colour and Gibbs was the obvious selection. The opening batsman spot remained a problem following the difficulties in England, and Bacher had failed twice in the first Test. 'I think it was actually my suggestion that he open the batting, if only because we couldn't do any worse. So he was picked and thank goodness for that, because look what he's achieved since.'

> 'I think it was actually my suggestion that he open the batting, if only because we couldn't do any worse. So he was picked and thank goodness for that, because look what he's achieved since.'

It was ironic that Gibbs was seen as a player to add a politically correct tinge of colour to the South African team. Quite apart from the physical fact that he is as pale of complexion as most white people, race has never been a big issue for him. At both his schools, St Joseph's and Bishops, his own cheery nature and his exceptional sporting talent made him a popular figure who did not endure any racial slights. His school friends, his girlfriends, most of his team-mates at provincial and national level, were white. He did not want to be seen as an affirmative action choice, a point of view that he put in politically indelicate language in an interview with Robert Houwing of *SA Sports Illustrated* at the end of the series in March 1999. In response to Houwing's ironic, 'Heck, it's tough being an "affirmative action" selection for the Proteas. Straight back to the ghetto after the game, eh Hersch?' Gibbs replies 'Ja, straight back to my shack in Khayelitsha, bru.' Houwing wrote that Gibbs said this 'with that staple, cheeky grin'.

The remark, made more in jest than as part of a serious interview, was widely reported. So was a more thoughtful but hardly discreet comment in the same interview on the furore over affirmative action. 'I don't want to say it's ludicrous ... but not that far off! I just made up my mind that once they'd chosen me I was going to make the most of it and play my heart out. I knew there was a vacancy within the top six and perhaps it wouldn't come up again. I can't be bothered with this affirmative shit, really. If people are talented and given the opportunity in life, it's up to them how they deal with that opportunity. Everything in life takes time; very few can just come in and cope with a situation and automatically come out successful. But this is a land of opportunity and if you're the right colour these days there will be opportunities that can make or break you. Seize them while you can; they might not come up again. That's my only message, really, to others in a similar position.'

There was definitely no time to consider political niceties when he surveyed the pitch on which he would have to face Courtney Walsh and Curtly Ambrose, two great opening bowlers. For many years Port Elizabeth had offered benign batting conditions but the surface for the West Indies Test continued a more recent trend which had started when Australia had played there two seasons previously, with plenty of grass and the promise of extravagant help for the pace bowlers of both sides.

'The practice pitches on the B field at St George's Park are among the best in the country, really good for batting, so it was quite a shock to see what was there in the middle,' says Gibbs. He did not let the conditions worry him, however. 'I went in with the attitude that I had nothing to lose. The way I saw it, the only spot open for me was opening batsman.' He also had the assurance from both Hansie Cronjé and coach Bob Woolmer that he would be in the side for the rest of the series, while opening partner Gary Kirsten offered him support, encouragement and practical advice.

'I started my career with Herschelle when he was in and out of the Western Province team, and then he was playing for Province while I was playing for South Africa,' said Kirsten. 'When he came into the South African team he was batting down the order. Then he was opening the batting. I was probably a bit of help because I had been through the same thing, I also hadn't been an opener at the start of my career.'

Gibbs didn't have long to wait to find out how he would cope first time up. Lara won the toss and sent South Africa in. As expected, the ball moved sharply off the pitch but Gibbs was off the mark with a confident push into

The big breakthrough

the covers off Walsh. He did not add to those runs, however, before he was bowled by the West Indian veteran, the ball thudding into the top of his pad from an inside edge before trickling back into the stumps.

Although St George's Park was an extreme example, Kirsten reckons batsmen have had it tough in South Africa. 'Especially against teams which we think will struggle against the bounce and sideways movement, we have tended to prepare wickets which will suit our seamers. If you bat up front you're going to be faced with some moisture and some lateral movement. That has caused some inconsistency in our batting.'

Gibbs's second innings was equally brief. He made four before he was caught off the other member of the great West Indian duo, pushing Ambrose to short leg. This was no match for batsmen, though, and it was all over in less than three days. The West Indies were bowled out for 121 and 141 and South Africa won by 178 runs.

On the second evening Gibbs saw an example of Hansie Cronjé the enigma. 'He had a humorous side to him but you could never figure out whether he was being serious or not.' South Africa had already lost five wickets in their second innings. In cricketing parlance these players had become 'small bags' because for the remaining days of the match they wouldn't need their 'coffins', laden with bats and batting equipment; all they required was a small bag for their whites. The 'small bags' were in a group who went to a steakhouse, renowned as much for the visual attractions of its waitresses as it was for the quality of its food. 'There was a rumour that there was this room where apparently you could take the waitresses if you wanted a bit more than food. We had a party, Hansie was encouraging this myth and we all had a good time.' The story about the room is, as far as the players know, nothing more than legend.

Conditions in Durban were hardly more promising for batsmen, with another well-grassed pitch giving every encouragement to the bowlers of both sides. After losing two Tests in a row, the West Indies made five changes, bringing in every member of the touring party who had not played at Port Elizabeth. Once more the captain winning the toss put the opposition in and it was Cronjé's turn to unleash his bowlers first. The West Indies were bowled out for 198 and Kirsten and Gibbs had 16 overs of batting on the first day. There was some early luck for Gibbs, who edged Ambrose over the slips for four before he played a glorious cover drive off the same bowler to the longest boundary on the ground. By close of play he was on 26 and South Africa had made the best start by either side in the series so far, 46 for no wicket. The second day started promisingly and Gibbs took the total to 57 and his own score to 35 when he punched Franklyn Rose off the back foot through the covers for four. He was out next ball, however, clipping a catch to short midwicket. It was a soft dismissal. South Africa took a first innings lead of 114, mainly through a fine 87 by Jonty Rhodes.

It was in the second innings of the Durban Test that Herschelle Gibbs stepped over the line that separates the players jostling for the attention of the selectors, forever anxious about their places in the side, from those who have reason to feel a sense of security about their tenure. First, it was his fielding that lit up the South African performance. A routine catch at square leg ended the innings of makeshift opener Junior Murray before Shivnarine Chanderpaul was joined by Brian Lara. The two best West Indian players were together and for the first time in the series it seemed that the tourists might gain a significant advantage. The boundaries were peppered and the bowlers were flagging as the two left-handers put on 160 for the third wicket, taking their side to an overall lead of 87. Another hour or two of this and the West Indies could have forged a winning position. Then came the key moment of the match. David Terbrugge pitched short and Lara, on 79, pulled powerfully. It seemed sure to be another four runs but in a blur of white-flannelled motion Gibbs, fielding at midwicket, who had started to go to his right in anticipation, flung himself to his left and held a sensational catch in mid-air at full stretch.

Woolmer believes the catch was the making of Gibbs. 'That to me was the defining moment of his career. The confidence that came with that catch and the way he played after that, the way he batted, turned him into a Test match cricketer.'

Gibbs disagrees. 'The worst batters in the world have taken brilliant catches. If you are picked as a batsman your job is to make runs.'

He admits, though, that his efforts in the field were a boost to his confidence. 'I like fielding in Durban because it's always humid. You feel loose and you're sweating because it's nice and warm.' He tends to lick his hands to keep them slightly moist, 'a habit that I got from rugby, because the ball seems to stick better that way'. In Durban's climate, such action is hardly necessary.

The big breakthrough

Chanderpaul was out for 75 five balls later and the West Indies were on a slide that was all too characteristic of their performances on tour. Five wickets fell for 13 runs and one of the men out was Daren Ganga, who mistimed a pull off Shaun Pollock. Gibbs sprinted five metres from midwicket and dived, with the ball dropping over his shoulder, to take a left-handed catch. 'That was actually the best of the lot,' he said. 'We practise catches like the Lara one day in and day out.' There was yet another catch for Gibbs when Rose skied Pollock to mid-on.

At close of play, with the West Indies eight down, Gibbs managed to please the maker of an energy drink, who regularly sent supplies to the team. Asked by journalists how he had managed to fling himself through the air to hold the catches, he quoted the advertising slogan for the drink, 'Red Bull gives you wings.'

He had been told that his four catches in an innings equalled the South African Test record for a fielder. When Curtly Ambrose was batting the next morning, Gibbs was fielding at mid-on and Cronjé at mid-off. 'I said to Hansie, anything that goes up, leave it to me.' Ambrose skied the ball but the catch went straight to the captain.

South Africa needed 146 to win the match and the series. The Gibbs who walked out to bat with Kirsten to chase the modest target was brimming with confidence. The fast bowlers were seen off and he skipped down the wicket to the leg-spinner, Rawl Lewis, and hit a six over long-off. He was dropped in the next over when he skied Lewis to square leg and there was a mix-up as both Ganga and wicketkeeper Ridley Jacobs went for the ball. Having escaped, he seemed set for his half-century until he played across the line against Carl Hooper, bowling his off-spinners from around the wicket, and was leg before for 49. He was the only man out before South Africa sealed the victory but photographs of celebrating South Africans in the dressing room show Gibbs in the forefront of festivities. He had become a real Test cricketer.

The confidence carried through to the fourth Test at Newlands, his first in his home town. He knew he belonged in the highest company and he was no longer inhibited by fear of failure. He made a solid 42 after Kirsten was out to the first ball of the match. It didn't matter that the series was over as a contest; the gates were closed before lunch on the first day as Capetonians made the most of the 2 January holiday and the chance to see a winning team in action. Once again, South Africa swept to victory. Jacques Kallis and Daryll Cullinan both made centuries and Kallis went on to dominate the match, hitting an unbeaten 88 and taking five wickets in the second innings. Gibbs didn't grab any headlines but he timed the ball sweetly as he made 25. He was disappointed that he failed to go on to a big score in either innings. 'I think sometimes I have been guilty of trying too hard in front of my home-town supporters. Nothing would give me greater pleasure than scoring a century at Newlands.'

South Africa completed a 5-0 clean sweep by winning the final Test at Centurion and again Gibbs made a contribution. Nixon McLean had him caught at third slip for two in the first innings but he made a splendid 51 with nine boundaries in the second.

South African cricket was on a high. They were only the seventh side in history to gain a clean sweep in a five-Test series and it was the first time the West Indies had been on the receiving end. In their glory days in the 1980s, they had handed out similar beatings three times, once under Clive Lloyd, who now contemplated gloomily from his manager's chair the disintegration of West Indian pride.

There was an undercurrent to the South African celebrations, however. Ali Bacher and Hansie Cronjé talked earnestly while waiting for the post-match presentations to begin. That this was no exchange of bonhomie could be seen by the look of anger on Cronjé's expressive face and the seriousness with which Bacher was speaking to him. In the moment of triumph, Bacher, then the managing director of the United Cricket Board, had reminded his captain that the politicians wanted more than just a single, pale-faced player of colour in the South African side. The demographics of the country would have to be better represented in the squad that would shortly be announced to play in seven one-day internationals.

Bacher later met with all the players in the team room at their hotel. Cronjé threatened to resign rather than have players foisted on him who did not deserve international caps. According to the captain, every international game was important and caps should only be worn by those who had earned them. Gibbs recalls, 'Ali kept on saying, "This is the country we are living in and this is the team we have to play," and Hansie kept on insisting the best team had to be picked.' Gibbs offers an interesting insight to support a view that Cronjé's strenuous resistance may have had something to do with the fact that he had become accustomed to getting his own way. 'Ali had obviously given Hansie a lot of say regarding selection and the team in general. Being the captain, Hansie wanted the best team and he wanted to keep on winning.'

Although Gibbs says the players all backed Cronjé, he adds that change 'was something the players had to accept sooner or later'. From his own point of view, he says, 'I've been a firm believer all my life of making the team on merit.' However much his own selection may have been the subject of controversy and linked to the racial issue, he was able to look at it in purely cricketing terms and to focus on the challenge of opening the batting. 'The discussion never really bothered me. I've always believed I had the potential and talent to adjust to any particular position. As I saw it then, nobody in the country was firing as an opening batsman, so there was an opportunity.' He says, though, that the 'quota' issue remains an area of concern for black players who come into the team. 'They want to know and to believe it themselves that they are actually good enough to make it on merit.'

Several days later, Bacher and Cronjé had a private meeting in Johannesburg and Cronjé withdrew his threat to resign. As later events would show, a serious rift had developed which would never be satisfactorily healed. An unwieldy squad of 17 was announced for the one-day series, although only two further players of colour were added, fast bowlers Victor Mpitsang and Henry Williams, who were to play in only one match each.

Gibbs played in five matches, with Mike Rindel getting some game time when he was rested, and made an important breakthrough in the fourth international in Port Elizabeth when he made his maiden international century. It was an excellent innings of 125 off 146 balls on a slow pitch, marked as much by good judgment and restraint as it was by sparkling strokes. 'It was a great relief, more than anything else,' he told journalists afterwards, an understandable comment for a player whose previous best one-day international score was 35. Batting with him for much of his innings was Cronjé, who helped his young partner stay focused. 'I told Herschelle we had had quite a few fifties in the series but that nobody had gone through to make a century and we needed him to bat through the innings.'

Looking back, Gibbs says, 'We lost two early wickets so we were in trouble when Hansie joined me. I played very much within myself. I learnt a lot about playing the slog-sweep during that innings from watching how Hansie played against Keith Arthurton.' Most important, though, was to reach three figures. 'The further I got into the innings, the more I was able to work the ball around and keep the score moving. I had played a lot of games for South Africa by then and it was a great relief. People only start judging you when you have made a century.' He suffered from cramp in the late stages of his innings. 'It got to me in about the 42nd over and I was out in the 45th.' Having suffered several times since, he believes it is something which cannot be prevented. 'A lot of players suffer from it. When it's hot you sweat a lot, especially wearing a helmet and playing in the green clothes. You can only replace a certain amount of fluid at a time.'

With the West Indies disposed of 6-1 in the one-day series, the next challenge was a tour of New Zealand. Soon after that would be the big one, the 1999 World Cup. Herschelle Gibbs no longer had to worry about whether he would be in the team. He was now a certainty for both tours.

The slow pitches of New Zealand made batting awkward for South Africa's strokeplayers and they struggled in the one-day matches. Gibbs opened the batting in the first international in Dunedin and made 16 before being bowled off an inside edge by Geoff Allott, New Zealand's bustling left-arm opening bowler. South Africa were beaten and Lance Klusener opened with Kirsten in the next match in Christchurch. Gibbs was left out.

'We wanted to try other combinations,' Woolmer explained. 'We were always going to play Herschelle, all we were trying to do was work out strategies for the World Cup. We explained to the players that whatever we did should be seen in that light, so please bear with us. We were trying different pinch-hitters in different positions and we were playing two spinners because we were on turning pitches. Herschelle was very much part of our plans, to attack the new ball with skill up front, but we didn't feel in the conditions in New Zealand it was necessary to do that then.'

Kirsten and Cronjé took South Africa to victory in Christchurch and the same team played in the next match in Auckland, where New Zealand won comfortably. It was a worrying time for the tour management as they battled to gain the ascendancy over a tough one-day side. Once again, bigger issues were at stake. Unnoticed by most people in the touring party, South Africa had yet again chosen an all-white team. There were howls of outrage from back home and Bob Woolmer fielded a call from Raymond White, president of the UCB, telling him the tour selectors were 'out of order'. White, who himself was to be forced to resign over accusations that he was not doing enough for racial transformation, issued a statement criticising the tour selectors for not adhering to the board's directive to field players of colour. Ali Bacher received an anguished midnight phone call from Hansie Cronjé. Woolmer later revealed that he and Cronjé were so incensed that they wanted to resign from the tour selection panel, which consisted of themselves and vice-captain Shaun Pollock. If the board wanted to dictate selection policy from across the ocean perhaps they should be picking the team too.

Gibbs backed the team management, telling the media, 'You must earn the cap.' He was satisfied that being left out of the one-day side was merely a matter of searching for the right combinations.

There was another controversy as the third match ended in acrimony. Pat Symcox, playing in what was to be his last match for South Africa, was bowling to Nathan Astle when six runs were needed to win. Astle was on 96. It was exactly the same situation that would occur four seasons later when Gibbs faced Alok Kapali of Bangladesh in Benoni. Symcox did what Kapali was to do, spearing the ball down the leg-side for four wides. Astle had not dominated the scoring to the extent that Gibbs would in Benoni but he was able to find the happy ending, hitting the next ball for four to bring up his century with the winning runs. It was alleged that the ever-combative Symcox had deliberately bowled the wide after telling Astle, 'You're not going to get your bloody hundred.' The same allegation would be made by disappointed South Africans about Kapali. It was a sad day for South African cricket. Symcox, already 38, had added steel, wisdom and wit to the South African cause but he was to announce his retirement ahead of the World Cup. Father Time, sport's most unrelenting foe, had caught up with him. Symcox admits that it was a deliberate wide but says it was Cronjé's idea. 'I said to him, "What do we do now?" and he said, "Bowl him a wide, stop him getting a hundred."'

Controversy took a back seat as there were three Tests to be played before the remaining three one-day games. Most of the top order took the chance to hone their batting skills in a three-day match against Northern Districts in Hamilton, with Gibbs helping himself to 57 and 85.

The first Test was played at Eden Park in Auckland, more famous for hosting rugby matches, on a pitch laid diagonally over a field which was far from ideal for cricket. The pitch itself wasn't much good, either. In a desperate attempt to prevent it from breaking up because of damage from a fungus, the ground staff applied wood glue. This literally bound the surface together and was so effective that bowlers toiled without any assistance for five days. Gibbs made a solid 34 before spending the next two days watching the other batsmen cash in. Kirsten made a century and Cullinan a South African record 275 not out, one more than Graeme Pollock had made against Australia at Kingsmead 29 years earlier. Cronjé declared, immediately after Cullinan reached his milestone, on 621 for five, one run short of the South African record total set in the same innings as Graeme Pollock made his 274. Although South Africa were able to enforce the follow on, they had only a day to bowl out New Zealand again. It was not enough.

Gibbs made a rare duck in a match against New Zealand A at Lincoln but took another major step up in his career during the second Test in nearby Christchurch. After New Zealand were bowled out for 168 he settled in for the longest innings of his life. At the end of the first day he had been batting for 24 overs and scored just 15. 'Gary said to me he had never seen me so disciplined, so tight.' After a rain-delayed start the next day, he and Kirsten took their first wicket stand to 127. He was joined by Jacques Kallis. Scoring quickly was difficult but both men batted patiently, with runs being scored at just over two an over. Shortly before the end of the second day, Gibbs reached his first Test hundred but not before an anxious wait. He was stuck on 97 for 38 minutes and the light was fading rapidly before he struck Allott through the covers for four. 'They had just taken the second new ball and Allott bowled particularly well,' he recalls. His century had taken him 381 minutes and he had faced 268 balls. This was anything but the free-scoring Gibbs who had flattered so often only to fail to convert promising starts.

Overnight he had the chance to set himself new goals. 'I said to myself that I had to try to play again the same way I had done for my first 100 runs.' He was delighted to share a big partnership with Kallis, and remembered their stand of 257 against Natal two seasons earlier against a strong attack. 'At the time we said to each other that we would like to do that in a Test match.'

Only 40 balls were bowled on the third day and play started late again on day four. Once more Gibbs and Kallis resumed. On and on they batted. Kallis reached his century, Gibbs went to 150. He gave his only chance on 165 when Horne put down a difficult offering at cover off Nash. South Africa were well ahead but Cronjé could not afford to declare because the light was poor and New Zealand would surely be able to get off the field before the South African bowlers made any inroads. When play eventually became impossible, Gibbs was on 211 not out, Kallis on 148 and the total 442 for one. The Western Province team-mates had put on 315 for the second wicket, a South African Test record and the third best partnership for any wicket. Cronjé declared overnight but rain had the final say.

'That was a turning point,' says Kirsten. 'He batted extremely conservatively, very tight and very good outside off-stump and I thought, he can face the new ball. With his flair, that makes him a really good player up front. I knew then he could make it.'

Gibbs was among the elite of South African cricket. He had made the sixth highest score for his country and was among a group of nine who had scored Test double centuries. A somewhat surprising statistic was that in batting for 659 minutes, a minute short of 11 hours, he had played the longest innings for South Africa. His Test batting average had climbed above 30 for the first time since his debut innings in Calcutta.

There was time for some off-field entertainment in Christchurch, on what he terms his 'French date'. He invited a local young lady to join him for dinner. 'I love my French champagne. It's obviously expensive but every now and then I like to treat someone. So I ordered a bottle. I had eaten a burger for lunch and was going to have another one but I decided not to. So I just ordered the French fries. That's why I call it my French date – French champagne, French fries and French kissing afterwards.'

> 'So I just ordered the French fries. That's why I call it my French date – French champagne, French fries and French kissing afterwards.'

His cricket form carried over to the third, decisive Test at the Basin Reserve in Wellington, the only Test of the series played on a ground built especially for cricket. After New Zealand were bowled out for 222 by Shaun Pollock and Steve Elworthy, who was standing in for the injured Allan Donald, Gibbs made a fluent 120 off 250 balls and Daryll Cullinan made another century. South Africa went on to a convincing victory but not before there was an unkind final twist in a tale of Test triumph for Gibbs. With South Africa needing 16 to win, he was run out for nought when he was sent back by Kirsten after playing the ball to mid-off and setting off for a run.

There may have been some rough justice in what happened to him in the second innings. He had incurred the wrath of the team management and some of his team-mates by returning in the early hours of the fourth day of play. He had made a century and it was a Saturday night. Most of the group he went out with returned to the hotel at a reasonable hour, but he stayed on with some of the non-playing tourists. It was Nicky Bojé's birthday, 'so we had to have a drink to celebrate that'. One drink followed another into the early hours. 'There were some members of the fairer sex there and I got to know one quite well.' He went to her house, finally catching a taxi back to the team hotel. It was 6.30am and the team bus was due to leave for the ground at 8.30.

Unbeknown to the late-night reveller, Peter Pollock, the convenor of selectors, was already up. As Gibbs, dressed in jeans and showing the effects of a night on the town, got out of the lift on his floor, he met Pollock. 'I'll never forget his face. He had his reading glasses on and he dropped them to look at me.' He knew he was in trouble. He thought of concocting a story but was unable to come up with anything plausible. His case was not helped when he twice dropped Nathan Astle, who went on to make New Zealand's top score of 62, off the bowling of Shaun Pollock, the vice-captain. 'In the warm-up I had been diving everywhere and catching everything but out in the middle Astle hit me two catches in the covers. The first one was slightly difficult but the next one was straightforward.'

A disciplinary hearing was called. He had to apologise to his team-mates and was told the management had given serious thought to sending him home. He was fined R5 000.

Of his batting in New Zealand, he says the realisation that he could play long innings was important. He remembers his balance as feeling particularly good, especially in the third Test, but believes he has advanced technically since then. 'My head's in a much better position these days.'

There was a one-day series to complete. South Africa won two of the matches, with one washed out, to take the series 3-2. Gibbs had scores of 52 and 47 among four innings, with the fourth match in Napier having to be replayed after rain on the first day. It was in the replay that Lance Klusener set the scene for what was to be a sensational year when, with four needed off the last ball, he hit a low full toss from Dion Nash for six. The World Cup lay ahead.

CHAPTER **ELEVEN**

Dropping the World Cup

The 1999 World Cup was always going to be a watershed event for South African cricket but no-one could have foreseen just how much drama and heartbreak there would be for the South African team and for Herschelle Gibbs in particular.

Bob Woolmer had planned meticulously since the 1996 tournament ended in bitter disappointment with defeat by the West Indies in Karachi. His contract was to expire after the World Cup. Also moving on would be Peter Pollock, the convenor of selectors. Woolmer, Pollock and Hansie Cronjé formed a highly successful triumvirate, who had taken South Africa to the top of the world rankings in one-day cricket and to second place behind Australia in the Test version of the game.

Expectations were high as Hansie Cronjé led his 15-man squad into the 1999 tournament. At his command he had a proven team which fulfilled Peter Pollock's view that a good one-day side should contain nine good batsmen and six quality bowlers. The retirement of Pat Symcox left them short of a match-hardened spin bowler, with Nicky Bojé not yet having developed into the player he would become, but it was an immensely strong team. Lance Klusener, Shaun Pollock and Mark Boucher were vying for batting positions seven to nine, with any of the trio capable of moving up the order to be a pinch-hitter. When the side was at full strength, the bowling, spearheaded by Pollock and Allan Donald, had six men who could be classed as front-line practioners, giving Cronjé options in case one should prove expensive. The fielding was close to fabulous with Rhodes and Gibbs in the covers setting the standard.

The tournament started in mid-May, early in the English season, and the pitches were lively. The Duke balls used in England, with their prominent seam, swung and moved off the pitch alarmingly at times, with the result that bowlers found it almost impossible not to concede wides because the ball often did too much. Opening the batting was hazardous, especially in the early stages of the tournament but Gibbs's failures in the first two matches, against India and Sri Lanka, did not endanger his place and he showed his class with a splendid 60 after South Africa were sent in by England at the Oval. He and Kirsten put on 111 for the first wicket, and huge numbers of South Africans, many of them living or working in England, cheered the team to a crushing 122-run win over the host nation.

'I had been a bit nervous going into my first World Cup but that was a good innings,' said Gibbs. 'The opening partnership set it up for the team because the pitch deteriorated after that.'

As an event, the World Cup lived up to expectations for Gibbs. 'There was a great atmosphere and so much interest and hype. What struck me about our guys was that even though we were among the favourites, if not the favourites, they were very calm. It was as though they believed they could win.'

An easy win over Kenya followed in Amstelveen, on the outskirts of Amsterdam in Holland, and South Africa were assured of finishing top of Group A.

An unexpected setback against Zimbabwe in Chelmsford was to have far more serious repercussions than any of the players could imagine at the time. There may have been an element of complacency in the South African camp as they had already won their group, while Zimbabwe needed to win the match to reach the Super Six stage.

Neil Johnson qualified for Zimbabwe by birth but was educated and played most of his cricket in South Africa. He played for South Africa A before throwing in his lot with Zimbabwe, reckoning that the chances of playing full international cricket for South Africa, competing with the likes of Pollock, Kallis and Klusener for an all-rounder's berth, were not good. On this day, though, he outshone all of his erstwhile rivals, hitting 76 and then wrecking the South African top order, taking three wickets as they crashed to 40 for six. At that stage, Gibbs's nine was the highest score. Pollock and Klusener both managed half-centuries but Zimbabwe won by 48 runs. 'I don't know whether the guys took it a bit for granted,' says Gibbs. 'Zimbabwe batted nicely up front and then we couldn't get any runs. Their bowlers got it in the right place and we lost too many early wickets. It was just a bad day.' Batting partner Mark Boucher blamed himself for Gibbs's run-out, but they repaired their friendship over several drinks in a club that night.

England, having gone into the last of their first phase matches in second place in their Group, lost to India and were squeezed out of the top three on run rate behind India and Zimbabwe. It was a blow to the English organisers, as local media interest dived with the elimination of the hosts. It was also a blow to South Africa. Instead of starting the Super Six with two wins over fellow qualifiers to their credit, the loss against Zimbabwe meant they carried through a defeat as well as a win. Zimbabwe did not have enough players of quality to pose a consistent threat and their presence in the Super Six provided other teams with a wonderful opportunity to win points and improve their net run rates.

South Africa's first Super Six match was against Pakistan at Trent Bridge and they looked in danger after their opponents made 220 for seven despite overcast, seaming conditions. Shoaib Akhtar, the 'Rawalpindi Express', was, together with Klusener, the sensation of the World Cup. His third ball to Gibbs was delivered at blistering pace and Gibbs steered it involuntarily to backward point. 'It was like it was nervous energy made me play that shot. He was obviously bowling with serious pace and I might have been a bit nervous facing him. When I played against him in Sharjah the next year I didn't have too much trouble.' He was out for nought; 93 miles an hour read the speed gun. In kilometres an hour it was around 149. Hansie Cronjé, not renowned for his ability against genuine pace, batted at number three. 'I don't know what he was thinking,' chuckles Gibbs. The captain top-edged Shoaib and was caught at third man. South Africa crashed to 58 for five before Kallis and Pollock staged a recovery, with Klusener providing what his team-mates had come to expect, a blazing burst of scoring towards the end, as he and Boucher saw the side home.

Gibbs had not performed to expectations but he and Kirsten set South Africa on the way to an easy win over New Zealand at Edgbaston, putting on 176 for the first wicket. Gibbs made 91 before being bowled by an in-swinging yorker from Geoff Allott, the left-armer who would finish as the tournament's leading wicket-taker.

Australia, meanwhile, were beginning to put some form together. They had started the tournament poorly, losing two of their first three matches, and scraped into the Super Six, which they entered without any points. They had to win all their three Super Six games to reach the semi-finals.

The last Super Six game was between South Africa and Australia at Headingley in Leeds. For the South Africans there was the considerable incentive of sending their most potent rivals home before the knock-out stage. If they won, they would finish top of the table and meet Zimbabwe in the first semi-final at Old Trafford, with every prospect of avenging the defeat at Chelmsford.

A major snag, though, was that Jacques Kallis had strained an abdominal muscle against New Zealand and would not be able to play against Australia. Who was to replace him? The logical choice would have been Alan Dawson, the feisty Western Province swing bowler. Dawson, though, had not played at all. Nor, for that matter, had Dale Benkenstein or Derek Crookes, victims of a policy which had failed in Pakistan in 1996 and was to prove disastrous in England.

In Pakistan, South Africa had stuck to essentially the same batting order in all their round robin matches, including their last game against Holland when they were already assured of finishing in first place in their group. The same batsmen gorged themselves time and again. When early wickets fell in the quarter-final against the West Indies, a succession of men who had barely had a hit during the tournament came to the crease and could not rescue a side chasing a big target. Brian Lara had made a century and a spin-based bowling attack, with Allan Donald controversially left out, was unable to keep the batting in check.

Cronjé remained an advocate of playing the strongest team at all times, and Woolmer had initially agreed with this view. 'In Pakistan the same three people selected the team, Cronjé, me and Peter Pollock. Then I was in favour of picking the best team all the way through and so was Hansie. So that is what happened until we stupidly left out our best player, Donald, against the West Indies. I say stupidly but we spent three hours discussing it, so it wasn't done lightly.'

In reflecting on the mistakes of 1996, Woolmer was prepared to be more flexible in 1999. 'When we got to the Kenya match, I said this was the time to change the team. We needed to give the other players a run. Hansie was adamant he wanted the best team. It was a pity because we still would have beaten Kenya and then three or four players would have been rested. They would have been eager to play the next game and we probably wouldn't have lost against Zimbabwe.'

Kallis had bowled well during the World Cup and his absence for the Australia match was crucial. If Dawson had played against Kenya he would have had some form ahead of Headingley. Instead, the decision was to go with Bojé, who had only played in the first game against India. The combination of Pollock and Elworthy with the new ball, backed up by Donald and Kallis, had been ideal, but now the balance of the side had been upset. Klusener had bowled his fair share of overs and would have to become the fourth front-line bowler. Cronjé had bowled himself more lightly, and he and Bojé would have to share the fifth bowler's duties.

In his account of the World Cup, Steve Waugh, the Australian captain, described how his team had identified Cronjé and Bojé as a potential weak link. They were to exploit it ruthlessly.

First, though, South Africa put up one of their best batting performances of the tournament on a pitch which was not renowned for high scores. Kirsten and Gibbs started cautiously but the tempo lifted when Cullinan, batting at number three, joined Gibbs. It was one of Gibbs's outstanding innings as he went to his second one-day international century, making 101 off 134 balls before being bowled when he stepped away in an attempt to hit McGrath through the off-side. Rhodes and Klusener hit out in the closing overs and a total of 271 for seven had South African supporters in jubilant mood when they chatted between innings. Herschelle Gibbs had hit a high point in his career.

'I had befriended a lady in London and she drove up to Leeds to spend a few days with me. She was there on the morning of the Australia game. My first thought when I woke up was a hundred. It had never happened to me before. I went to the ground almost knowing I was going to get a hundred. It was an amazing, positive thought process.'

When Australia slipped to 48 for three, South Africa looked set for the high road to the final as Super Six winners, with a semi-final against Zimbabwe their reward. Steve Waugh and Ricky Ponting stabilised the innings but it was slow going. After 21 overs, Australia's total was 68. They needed 204 off 29 overs, a required rate of more than seven an over. Thirteen runs were taken off a Klusener over, then 10 from Donald. Even so, midway through the innings, the total was only 97. The required rate was still seven an over. The real problems started when Bojé and Cronjé bowled in tandem. Bojé conceded one run off his first over as he was assessed by the batsmen, but was then hammered for 28 runs off his next two and did not bowl again. Cronjé conceded 17 off his first two overs and ended up going for 50 off seven. Eighty-two runs were scored off 10 overs and, according to Waugh, the South Africans 'cracked', with the most obvious signs of distress coming from the normally in-control Cronjé, who became 'quite animated and agitated as the game began to turn in our favour'.

Gibbs had developed a habit of releasing the ball almost as soon as he completed a catch, flicking it casually over his shoulder or simply letting it fall to the ground. The first time he remembers doing it was in a day-night match in Melbourne in 1997/98. 'I let go of the ball very quickly because I wanted to go to the toilet, so as soon as I caught it I was on my way to the dressing room. I remember Bob saying, "For God's sake, Herschelle, put the ball in your pocket or something," as I went back onto the field.

'We had warned Herschelle about it,' said Woolmer. 'I said to him during the West Indies series that it's going to come back and haunt you one day. [Assistant coach] Corrie van Zyl told me in New Zealand, "We've got to stop Herschelle doing this," so we sat him down and spoke to him about it.' The player's response was not whole-hearted. 'He said, "It's just me, coach," but he did say he'd try not to do it again.'

The Australians, who seldom miss a trick, had noticed the habit. At a team meeting before the game Warne suggested that if anyone was caught by Gibbs they should stand their ground if he released the ball quickly. In his autobiography, Warne says his team-mates laughed at him. Steve Waugh did not mention Warne's contribution afterwards but he undoubtedly made a mental note.

The key moment came in the 31st over when Waugh, on 56, chipped Klusener to midwicket with the total on 152. It was a simple catch and Gibbs moved smoothly to the ball. It went into his hands and he started his celebratory flick. Scarcely had the ball been taken, though, before it slipped from his grasp as his knee bumped his right hand. Waugh stood his ground. Peter Willey, the umpire at the bowler's end, looked across at Srinivas Venkataraghavan, the square leg umpire. 'Venkat' thought the catch had been taken but Willey was not sure. As ever in cricket, the benefit of the doubt went to the batsman.

Waugh went on to make 120 not out in what he described as the sort of innings he had dreamed about. As brilliantly as Waugh played, with two overs remaining Australia still needed 15, and they completed a five-wicket win with only two balls to spare.

'That one catch made all the difference,' said Woolmer. Unusually for him, Woolmer challenged Gibbs in the dressing room afterwards, instead of allowing emotions to cool. 'What happened there, Herschelle?' he asked. According to Woolmer, 'He started to make excuses but I said, "No, think about what you did and come back to me later." About 10 minutes later he came up to me and apologised.'

Afterwards it was reported that Waugh, never short of a pithy comment on the field, had said to Gibbs, 'How does it feel to have dropped the World Cup?' Waugh himself said in his book about the World Cup that this was no more than 'a nice story' that the press had picked up. His version was more prosaic but no less brutal: 'I hope you realise you've just lost the game for your team.' Gibbs says he doesn't remember Waugh saying anything. 'I ran past him at the end of the over. I would remember if I had heard him make any comment.' He was, he admits, in a state of shock, realising he had made a crucial error, and may not have taken in any verbal asides.

It was a devastating defeat, as it meant the teams had to meet again in the second semi-final at Edgbaston four days later. Instead of finishing top of the Super Six table, South Africa had slipped to third, level with Australia but with an inferior net run rate. In the event of a tie or a no-result, Australia would go through to the final. Zimbabwe, instead of being potential cannon fodder for a revenge-hungry South African team, were on their way home.

The psychological momentum had swung. Australia, given a new lease of life, were buoyant. South Africa, having climbed a mountain only to fall short of the summit, had to start all over again against the toughest competitors in world cricket. 'We didn't leave Leeds a very happy team and I was obviously bearing the burden of the team's disappointment,' said Gibbs.

In the build-up to the Edgbaston match, Gibbs showed journalists a swollen middle finger on his right hand, caused by a blow while batting against Paul Reiffel. The pain-killing spray used to dull the pain had numbed the finger for the rest of the match. 'By the time I finished batting I could not feel anything in the finger.' Of the catch, he said, 'It may look in slow motion as though I had control of the ball but it was not so. It was almost as though my hand did not want to close. I couldn't feel the ball in my hand. I tried to close my hand around it but it was on the ground before I knew what happened.'

Some time later, he told Scyld Berry of the London *Sunday Telegraph*, 'In quiet moments, my mind goes back immediately to what happened and I break out in a cold sweat. I've had a few cold sweats.'

> 'In quiet moments, my mind goes back immediately to what happened and I break out in a cold sweat. I've had a few cold sweats.'

Woolmer has studied the videotape of the incident. He remains convinced that Gibbs was showing off. 'He meant to throw it up. He took it on the run and as he started to toss it in the air his knee hit the hand.'

Gibbs has also watched the tape, but for the most part he stands by what he said at Edgbaston, although he admits there was an element of showboating as the catch came his way. He was moving in the direction of the main grandstand, where the Australian dressing room was located. 'My first thought was to show them the ball after I caught it, to show them the game was over. When you look at it in slow motion it does actually go in but I never actually felt it go in properly. When I take a step is when I drop it. It was a dropped catch and it was obviously a really expensive mistake. It lingers with me to this day and it always will.' He is more careful these days about leaving no doubt that a catch has been taken, but says that holding a catch in a crucial situation remains an adrenaline-driving experience. 'You are just so pleased that you have taken a wicket that you have to celebrate.'

The semi-final at Edgbaston has been described as the greatest one-day match yet played. It is a fair assessment. Two high-quality teams, playing for the greatest prize in the game, slugged out a battle of fluctuating fortunes which ended in sensational fashion.

South Africa were well pleased with their effort in bowling out Australia for 213. Kallis was back in the side and bowled superbly, despite feeling pain from his abdominal injury. He conceded only 27 runs in 10 overs and took the important wicket of Adam Gilchrist. The main destroyers were Pollock and Donald, who took five and four wickets respectively. Once again, as South African supporters discussed the match during the break between innings, the mood was one of optimism and excitement.

South Africa's innings started splendidly. Gibbs was in magnificent form, hitting six boundaries as he hurried to 30 in an opening stand of 48 with Kirsten. Glenn McGrath, normally so miserly, conceded 23 runs off five overs and was taken off. In his place, in yet another example of Steve Waugh's exceptional captaincy, came Shane Warne. The great leg-spinner had been so disappointed with his form during the early stages of the World Cup that he told team-mates he was thinking of retiring from cricket. He had bowled well at Headingley, however, and Waugh knew there was no better man in a crucial situation. It meant Warne would have to bowl three overs within the first 15, without the protection of more than two fielders in the deep. Warne's seventh ball was the turning point of the match. His renowned drift, with the ball dipping towards leg, unbalanced Gibbs and a brutal leg-break spun across the batsman and hit his off-bail.

In an interview with Australia's *Sunday Telegraph* two years later, Warne rated the Gibbs dismissal at number two in '10 magic moments'. He described the delivery as 'the most lavish leg-break in my armoury'. He rates his number one dismissal bowling Mike Gatting at Old Trafford, in 1993, with his first ball in an Ashes Test.

'It was the perfect leg-spinner,' says Gibbs. 'It wasn't full enough to sweep and it wasn't short enough for me to go back.' As the ball swerved towards the leg-side Gibbs lost his balance. 'If your balance isn't right you get outside the line of the ball and your left pad gets in the way of the bat. That particular ball spun so sharply that I was completely amazed when the Australians went up.

I thought there was no way the ball could hit the stumps. I looked back and I saw my off-bail was missing.'

In his next over Warne bowled Kirsten, who missed a sweep, and two balls later Cronjé was given out, caught at slip off a ball which went off his boot. Kallis and Rhodes brought South Africa back into the game but all seemed lost when McGrath bowled Boucher, and Elworthy was run out in the 49th over. South Africa were 198 for nine. Sixteen runs needed, eight balls left. Elworthy's sacrifice in going for a second run after Klusener hit to long-on meant Klusener was still on strike. The next ball was hit hard and low to long-on and Reiffel could only parry it over the boundary for six. A single kept Klusener on strike for the final over, bowled by Damien Fleming. The first two deliveries were hit with savage power to the off-side for fours. Waugh stopped the game and brought all his fielders up to save a single. It was inspired captaincy. Donald was almost run out, backing up, as Klusener hit the next ball to mid-on. Then Klusener hit to mid-off and started running. Donald was watching the ball and set off fatally late. Mark Waugh flicked the ball to Fleming, who, realising that Donald had no chance of getting to the other end, rolled it down the pitch for Gilchrist to make the easiest of run-outs. The match was tied and South Africa were out of the World Cup.

> 'The next thing is he came running in and he just swore. I said, "What, what?" and he told me about the run-out. That's when I went out to look and I saw Lance walking off the field. I saw Hansie and he had his head in his hands.'

Gibbs is a nervous watcher and he stayed in the physiotherapist's room for about the last 30 overs. 'I was far too tense to look at it. I was listening for sounds to judge what was going on. I couldn't even look at the television. I could see Nicky Bojé, who was the 12th man, and I was watching his reactions. Then as it got really tense I blocked my ears with my hands. I saw Nicky jumping up and down and he told me Lance had hit a great four. He said, "He's hit another one." Then he told me Allan was nearly run out. Next thing he came running in and just swore. I said, "What, what?" and he told me about the run-out. That's when I went out to look and I saw Lance walking off the field. Hansie had his head in his hands. There was complete silence for about an hour-and-a-half. At Edgbaston the change rooms are opposite each other.

In the Australian room it was like there was a pop concert going on. That just made it worse for us.'

The veterans of that epic contest seldom talk about the nightmare of Edgbaston, 'although occasionally someone who has just come into the team will ask us what it was like'. Gibbs still wonders at the thought processes that were going on. 'You can never blame one guy in a situation like that but the task seemed so easy when it came down to one run off four balls. I've never asked him the question but the guy that's playing heavenly cricket at that stage, Lance Klusener, has got all the fielders up in the circle and we only need one run. He could easily have hit another boundary.'

CHAPTER **TWELVE**

The captain makes a deal

After the disappointment of the World Cup, there was a danger that South African cricket would nurse a hangover during the 1999/2000 season. What could not be foreseen was that the game would be hit by its biggest scandal, with Hansie Cronjé the central figure and Herschelle Gibbs among those implicated.

There were rumblings at the start of the season when Rushdi Magiet, who succeeded Peter Pollock as convenor of selectors, announced a squad for a four-nations one-day tournament in Kenya. Cronjé was confirmed as captain only until after the second of five Tests against England later in the summer. Effectively, it was an appointment for half a season. Cronjé was so depressed immediately after the devastating World Cup elimination that he had hinted he might quit. Even so, the perceived lack of confidence from the new selection panel stung deeply.

The South African captain's response was to sign a contract to coach Glamorgan in English county cricket for two seasons from 2000. This made him unavailable for a tour of Sri Lanka during the same year, though Cronjé had not consulted the United Cricket Board before talking to the Welsh club. Questioned on an apparent breach of courtesy and ethics, Cronjé said he did not believe he had any security of tenure beyond the expiry of his UCB contract in April 2000.

Ali Bacher stepped in as a negotiator. He had a meeting with Cronjé and afterwards read out a statement in which Cronjé 'expressed his keenness to play an important role in the transformation of South African cricket through a process that will also ensure South Africa remaining a top nation in world cricket'. Cronjé and Magiet sat down together and jointly told the media they had resolved their differences. Bacher made contact with Glamorgan and extricated Cronjé from his commitment. Glamorgan, not surprisingly, were angered at the unravelling of a deal which the county understood to be not only signed but sealed.

If Cronjé was disillusioned or any less committed to his captaincy, it was not noticed by Gibbs. 'You could never really sense if he was unhappy or whatever. In that regard, he was a true leader.'

In Kenya, South Africa lost their first match to India. They were tied in knots by Sunil Joshi, a left-arm spinner, who took five for six on a tricky pitch, and were bowled out for 117 after Gibbs and new cap Boeta Dippenaar had put on 32 for the first wicket. South Africa went on to a comfortable nine-wicket win against Zimbabwe after Gibbs and Lance Klusener set them on their way with a 125-run opening stand off only 18,4 overs. Gibbs made 48 before retiring hurt with a freak injury, straining a tendon under his right toe as he turned quickly to regain his crease. He missed a match against Kenya but returned for the final against India. Still struggling because of the injury, he made a mature 84 off 124 balls. South Africa gained revenge for their round robin defeat and Gibbs was named man of the match.

What had seemed to be a minor injury kept Gibbs out of home-and-away Tests against Zimbabwe. South Africa gained innings wins in both matches, and the tour proved a satisfactory tune-up for the main event of the summer, a five-Test home series against England.

The first Test at the Wanderers had a sensational start after Cronjé sent England in. Shaun Pollock and Allan Donald, first and second on the world Test bowling rankings, reduced England to two for four wickets in overcast conditions on a lively pitch. Only India, who had been none for four against England at Headingley in 1952, had lost four wickets for fewer runs in a Test innings. England were bowled out for 122.

Gibbs produced just the innings that was required on a pitch which still had plenty of 'juice', playing only those balls which needed to be played and waiting to take advantage of rare loose deliveries. He made 85 off 222 balls, and he and Daryll Cullinan, who made a century, put on 96 for the third wicket. 'That was probably the best innings I had played up to then. There wasn't much that I could put away, so it was an innings of patience and my technique was very tight. I had improved vastly in a couple of years. I was disappointed not to get a hundred but it was an important innings for me.'

For the first time in 116 Tests, South Africa beat England by an innings. Mike Atherton, the hero for England at the same ground four years earlier, when he saved his side by making 185 not out in the second innings, made a 'pair'.

The second Test in Port Elizabeth was drawn. Gibbs made 48 in the first innings before being run out in a mix-up with Cullinan.

While Gibbs was in good form, his opening partner, Gary Kirsten, was struggling. He failed again in the first innings in Durban, as both he and Gibbs were early victims of Andrew Caddick, who took seven for 46 in an inspired performance. South Africa were forced to follow on 210 behind before the close of play on the second day. Gibbs helped Kirsten put on 41 for the first wicket in the second innings and Kirsten went on to play an epic role, making a South African record-equalling 275. He far exceeded Gibbs's record for the longest innings for South Africa, set in New Zealand the previous season, by batting for an extraordinary 878 minutes, the second-longest innings in Test history.

More splendid bowling by Donald and centuries by Jacques Kallis and Cullinan were the cornerstones of a series-deciding innings win in the fourth Test at Newlands. Once again Gibbs promised much to his home town supporters, scoring 29 in a fluent innings before steering a catch to backward point.

The fifth Test at Centurion was severely hit by rain. South Africa were 155 for six when bad light stopped play on the first day. There was no play on the next three days. With play aborted again on the fourth day, there was a meeting between Bacher, the two captains, match referee Barry Jarman and the umpires to discuss what might be possible. One option was to play a one-day international but this was ruled out because of sponsorship agreements. When the meeting broke up, it seemed the best that could be expected was that both teams would go through the motions on the final day.

The captain makes a deal

The sun finally came out and there was a surprise for the South African players. 'Hansie called us together and told us he wanted to set England a target,' says Gibbs. Cronjé proposed to offer England captain Nasser Hussain a deal. If Hussain forfeited England's first innings, South Africa would reciprocate by giving up their second turn, making it into a one-innings match. 'I didn't even know you could forfeit an innings,' said Gibbs, 'so that in itself was an eye-opener for me. There were quite a few guys in the team who said, "To hell with this, we can just bat out the game and shut them out."'

Most of the players seemed to feel that a Test match should not be subject to such manipulation. Test match victories were meant to be earned with sweat and blood, not a few blazing strokes or a flurry of wickets on a single day. Mark Boucher told the King Commission later in the year, 'I was against it. I think the majority of the side were against it.'

> The sun finally came out and there was a surprise for the South African players. 'Hansie called us together and told us he wanted to set England a target...'

Cronjé's powerful personality prevailed. 'Hansie kept on saying, "They won't get the runs," but I could see the uncertainty on the faces of the guys. Giving England even a little chance of winning didn't go down well with them,' said Gibbs, who was swayed by his captain's argument. 'I didn't think they could win against our bowling attack if they had to score three-and-a-half, four runs an over. I went along with it because to win the game you had to take the chance of losing. I backed our bowlers to get them out.'

Hussain was initially wary but after seeing there were no perils in the pitch during the first half-hour of play, he sent word to Cronjé that he had a deal. Cronjé duly declared, two innings were forfeited for the first time in Test history, and England were required to score 249 off 76 overs.

What ensued was an enthralling day's cricket, which England won by two wickets with five balls to spare. South Africa were hampered by an injury to Paul Adams, who broke a finger early in the innings when he dived in an attempt to stop a boundary and slid into an advertising board.

In his autobiography published in 2002, Mike Atherton claims that Hussain was muttering darkly that he had been 'conned' when England slipped to 102 for four halfway through the innings. Michael Vaughan was sent out and told to play safe. Could the match yet end in a draw? Atherton believes that

Cronjé's decision to bring on part-time bowler Pieter Strydom was a decisive moment. There was a spurt of scoring and England again pressed for victory.

A careful review of the record shows that there was in fact a double change. Cronjé came on to bowl his medium-pacers when the total was 171 for four, when England still needed 78 off 20 overs. Strydom then came on in the next over. His second over cost nine runs, including a six by Alec Stewart, yet Cronjé kept him on. His six-over spell cost 27 runs. Cronjé only conceded 15 off five. Was it a bold ploy by a captain trying to win? Or a cynical move by a man who had undertaken to ensure there would be a result? Only Cronjé could know.

It was an unhappy South African dressing room afterwards. 'There was a lot of anger,' said Gibbs. 'The guys were saying, "Why did we ever give them a chance?" It didn't go down very well. They don't like losing, especially against England.' Cronjé was 'quite calm, although I am sure he was disappointed'.

Raymond White, the president of the United Cricket Board, attended the post-match press conference specifically to applaud Cronjé for his bold move, which he said had been for the good of cricket. Cronjé himself seemed unhappy about losing. Always conscious of records and milestones, he was aware that defeat, even in such contrived fashion, meant that South Africa had failed to extend a record-equalling sequence of 10 successive Tests without a loss.

Only later did it emerge that Marlon Aronstam, a Johannesburg bookmaker, had somehow managed to get through to Cronjé on his cellphone, which many journalists knew was not easy to do. Aronstam convinced the captain to 'make a game of it', for which Cronjé later received a total of R53 000 as well as a leather jacket for his wife.

Thereafter, according to cellphone records, there were more than 150 calls between the various numbers of Aronstam and Cronjé over the next several weeks.

It was a season of clandestine dealings. Yet another man who seemed able to make frequent cellphone contact with Cronjé was Hamid 'Banjo' Cassim, a Johannesburg sweet shop owner who ingratiated himself with the team through gifts of biltong, the South African dried meat snack. An unconvincing witness at the King Commission, he was unable to explain adequately his role in the dealings between Cronjé and Sanjeev 'Sanjay' Chawla, an Indian citizen living in London. Cassim introduced Cronjé to Chawla in an Umhlanga Rocks

The captain makes a deal

hotel, near Durban, two nights before South Africa lost to Zimbabwe by two wickets off the last ball in a limited overs international at Kingsmead. Cronjé received a cellphone box stuffed with United States dollar bills, supposedly in return for providing information about pitch conditions and team selections during the series.

Cassim's precise role in the match-fixing scandal was one of the mysteries left unsolved by the winding up of the King Commission before every investigative avenue had been pursued. Handed in to the inquiry was a list of cellphone calls made and received by the 'biltong man' between November 1999 and April 2000. They included 180 calls to Cronjé, 146 of them during the triangular one-day series. Cronjé phoned back 11 times.

It was not only Cronjé who Cassim tried to contact. Eight other players, as well as members of the management team, were telephoned. With 14 calls, Gibbs was relatively low on the list, although by returning three calls, he responded more often than most. Cassim claimed to be friendly with several of the players and said he had received words of support from Gibbs, who told him, 'Hamid, be strong. We know what type of a character you are.' Paul Adams was phoned 30 times and Lance Klusener 28 times. Neither called back. One man who did call Cassim was Sanjeev Chawla, 29 times between 29 January and 1 February. Cassim introduced Chawla to Cronjé on 31 January.

The players who gave evidence at the King Commission said they did not know much about Cassim other than as someone who was seen frequently around the team, mainly in the vicinity of the dressing room or the nets at the Wanderers, who handed out biltong, and who sought complimentary tickets from the players.

'There was nothing odd about the man,' says Gibbs. 'He never spoke of money or anything like that. He was just someone who knew Hansie and a few of the other guys in the team. He wasn't loud, he'd say hello to the guys and that would be it. He loved giving away biltong and would always ask if we wanted some.'

As for the calls, Gibbs says all he can remember is that Cassim asked for tickets 'once or twice'. Cassim got through to the player when he was in Dubai later in the season, after the tour of India, again asking for tickets.

South Africa did not play consistently during the triangular tournament. Going into the last round of league matches, all three teams had two wins

131

and two defeats, one each against both their rivals. South Africa made sure of playing in the final by beating both the two touring sides and they went on to win a low-scoring, rain-hit final against England. It was a quiet series for Gibbs, apart from an innings of 65 in the first match against Zimbabwe.

Gibbs said he was unaware of any attempt to manipulate results or match situations during the series. 'We'd see Banjo from time to time but if there was anything going on it was very discreet.'

Since the King Commission, Cassim has stayed away from the team. 'I haven't seen him once since then,' says Gibbs.

Within a week of the triangular final, the South Africans were in Mumbai at the start of their second Test tour of India.

CHAPTER **THIRTEEN**

Triumph and corruption

A cricket historian who knew nothing about the subsequent match-fixing scandal might study South Africa's tour of India in February and March 2000 and conclude that it was Hansie Cronjé's crowning achievement as captain.

Winning a Test series in India has proved almost impossible for touring teams down the years. Not even the great Australian sides led by Mark Taylor and Steve Waugh have emerged victorious. South Africa, under Cronjé's leadership, had gone into the third match of a three-Test series all square three years earlier and were beaten heavily in the decider in Kanpur.

During the 1990s, India played 30 Tests at home and won 17, losing only five. They had not lost a series since Pakistan had been triumphant 13 years earlier, although Pakistan had shared a series in India in 1998/99 and then won a separate Asian Championship Test on Indian soil.

South Africa were originally expected to play three Tests in India but the itinerary was changed to meet a seemingly insatiable demand for one-day internationals. There would be only two Test matches, followed by five one-day games. Then both teams were due in Sharjah to join with Pakistan in a triangular tournament.

Gibbs made 53 and 28 in a satisfactory warm-up match against a Board President's XI at the Brabourne Stadium in Mumbai. He was out in both innings to Harbhajan Singh, a 19-year-old off-spinner, who took only two other wickets in the match and gave barely an inkling of the impact he would make at Test level within the next two years.

The first Test was at the Wankhede Stadium in Mumbai, no more than a few hundred metres from Brabourne. Both grounds occupy valuable real estate near Marine Drive, which sweeps around Back Bay, with the million-dollar apartments of Malabar Point at one end and the international hotels of Nariman Point at the other. It was at Wankhede where South Africa had suffered such disappointments in two one-day matches on the 1996/97 tour.

Although the pitch was nothing more than hard-rolled, red earth, there was some bounce for the fast bowlers, and India struggled against South Africa's fast bowlers in the first innings. Sachin Tendulkar made 97 in a total of 225. South Africa collapsed to 176 all out after Gibbs and Kirsten had put on 89 for the first wicket, Gibbs scoring 47 before being caught at slip off a Tendulkar leg-spinner. The visitors struck back through Donald, Pollock and Cronjé to bowl India out for 113 in their second innings. South Africa needed 163 to win.

Amid a cacophony of sound, Gibbs and Kirsten started the run chase with positive strokeplay, putting on 51. There was an eruption of noise when Kirsten was caught behind off Anil Kumble, the Indian leg-spinner who held the key to India's hopes. Jacques Kallis survived three lbw appeals in one over from Kumble before he settled down to play a crucial innings. Gibbs was at his best as he moved to 46 with nine boundaries. After square-cutting a rare loose delivery from Kumble for four, he was caught at short leg off bat and pad off the next ball, a top-spinner which bounced and hurried through. As in the first innings, the loss of Gibbs brought a flurry of wickets and South Africa slipped to 128 for six. Kallis stood firm, though, and Boucher joined him to seal a thrilling four-wicket victory.

'It was an unbelievable feat, the guys were completely overwhelmed,' said Gibbs. 'It was nerve-wracking because the pitch was playing in their favour and turning quite a bit.' Boucher's aggression proved decisive as he hit an unbeaten 27 off 32 balls. An image that Gibbs will carry with him is of Allan Donald racing onto the field to hoist Boucher in the air after the winning runs had been hit. Donald, who had originally not planned to go to India, knew just what an achievement it was to win there. At worst, South Africa would share the series.

The players were apparently unaware that the sinister Cronjé-Chawla axis was in operation, the captain having been supplied with a cellphone by Chawla. According to his statement to the King Commission, Cronjé was receiving calls from both Cassim and Chawla, sometimes as late as 2am and 3am. They wanted him to involve other team members and manipulate results.

There was a sequence of strange overtures by Cronjé to players. Before the Test in Mumbai, he spoke to Pieter Strydom, who had made his Test debut in Centurion. 'Hansie said I could make R70 000 if South Africa got less than 250 in the first innings.' Taken aback, Strydom, who knew Cronjé was a practical joker, said he wasn't interested but that he might consider it if he had played in 80 or 90 Tests. As it was, he was about to play in only his second Test. 'As I left the room, I thought maybe I had passed some sort of test.' Later, Cronjé nudged him. 'How about R140 000?' He assumed the captain was joking.

In his statement, Cronjé said Strydom's account was true. 'At the time of speaking to him I was already wracked with guilt and his remarks about doing his best for South Africa shamed me.' Not enough, though, to stop Cronjé from making another approach, this time before the second Test in Bangalore. Room-mates Boucher and Kallis were offering around some excess pasta. Several players came into their room, including Cronjé and Lance Klusener. Boucher told the King Commission, 'While we were sitting down and all the rest of the guys had left, it was with Jacques, myself and Lance in the room, and he just managed to mention, in a joking way, that he had been phoned, and anyway, he asked us if we were like keen to – I'm not sure of his exact words but it was along the lines of fixing a game. And that's it – it lasted for 10 or 15 seconds – and we just dismissed it. And then he carried on eating his food, and then the guys left the room.'

Boucher said that at the time the three players thought it was a joke. Asked whether, looking back, he thought Cronjé might have been serious, he said, 'In hindsight, probably that could have been the way that he might have wanted to approach us.'

According to Kallis, 'We said we were not interested and told him to get lost but in harsher words.'

Whatever was happening in the hotel rooms, or being discussed on the telephone between Cronjé and Chawla, on the field in Bangalore South Africa produced one of their most memorable performances. Opting for a pace-based attack after playing two spinners in Mumbai, South Africa bowled India out for 158. With only five overs left at the end of the day, India used Kumble as an opening bowler and Gibbs was trapped leg before off the last ball of the leg-spinner's second over. He saw it as an opportunity missed. 'It was a good pitch, not as dry as the one in Mumbai and it didn't turn as much.' The rest of the batsmen dug themselves in and South Africa went on to win by an innings and 71 runs. Nicky Bojé, who was only on tour because Paul Adams was injured, was the hero in his second Test, making 85 as a nightwatchman and taking seven wickets.

Gibbs recalls that Kapil Dev, India's coach and former legendary all-rounder, was grudging in defeat. 'He said, "You can't really call two Tests a series," so we said to him, "Put on another game and we'll beat you in that too."' Despite Kapil's carping, it was an exceptional achievement. No side had won two matches in a series in India since David Gower's England won a five-match series 2-1 in 1984/85. 'It was a great experience and something Graham Ford can be really proud of,' said Gibbs. Ford was on his first tour as coach after taking over from Bob Woolmer.

A five-match one-day series started in the hot and humid southern coastal city of Kochi, with Sourav Ganguly assuming the captaincy after Tendulkar had stepped aside. In Kochi, Chawla emerged from the shadows, staying in the same hotel as the South African team. Cronjé was under increasing pressure to involve more players, he said in his statement to the King Commission. Chawla telephoned him on the morning of the first match and Cronjé told him South Africa would lose and that he had spoken to other players, although, according to Cronjé, this was untrue. Gibbs says he never met Chawla and did not know he was in the hotel.

In front of a crowd of 60 000 in a multi-purpose stadium, with short boundaries on either side of the pitch, Gibbs and Kirsten batted magnificently to set a South African first-wicket record of 235. Gibbs made 111 and Kirsten 115, with Gibbs setting the tone by hitting Ajit Agarkar for two sixes over cover in the third over of the game. Kirsten remembers Kochi as one of his best partnerships with Gibbs. 'We often talk about it. It was probably the hottest day's cricket I've played in. I remember it because I outlasted him in terms of physical endurance. We were both absolutely stuffed afterwards.'

Gibbs recalls, 'The game started quite early and I remember the sun was just above the stadium when we arrived to warm up. There were already 30 000 people in the ground. It got seriously hot. With the coloured clothing on, it was unbearable. When we both got to about 60 or 70 we would hit the ball to the sweepers on the boundary and we had to walk between wickets, we were so tired.'

Physiotherapist Craig Smith had to make frequent trips onto the field to give the batsmen ice packs to put on their heads to cool them down. The umpires, anxious about getting the overs bowled on time, at first refused to allow water to be brought out but the Indian fielders were also suffering and the officials had to relent.

> Kirsten remembers Kochi as one of his best partnerships with Gibbs. 'We often talk about it. It was probably the hottest day's cricket I've played in.'

Astonishingly, despite making 301 for three, South Africa were beaten by three wickets. Fast bowler Mornantau Hayward bowled only six overs before having to leave the field with heat exhaustion, and he was put on a drip. Cronjé claimed that he had 'honestly tried to win the match'.

In totally different conditions, in the industrial city of Jamshedpur, on the other side of India, South Africa were bowled out for 199 in the second match and lost by six wickets. They won by two wickets in Faridabad, near Delhi, but lost the series when they went down by four wickets in Baroda as a pattern continued of the side batting second taking the honours. Gibbs's scores were 27, 19 and 31, all made at close to a run a ball.

The series was decided. There was one match to play, in Nagpur.

What happened on the morning of the match was described at the King Commission by Herschelle Gibbs when he was questioned by Mike Fitzgerald, an advocate acting on behalf of the players.

Gibbs: It was quite early in the morning, the morning of the last one-day game because I distinctly remember it was 19 March which is my mother's birthday, and Hansie came into my room. I was sharing a room with Henry Williams. He had this huge grin on his face. He then he came to me and Henry had just

	finished showering or whatever and he was coming out of the bathroom when Hansie said to me that somebody had – he'd been on the phone with somebody, or somebody had phoned him and they were prepared to offer myself $15 000 if I made less than 20. At which I said, 'Yes.'
Fitzgerald:	[Gibbs's final sentence was blurted out so quickly that Fitzgerald had not heard it properly] What was your response to the offer?
Gibbs:	Pardon?
Fitzgerald:	How did you respond to the offer that was made to you?
Gibbs:	Well the first thing that came to mind, without even thinking about what he'd actually asked me, I immediately thought about my mother because I know just before we went to India my parents were thinking of, or were divorced and my father at that stage had a temporary job and I knew that ever since I heard him talking of the divorce that I would have to look after my mom for the rest of her life and at that stage my father wasn't in a position really to help her out. And that is why I probably said, 'Yes,' or I said, 'Yes.' He then approached Henry and he asked Henry that – well he didn't ask Henry, he said that the same guy, he didn't say, mention any name, would give him the same amount of money, $15 000, if he went for not less than 50 runs in his 10 overs. At which Henry also said, 'Yes.' I then told him if you can get more money then do so. And he said – and the team mustn't get more than 270.

The sheer matter-of-factness about the way Gibbs made his confession was almost as startling for observers at the hearing as the revelation itself.

Looking back, more than two years later, Gibbs said the approach was a complete surprise. He had always had complete confidence in his captain. 'Everybody had so much respect for him, we all thought that whatever decisions he made were the right ones.' At no stage during the preceding four games did he think the captain was trying to do anything other than win every match.

Referring to the 'huge grin' on Cronjé's face when he entered the room, Gibbs says, 'That was the thing about Hansie, you never knew whether he was being serious or joking.' His explanation for bowing to temptation remains as given at the King Commission: 'I knew I would have to support my mother for the rest of my life. I had only been playing for South Africa for four years. Any money that could come my way, I'd take it to help pay off the house as quickly as possible.'

He admits he had no immediate thoughts about the consequences. 'I agreed to it.'

By then Williams had emerged from the bathroom. 'He spoke to Henry and then we had a little group discussion. We asked Hansie if he could get more money and he said he would try, he would talk to his mate.' The details decided, Cronjé left, with an admonishment to both players not to tell anybody about their meeting.

Surrounded by his team-mates on the bus to the ground, Gibbs thought to himself, 'Whoever is going to know? Cricket being the game it is, there are no guarantees that you are going to get runs.' He remembered, though, that Nagpur had an especially good batting pitch, the one on which he had scored 200 not out and 171 against India A three seasons earlier. In the dressing room, there was an air of conspiracy between the three collaborators after India won the toss and it was decided that South Africa would bat first. 'I looked across at Hansie and we both had these little grins on each other's faces. I looked at Henry and he grinned too.'

He went out to bat, still thinking about his captain's offer, but the plot unravelled almost immediately. 'I just hit everything in the middle of the bat from ball one.'

Gibbs told the King Commission how he hit two fours off the first two balls he faced and thereafter 'batted like a steam train'.

The author was able to view a tape of the full innings.

Kirsten took a single off the second ball by Javagal Srinath. Gibbs stood tall to the next ball and thrashed it past cover for four. He swung at the next and it flew off a thick bottom edge to fine leg for another boundary. He hit across the line at his third delivery and was struck on the thigh. He patted the last ball of the over back to the bowler.

He faced one ball after Kirsten was run out in the next over, which was bowled by Venkatesh Prasad, before flicking Srinath to square leg for four and pulling him for a single. He charged down the wicket to Prasad and took a single to mid-wicket. It was stirring stuff. 'Boy, Gibbs is in an aggressive frame of mind,' boomed Tony Greig on the television commentary. 'Gibbs is South Africa's Gilchrist, he's South Africa's Jayasuriya.' He took another single off Prasad. He faced only one delivery from Srinath in the fifth over and, flat-footed, cracked it in the air, just out of reach of cover, for four. His score was on 19 after 10 balls. To meet his obligation to Cronjé, he needed to get out without scoring any more runs.

Facing Prasad again, he put his foot down the wicket and flicked the ball to fine leg for yet another boundary. He had faced only 11 balls and his innings had been a blur of unusually aggressive shots. He charged Prasad again and smashed the next delivery over cover for four more. His score was 27 off 12 balls.

Anil Kumble was brought on and immediately had Neil McKenzie caught behind. In the same over Gibbs, on 27, pushed a catch back to Kumble but the bowler put it down.

What was going through his mind? It appears that natural instincts took over once he was at the crease. On the one hand he was thinking of the bribery offer, on the other he remembered his run feast at the same ground on the previous tour. 'When I hit those first two balls for four I thought I could do something serious here. I was enjoying it so much, I was batting like a man possessed. I was hitting the ball so sweetly. I was playing quite a few cross-batted strokes, there was nothing I could do wrong. One of the Indians asked me, "Are you in a hurry or something?"'

Of the dropped catch, he said, 'I was trying to hit over the bowler's head and didn't get to the pitch of the ball. I was relieved. It was quite a nice feeling because you hardly ever get dropped.'

More than two years after the incident he was convinced his score was on 18 when he was dropped, despite the irrefutable video evidence to the contrary. He had used the missed chance as an excuse to himself and Cronjé for not keeping his side of a corrupt deal. 'I thought I played into the whole thing. For me, that chance saved my bacon. I thought I hit a realistic caught and bowled to Kumble.'

What was striking during two separate interviews on the incident was the way a serious issue of morality and a naive, almost child-like enjoyment of batting in favourable conditions became merged in his stream-of-consciousness replies.

It would have been fascinating to study the body language of the two batsmen when Cronjé joined Gibbs at 66 for three, as the deal with Chawla was going horribly wrong. Unfortunately, though, during what was presumably an advertisement break in India, the television cameras stayed focused on the Indian fielders. At the end of the over, it could be seen from the stump camera, in another break from commentary, that Cronjé and Gibbs had a lengthy conversation which only ended when Srinath, who was brought back into the attack, was ready to bowl.

At the King Commission, Fitzgerald drew from Gibbs what happened when Cronjé joined him. 'Obviously as Hansie walked in I then was reminded of what discussion took place in the hotel . . . after he had faced a few balls I came up and I said, "Now you know what's going to happen here? I've got 30 or 40 already and you know what's going to happen?" And he just said to me, "Well, there is nothing we can do at this stage, you are just going to have to keep on batting," and he then also decided, he got on with the bowling and he was batting at a ferocious sort of pace and a few more overs went by and then I asked him, "Okay, well, what are we going to do?" And he then said, "Well, if either one of us has to go out it will be me," and obviously referring to me he just said, "You just carry on batting."'

Gibbs raced to 50 off 30 balls, the quickest half-century of the series, and Cronjé shook his hand. On 53 he was dropped by Tendulkar when he hit a searing drive off Sridharam Sriram to short cover. Cronjé thrashed 38 off 31 balls before falling to a stupendous reflex catch by Dravid at a wide slip position. Gibbs went on to score 74 off 53 balls, with 13 fours and a six, before he was run out by a direct hit from Sriram at cover after Boucher called for a quick single.

It was an innings of high-risk strokes. Were they, though, notably more risky, reckless or played with intent to get out than when he hit two sixes in the third over in Kochi? Or when he raced to 37 off 31 balls in Baroda? Gary Kirsten has an interesting insight. 'The difference was that those sixes over cover in Kochi were good cricket shots. The way he played in Nagpur he was playing across the line, trying to hit it over midwicket from outside off. When I watched it, having got out early, I thought it was another great Herschelle innings but later I began to think back. Then I thought, in hindsight, it was over the top in extravagance, in terms of the shots he tried to play.'

At the King Commission, the questioning on the incident came to an end.

Fitzgerald: Mr Gibbs, you described it, when the offer was made to you, you accepted it immediately. Did you consider then the consequences of what you were doing?
Gibbs: Not at all. As I said the first thought that came into my mind was my mother and obviously looking back now it was probably one of the most stupidest decisions I have ever made and I do regret that. You know I obviously feel that I let my country and my team-mates down and probably family as well.
Fitzgerald: Just for the record, you never got the $15 000?
Gibbs: No.

South Africa surged past the 270 discussed by Cronjé, finishing with 320 for seven. While they were batting together, Cronjé told Gibbs the deal was 'finished'. Before they went out to bowl, the captain told his players, 'We have to win this thing.' Williams, suffering from a recurrence of a shoulder injury, sent down 11 legal balls and six wides before going off the field because of the injury. A seventh delivery that would also have been called wide was hit by Ganguly to backward square leg, and Williams had figures of one for 11. It was his last match for South Africa.

Tendulkar and Dravid put on 180 in an electrifying second-wicket partnership but South Africa won by 10 runs. An inspired run-out of Kumble by Gibbs, who hit the stumps from side-on after diving and throwing under-arm, was a decisive moment. It was the ninth wicket and the last man was out three balls later.

On the way home from India, South Africa took part in a three-team tournament in Sharjah, playing against India and Pakistan. Cronjé reminded Gibbs to 'keep quiet' about what had happened in Nagpur. 'He told me he was in trouble because his mate had lost a serious amount of money on that game.' In Sharjah, Gibbs had his own room. 'Hansie came in once or twice to make a call.' He used the room telephone. 'He never said who he was phoning. I didn't mind him using my phone but I found it a bit peculiar.' It was especially strange because Cronjé had a cellphone used by many of the players to make international calls to family and friends. 'Hansie said this phone had been put in his room. He didn't know where it had come from. The guys used the phone a lot.'

Gibbs made an unbeaten 87 in the first match against India as South Africa achieved a target of 165 without losing a wicket. He was out first ball, caught at slip off Waqar Younis, during a win against Pakistan. Out for eight in a second match against India, he batted through a dismal innings of 101 all out against Pakistan, making 59 not out, as a below-strength team lost by 67 runs. Cronjé was one of five regular players who rested. Their winning momentum interrupted, South Africa lost the final against Pakistan by 16 runs. Gibbs made just five.

The South Africans returned home to prepare for a three-match challenge series against Australia. But what promised to be an enthralling encounter was to be overshadowed by scandal.

CHAPTER **FOURTEEN**

Scandal and suspension

The news flash from Agence France-Presse in New Delhi seemed so far-fetched that it was almost impossible to believe. Indian police had accused South African cricket captain Hansie Cronjé and three team members of match-fixing. Charges of criminal conspiracy, fraud and match-fixing had been registered against Cronjé, Herschelle Gibbs, Nicky Bojé and Pieter Strydom.

The news broke on Friday, 7 April 2000. The immediate reaction was one of disbelief and denial. Cronjé told Ali Bacher that the allegations were 'absolute rubbish'. The United Cricket Board's managing director put out a statement on Cronjé's behalf and undertook to deal with the media. The captain switched off his cellphone and the UCB kept in touch with him through his wife, Bertha.

Bacher phoned Gibbs and, typically, asked the player some preliminary questions. 'Do you respect me, would you lie to me?'

'Yes, no,' were the replies.

'Have you ever been involved in match-fixing?'

'No.'

Bojé and Strydom also told Bacher there was no substance to the allegations.

Scandal and suspension

The sensational story broke as Australia, the World Cup champions, were preparing to travel to South Africa for a three-match challenge series, which would be reciprocated later in the year by three matches in the Colonial stadium, an indoor arena in Melbourne. The Australians arrived in Durban on the Sunday, while the South Africans were playing a day-night practice match at Kingsmead.

Bacher had arranged a press conference during the dinner break. Half an hour before the conference, a meeting was held in the members' dining room. In attendance were Bacher, Cronjé, Gibbs, Bojé, team manager Goolam Rajah, UCB communications manager Bronwyn Wilkinson and the organisation's legal adviser, Clifford Green. Not present was Pieter Strydom, who had not been selected for the matches against Australia.

Cronjé made three points. He had never been involved in throwing a match, anyone could look at his bank accounts to see if he had received any money and he had never approached any player to throw a game.

The allegations had been the main story in every South African newspaper and news bulletin since Friday. A lengthy transcript of telephone conversations between Cronjé and Sanjeev 'Sanjay' Chawla, allegedly recorded by the Indian police, had been widely published.

The most sensational extract implicated Gibbs.

Sanjay:	Is Strydom playing?
Hansie:	Yes, he is playing, yeah.
Sanjay:	Bojé?
Hansie:	Bojé is playing.
Sanjay:	Yeah, Bojé is playing ... and who is playing? Gibbs?
Hansie:	Gibbs and myself.
Sanjay:	Ya, what about anybody else?
Hansie:	No, I won't be able to get more.
Sanjay:	You won't be able to get more?
Hansie:	No.
Sanjay:	Okay just tell me. But you have only four with you and not anybody else?
Hansie:	No.
Sanjay:	Klusener and no-one?

Hansie: No. No. Impossible. Impossible. They were saying that they were already doing Cochin [Kochi]. The other guys are already angry with me because I have not received their money you know.
Sanjay: No. But I told you, I have already given him altogether 60.
Hansie: Okay.
Sanjay: And tomorrow I can deposit the money in your account. It is not a problem because of the time difference. Tomorrow itself I can deposit the money.
Hansie: Okay, I have spoken. Yes, everything is fine. Spoken to Gibbs and to Williams and Strydom. Everything is fine.
Sanjay: Already, okay. And how many runs for Gibbs?
Hansie: Less than 20.
Sanjay: Less than 20?
Hansie: Yeah.
Sanjay: Okay. So everything is according to plan. They have to score at least 250?
Hansie: Yeah.
Sanjay: And if you score 270, it is off?
Hansie: Okay. And financially the guys want 25. They want 25 each.
Sanjay: Alright, okay.
Hansie: So that's 75 for those three and ... what can you pay me? I do not know how much you pay me ...
Sanjay: You say.
Hansie: If you give me ... 140 for everybody.
Sanjay: 140 altogether?
Hansie: Yeah.
Sanjay: Okay, that's fine.
Hansie: Okay.
Sanjay: And we will sort something out for the previous one as well.
Hansie: Okay, sure.
Sanjay: Yeah?
Hansie: Alright. So we definitely are on.
Sanjay: Okay and one last thing I want to ask you ... you know, just in case India bat first and if they get out for less than 250 and when you come in to bat for the second innings, is it possible that you could ask Gibbs

> to ... his wicket ... we will score him out and try and score slowly and not so fast so that you know ... maybe we can get out of it.
>
> Hansie: Okay.

At the time it was assumed the recordings had been made while the team was staying in New Delhi, before the match in Faridabad in which Gibbs was out for 19. It later emerged, however, that the conversation took place before the final match in Nagpur. One of the frustrating aspects of the whole affair was that South African authorities were unable to obtain authenticated copies of the tapes from their Indian counterparts, despite investigators from the King Commission flying to India. The context and accuracy of the tapes were never fully explained or verified. That, though, was in the future.

In Durban, there was huge interest in the press conference. Cronjé had not spoken directly to the media since the story surfaced. The members' dining room at Kingsmead was packed. Shortly before the conference Cronjé told Gibbs, 'Just deny that I ever approached you and we ever accepted an offer.'

Facing the media, Cronjé, looking strained, offered the same defence he had in the pre-conference meeting. He was supported by Bacher and UCB president Percy Sonn. Gibbs and Bojé simply denied any involvement.

Newspapers the next day focused on Cronjé's denial. 'Nothing to hide, says Cronjé,' was the banner headline in *The Mercury*, the Durban morning newspaper.

Doubts were expressed by the author, though, on the *Sunday Times* website on Monday.

> The most extraordinary statement since the Hansie Cronjé saga exploded came from the South African captain himself, more than 48 hours after the story broke that he and three team-mates faced criminal charges of match-fixing in India.
>
> Cronjé claimed at a press conference on Sunday night he had not read the transcripts of the tape recordings which New Delhi police claim to have recorded of conversations between Cronjé and an Indian bookmaker – even though most South African newspapers published substantial excerpts from the transcripts on Saturday and Sunday.

For someone facing the most serious allegations ever made against an international cricketer, this was at best a remarkable oversight. Studying all the available information would have seemed the obvious first step for Cronjé to take if he was to mount a vigorous assertion of his innocence.

Cronjé had a support group of United Cricket Board president Percy Sonn, managing director Ali Bacher and lawyer Clifford Green. If they did not discuss with him the content of the transcripts in some detail before the press conference they surely failed in their duty.

The South African defence of the national captain has been less than conclusive. Although there seems to be overwhelming support for Cronjé in this country, it would be naive to expect the rest of the world to be as charitable in its interpretation of events which have been on the front pages of newspapers throughout the cricket-playing world.

> **... Rajah told them of Cronjé's confession. The sense of shock was overwhelming for Gibbs. After the meeting he went alone to the dressing room and broke down in tears.**

Cronjé finally cracked in the early hours of Tuesday morning when he confessed that he had lied. In a hand-written confession he admitted receiving money from Chawla but claimed that no other players were involved. He was immediately suspended and withdrawn from the team by Ali Bacher and Percy Sonn, who had been entertaining two leading Australian officials at a private game reserve in northern KwaZulu-Natal. Bacher and Sonn returned to Durban immediately, and decided to ask the government to convene a judicial inquiry.

The South African team met for a morning practice at Kingsmead and Rajah told them of Cronjé's confession. The sense of shock was overwhelming for Gibbs. After the meeting he went alone to the dressing room and broke down in tears.

At lunch-time, Bacher, Sonn, Wilkinson and Green attended a team meeting. After outlining the seriousness of the situation, Bacher asked Gibbs to stand up. 'He asked me, "Herschelle, were you ever approached?" and I said, "No, no Doc, no I wasn't."' Asked at the King Commission why he had lied, he said, 'I was scared and I was doing as Hansie asked me to do.'

Scandal and suspension

When he switched on his cellphone after the lunch-time meeting, there were 75 missed calls. He was advised by Rajah to keep it switched off to avoid being harassed. 'That was the time I started to get a bit fidgety, not knowing what to do.' He couldn't speak to anyone. He tried to contact Cronjé but his phone was switched off too. 'I couldn't focus properly and I didn't sleep very well.'

The first match was the next day. During the morning, Gibbs was phoned by Rajah, who again asked him whether he had been approached. He continued to say no. Batting partner Gary Kirsten called him. Another denial. Kirsten then revealed that Pieter Strydom had told him that Strydom, Boucher and Kallis had been approached by Cronjé. Still Gibbs stuck to his story.

The match at Kingsmead was an emotionally-charged occasion. Pollock, the new captain, bowled brilliantly. His first three overs were maidens and he trapped Mark Waugh lbw for nought in the third over. Gibbs ran out Matthew Hayden, also without scoring, with a diving underarm direct hit from cover in the next over. Australia scrambled a total of 240. Gibbs was out to Glenn McGrath for nought when he played a forcing shot off the back foot to Steve Waugh at cover. Kirsten made 97 and South Africa won a remarkable victory by six wickets.

The series moved on to Cape Town. Back in his home town, Gibbs sought an escape from the pressure. He went to the Galaxy nightclub in Athlone and did not return to the team hotel until 3.30am on the morning of the match. 'I got a bit carried away and saw a few of my mates. I had a few Jack Daniels. I knew it was a day-night game. It meant I could sleep in but I felt a bit heavy the next morning for obvious reasons.'

Inevitably, Gibbs was spotted at the nightclub by someone who tipped off the newspapers. Once again, Cape Town's prodigal son was on the front pages. When a disciplinary hearing was convened in May he was fined R5 000, with a further R10 000 and a ban from three international matches suspended for a year.

After the unexpected triumph of Kingsmead, South Africa played poorly at Newlands on a difficult pitch. Again Gibbs was hopelessly out of form, scoring five off 17 balls before he was caught behind off McGrath. 'I just couldn't get McGrath away. A lot of people blamed it on the night before but

Gary struggled as well on that wicket.' South Africa were all out for 144 and Australia won by five wickets.

The deciding match was at the Wanderers in Johannesburg. In front of a packed crowd of 31 500, South Africa won by four wickets. Gibbs, batting at number three to accommodate Andrew Hall as a pinch-hitting opening batsman, failed for the third time, lbw for four when he padded up to McGrath.

That evening, Gibbs, due to have a meeting with Bacher later in the week, took a call from Cronjé. Gibbs said at the King Commission that Cronjé had told him, 'You can tell Dr Bacher that I approached you but we didn't discuss any figures, no amounts, and I still turned down the offer.' Cronjé said Gibbs should telephone Henry Williams so that he would tell the same story.

Still the doubts nagged at Rajah and Bacher. Once more Rajah telephoned. 'He wanted to know if I was being honest with him. I then said to him that Hansie did approach me but I didn't accept the offer and there were no amounts of money spoken of at all.'

The truth was starting to emerge.

Ali Bacher called Gibbs. 'He asked me, "Herschelle, would you ever lie to me? Do you respect me?" I think he asked me once or quite a few times the same question.'

Bacher asked once more whether Gibbs had been approached by Cronjé. 'I said, "Yes, but I didn't accept the offer."'

Bacher called a meeting the next day at his home in Sandton. Present were UCB vice-president Richard Harrison, Bronwyn Wilkinson, Clifford Green and two players, Strydom and Gibbs. Bojé was asked to attend but said he had never been approached and he did not believe it was necessary to be there.

Minutes of this meeting were handed to the King Commission. Strydom was questioned first. He revealed details of Cronjé's approach to him before the Test in Mumbai and told of his anxiety after the story became public. He had not been with the team but had phoned Cronjé, who told him not to worry because the tapes referred to the one-day games. He had also phoned Mark Boucher and Gibbs. Boucher told him about the meeting in Bangalore with Cronjé, Kallis and Klusener. Gibbs's response was to brush off the affair: 'Herschelle just laughed and said he had also been approached for the one-day game and was asked to get under 20.'

Gibbs says the conversation with Strydom was a night or two before the meeting at Bacher's house. 'When Pieter told me he had been approached by Hansie it was news to me.'

When Gibbs was questioned at the meeting, he told how Cronjé had arrived in the room he shared with Williams in Nagpur. 'He was laughing. He said there are some guys at me and they want you to score less than 20 and I said I'd never do anything like that. He was laughing. There was no money mentioned. I thought it was a joke.'

The whole truth remained concealed.

Afterwards Gibbs had lunch with Bronwyn Wilkinson at the Wanderers Club. According to Wilkinson, Gibbs asked her, 'If someone was asked and they did comply but they never got the money, can they still get nailed?' She asked whether that was in fact the case. He said it was not.

Gibbs gave his own version of the same conversation in his evidence before Judge King.

Gibbs:	We did have one or two Amstels [beers]. I said 'What happens if you did as they asked you to do, or you accepted the offer, but didn't do as they asked you to do?'
Fitzgerald:	And never received any money, what would happen?
Gibbs:	Correct, ja.
Fitzgerald:	And what was her response?
Gibbs:	I think she sipped on her Amstel.

Over the next three weeks Cronjé stayed in touch with Gibbs. 'He phoned occasionally, just to find out if anyone had been asking questions or anything.' Gibbs in turn contacted Williams, 'basically just to remind him to keep his mouth shut'.

The pressure was building up, however. Donné Commins, of the Octagon company, which managed Gibbs's commercial business, told him a judicial commission had been set up and that he would have to give evidence. 'She told me, if I knew anything, I must tell her.'

Still he did not reveal the whole truth. It was a difficult, stressful time. 'Your parents don't know, your friends don't know.' As was the case with Liesl Fuller's pregnancy, he did not share his burden with anyone. 'I'm not very open when it comes to the deeper side. People see a smiling face and a happy-go-lucky kind of guy but when it comes to serious things I keep it to myself.'

Judge Edwin King, former Judge President of the Cape, was appointed to head a judicial inquiry into cricket match-fixing and related matters. The evidence was being collated. It was time for the players involved to consult with lawyers.

On 22 May, Gibbs sat down with advocate Mike Fitzgerald and attorney Peter Whelan. He gave them the version of his story that he had told Bacher more than a month before. Williams also stuck to his story.

Nine days later, with the inquiry a matter of days away, he received a telephone call from Mark Boucher, the South African vice-captain, who asked him to have a drink at a bar in Cape Town's popular Long Street. Boucher was in town for a consultation with Fitzgerald and Whelan. In his statement to the King Commission, Boucher said, 'They told me that they thought that Herschelle was hiding something from them. They told me that it was imperative that Gibbs "come clean" and tell them everything.'

> '. . . he just said to me, "If you don't come clean now and you lie in court, you're going to go to jail. So, if you are hiding something, best you say it now."'

The two players sat down with Donné Commins. 'She obviously felt I was keeping something back,' says Gibbs. Commins had left by the time Boucher broached the crucial question. As Gibbs described it, 'He wanted to know if I'd been honest all the time, speaking to the attorneys and to Dr Bacher and to the media, and I kept on saying yes. And then he said, "Well if you don't come clean now – and I'm not saying that you're being dishonest . . ." he just said to me, "If you don't come clean now and you lie in court, you're going to go to jail. So, if you are hiding something, best you say it now."'

By the count of Jeremy Gauntlett, senior counsel for the United Cricket Board, Gibbs had lied to his employers on eight occasions. Twice, at least, Cronjé had actively encouraged him to mislead others.

Finally the truth was out. The first to be called was Commins, who lived nearby. 'I had only just left them. I was about to park at my house when the phone rang. I went straight back.' Then he called Whelan, who contacted Fitzgerald. Whelan hurried to the Long Street Cafe. Gibbs ordered a Jack Daniels. There was a lot of truth to be told.

The King Commission started its hearings on 7 June at the Centre for the Book in a large, wood-panelled room with a high, domed ceiling. There was huge media interest. Two journalists had travelled from Australia, while others arrived from England.

Gibbs telephoned Cronjé to break the news that he was going to tell the truth. 'He didn't get angry or anything. He said, "It's fine, I understand. Just be honest with them and tell them exactly what happened."'

For days on end, banner newspaper headlines carried the latest revelations. The first celebrity witness was Pat Symcox, who told how Cronjé had consulted him about a match-fixing offer before a one-day final against Pakistan in January 1995, soon after Cronjé became captain. Symcox gave his version of the meeting in Mumbai.

Gibbs arrived on day two and listened as Derek Crookes and Daryll Cullinan gave evidence. Security consultant Rory Steyn provided dramatic details of Cronjé's late-night confession in Durban.

The other players were dressed in largely conservative, dark outfits. Gibbs wore a flashy, high-buttoned light beige suit with a dark shirt and tie. He looked and felt anxious. He had been at the lawyers' chambers earlier to go through his statement one last time before he took the witness stand. Photographers and television cameramen jostled to take his picture. The room was packed. 'I was shaking. I couldn't even complete the oath, I was so nervous.'

At one stage he was close to tears. 'I could tell how much I had let the people down and let myself down. At the same time I knew I was doing the right thing, coming out with the truth.'

A stunned audience heard him confess how Cronjé had made him the offer in Nagpur and how he had agreed to take a bribe, how Cronjé had asked him to lie and how Boucher had persuaded him to tell the truth.

Afterwards he went back to the lawyers' chambers. 'I had a cigarette and a drink. I was so relieved it was over.'

His stint as a witness might have been over but the repercussions were about to begin. A huge headline across the front page of the *Cape Times* the next morning screamed, 'Gibbs runs out Cronjé.' The article reported that Gibbs was almost certain to be axed from the tour of Sri Lanka in July.

Williams gave evidence the next day and corroborated his room-mate's story. Perhaps the most telling sentence in his statement was, 'I had great respect for Mr Cronjé. I thought, if he can do something like this, why can't I?' He admitted, 'It was not right. I was stupid. I should have known better.'

In the early stages of the King Commission hearings it seemed there was a genuine zeal to uncover every unpleasant truth. The Gibbs revelations were probably the most newsworthy, while Cronjé's testimony was so eagerly anticipated that it was eventually broadcast live on national television.

The statement that became part of the commission record was greatly modified from his first, hand-written confession in which he denied having involved any other players.

The hearings were adjourned on 26 June. Two investigators went to India to seek further evidence and to try to obtain authenticated versions of the tape recordings made by the Indian police. They returned empty-handed.

In the meantime, Gibbs was withdrawn from the side that toured Sri Lanka in July 2000. He, Williams and Strydom had to appear before a three-man tribunal headed by former judge Mervyn King.

Gibbs went armed with testimonials from John Gardener, who had been his headmaster at Bishops, Arthur Turner, chief executive of Western Province, his former provincial captain, Craig Matthews, and his current captain, HD Ackerman.

Gardener described Herschelle as 'an ebullient, high-spirited, outgoing character' who 'does tend to leap before he looks'. He wrote that he hoped the tribunal would be able to 'temper justice with mercy, to combine deterrence with constructiveness, to balance the needs of the community and those of the individual in a tough-tender fashion'.

Turner wrote, 'Herschelle's loyalty and dedication to Western Province is certainly an example to other Western Province players and certainly more than I can say for certain current Western Province players in the national team.' He believed that the player had been 'sucked into this untenable position'.

Matthews related an 'over-riding feeling about him that he was incredibly impressionable. He really feels a need to be accepted and liked and has sometimes compromised himself in this pursuit'. Matthews added, 'He has made a few wrong calls that can be attributed to the folly of youth but he has many great attributes, which make him an inspiration to many.'

Ackerman wrote of a long-lasting friendship. 'In the last few months we have seen a change in "Scooter". As much as he tries to hide it from his friends,

Scandal and suspension

we can all see that he is not himself. His one true passion has been taken away from him and he needs it back. SA cricket needs Herschelle Gibbs.'

The tribunal's verdict was delivered on 28 August and the findings were announced by Michael Kuper SC.

Gibbs and Williams were banned from playing international cricket for the rest of the year. They were found guilty of conspiracy but not match-fixing as neither had gone through with the plan to under-perform. The bans, backdated to 30 June, would end on 31 December. Gibbs was fined R60 000 and Williams R10 000. Gibbs was given a heavier fine because he continually denied any involvement in the scandal, despite being questioned on numerous occasions by the UCB. 'Gibbs compounded the damage he had done,' Kuper said.

The committee considered a life ban for the two players but decided such a penalty 'would have gone beyond what is fair and proper'. An extenuating circumstance was that the players had been corrupted by Cronjé. 'Both players were heavily under the influence of their captain,' Kuper said. For this reason, they would be allowed to play domestic cricket while serving their bans from the international game.

International Cricket Council rules on match-fixing, which demanded a life ban for anyone involved in match-fixing, only came into effect on 20 April and therefore could not be taken into account.

Kuper said Gibbs never explained why he did not under-perform as agreed. 'When Gibbs came to bat he had closed his mind to the corruption. His was a temporary fall from grace.'

Strydom was acquitted on charges of contravening a rule forbidding betting on the outcome of matches, as a bet he had tried to place on the Centurion Test had been on behalf of Cronjé.

UCB managing director Ali Bacher told the press conference at which the bans were announced that Gibbs would lose earnings in the region of R756 000 because of the ban.

In a statement, Gibbs apologised for his actions and said he had 'come to appreciate fully my stupidity'.

Judge Edwin King released an interim report which summarised the evidence, then a second interim report which recommended some measures to monitor cricketers' actions.

In October, the general council of the UCB resolved to ban Hansie Cronjé for life from all activities of the UCB and its affiliates.

The King Commission did not sit again. In his final report, issued in June 2001, Judge Edwin King said the fact that action had been taken against Cronjé, Gibbs and Williams, and that some of his recommendations had been carried out, had enabled the commission to achieve its objective of investigating and reporting on match-fixing and related matters.

CHAPTER **FIFTEEN**

The Cronjé factor

Hansie Cronjé was a powerful and charismatic captain who had a profound influence on the players under his control. The extent of his power became evident during the corruption saga.

In summing up the evidence that had been presented at the King Commission, Judge Edwin King described the various attempts made by Cronjé to corrupt his team-mates. 'There is a common thread to these events where Cronjé sought to involve his team-mates in match-fixing or related matters and that is that the initial approach is made jocularly. It seems that this was Cronjé's *modus operandi*. He would sound out his colleagues, in a way which would enable him to say later, if the need arose, that he had only been joking. Herschelle Gibbs also testified that he was approached by Cronjé "with a huge grin on his face". In fact, Cronjé said in evidence that he felt shamed by Pieter Strydom saying that he wanted to do his best and thereafter "tried to pass off the whole incident as a joke".'

Professor Tim Noakes, South Africa's eminent sports scientist and the South African team doctor during their World Cup campaign in Pakistan in 1996, was made aware almost immediately after his appointment of Cronjé's power and the way he operated.

Addressing the players in Johannesburg in late 1995, some months before the World Cup, Noakes warned them of the harmful effects of drugs and told them that they would be tested for substance abuse before they went to the tournament.

He was shocked when Cronjé said at the end of his presentation, 'Your job is not to test us but to give us the drugs that can give us a competitive advantage.'

Recalling the incident seven years later, Noakes says, 'His statement immediately undermined my status in the team. I wasn't sure whether he was joking. At that stage I didn't know all of the players well enough to come back at him.'

Noakes, who has an infectious enthusiasm for pushing the boundaries of knowledge about sport, says Cronjé made it clear from the start that he did not regard him as part of the team. Noakes was planning to compile a diary of his experiences in Pakistan and wanted to interview players 'to find out what made them tick'. Cronjé refused to co-operate and ensured that the project foundered.

'He wanted total control, with no interference,' said Noakes, who believes the scandal of 2000 and the corruption of Gibbs had their roots in the meeting in Mumbai in December 1996. 'He got the team together and said, "Let's cheat." Everything came from that.'

In hindsight, Noakes believes that the 1995 incident was an indication that Cronjé wanted him to cheat as well. Cronjé's remark about acquiring drugs to help the team might well have been a test to establish whether Noakes was prepared to compromise his ethical standards.

Noakes says the players were so much under the captain's control that they were unable to judge him objectively. 'What astonishes me is the continued support that he has.'

Among those who refuse to condemn Cronjé is Herschelle Gibbs, even though his career was almost ruined by him.

As recently as 25 September 2002, Gibbs dedicated a century made against India in the ICC Champions Trophy to Cronjé because it was the late captain's birthday.

Bob Woolmer, who was coach during most of Cronjé's captaincy, is prepared to give him the benefit of the doubt. He says, 'I spoke to Hansie about this. He said he went in to Herschelle and Williams and offered them the money but he really wanted to see their reactions. He'd been talking to the bookie. Knowing Hansie as I do, he did it for a reason, he was testing other people and he was probably testing himself.

The Cronjé factor

'There was an immediate reaction, "Okay." Those two are naughty boys. Hansie said he was a bit taken aback at the time and fortunately nothing happened on the field. When the lawyers started taking statements, Herschelle told a lot of fibs to protect Hansie and then eventually said, yes, that he had been offered money.

'As Hansie says, it looks far worse when it's written down on paper than it was. He used to test people all the time. I spent my life being tested by Hansie Cronjé.'

Woolmer's generous view of the former captain is shared by many, as was shown by the fulsome tributes and the public outpouring of emotion after Cronjé died in an air crash near George on 1 June 2002.

It is, to paraphrase Tim Noakes, astonishing that so many people are prepared to ignore the clear evidence that was presented to the King Commission. It is particularly astonishing that Gibbs, whose career was so nearly ruined by Cronjé's influence, should have forgiven him so lightly. Gibbs's attitude is especially surprising in the light of the evidence which suggests that had things gone according to plan at Nagpur, Cronjé would have pocketed $110 000, more than seven times as much as Gibbs and Williams.

'Perhaps he tried to do down his own mates,' admits Gibbs, who adds, 'Even if he thought like that, for me it was good money anyway.' There was not so much as a stutter in his relationship with his former captain. After listening to Cronjé giving evidence at the King Commission, he went to the chambers of Cronjé's lawyers. 'I hadn't seen him for a few months. He kept on apologising. He said, "I'm sorry to have dragged you through all this." I said, "That's fine, don't worry, worse things have happened. It's finished, it's done." It was just nice to see him.'

Within two months, Gibbs spent a long weekend at Cronjé's home at the Fancourt golf estate near George, as he had been invited to play golf at the opening of Sparrebosch, another luxury golf development in nearby Knysna. The former team-mates played in a celebrity four-ball put together by Garth le Roux, a Springbok fast bowler from the rebel era. In South Africa, it seems, notoriety does not necessarily diminish the appeal of a celebrity.

Gibbs made his first hole-in-one during the game, when he hit a perfect nine-iron into the 130-metre 11th hole. It was the first 'ace' recorded at Sparrebosch. He had another round of golf with Cronjé when he and some friends went to Fancourt a month or two later.

They stayed in contact by telephone. 'He would phone or send me an SMS when I did well and we would have the occasional chat on the phone.'

Does he feel that Cronjé let him down? 'I never held it against him. We were like two naughty little kids. It had got us into trouble but it was over. I had been given my fine and my sentence. I was still going to be playing cricket and he wasn't. There was nothing for me to be unhappy about. Obviously my reputation went down a bit but I could change that by playing good cricket. It was like a six-month holiday for me.'

'Obviously my reputation went down a bit but I could change that by playing good cricket. It was like a six-month holiday for me.'

It is a reply that suggests Gibbs still does not fully appreciate the seriousness of the situation in which he found himself.

A few months before Cronjé's death, Gibbs and some other players met him for a drink in Johannesburg, where Cronjé had taken a job as a financial adviser with an equipment company, commuting weekly from George.

By coincidence, Gibbs was in George on the weekend that Cronjé died, making a personal appearance at the invitation of a company. 'I spoke to him on the phone on the Friday night, so I was probably one of the last people to speak to him. He said he would see me the next day for a cup of Mocca Java.'

They never did share a coffee. Later that evening Cronjé, who had missed a scheduled flight, climbed aboard a cargo aircraft used for a mail delivery run. On Saturday morning, after an aborted landing because of bad weather, the aircraft crashed into Cradock Peak in the Outeniqua Mountains.

'My phone started ringing early. At first I thought it must be a joke. My dad was one of the callers and he said Hansie had been in a plane crash.' Brian McMillan and his wife, Denise, were part of the group with Gibbs. That evening they went to the Cronjé home to comfort Hansie's wife, Bertha.

Gibbs's admiration remains undimmed. 'He was a great person. He had his faults but I had a lot of respect for him.'

There is almost universal agreement by those interviewed for this book that Cronjé's power over Gibbs was such that the player would have followed almost any suggestion made by his captain.

Basil Bey, his school rugby coach, said it did not come as a great shock to learn that his former star flyhalf had been involved in the Cronjé affair. 'We all knew Herschelle well enough to know he was going to slip sometime. I don't think there was any evil intent and I don't think he will ever be corrupt. There's a huge honesty about Herschelle.'

Springbok rugby player and former Bishops team-mate, Selborne Boome, says, 'Hansie obviously influenced Herschelle. I don't think it's something Herschelle would like to have been involved in but if Hansie was the leader and the guy who was supposed to know everything, if he told him it was okay ... maybe he was a bit naive.'

Robbie Fleck says he felt 'very sorry' for his friend. 'He's the type of guy who believes in people and can be influenced. I don't think he knew the full circumstances of what he was doing.' Typically, Fleck managed to provide some light relief. 'I gave him a call and told him, "If there's any chance you can't play cricket again, you can always come and play for the Springboks."' More seriously, Fleck thinks Herschelle has emerged as a better person. 'The whole experience has helped him mature.'

His school cricket coach, Grant Norton, agrees that Herschelle was especially impressionable. 'I wasn't surprised that someone got to Herschelle. I believe he was totally naive. He worshipped Hansie, who had backed him and given him confidence. He thought if Hansie said something was okay then it was. He came through it well. He grew up.'

Brian McMillan, who is among those who feels Cronjé was harshly treated, says the nature of professional sport is such that its participants need to make as much money as possible while they can. 'Herschelle was an easy target. Hansie wielded a lot of authority.'

Where Gibbs and the admirers of Cronjé are correct is that he was an inspirational captain. He led South Africa in 53 Tests between 1994 and 2000, of which 27 were won and only 11 lost. In 138 one-day internationals, there were 99 wins and 35 defeats. It is a record that stands comparison with the best captains in the history of the game.

History, though, will not judge him on results alone.

CHAPTER **SIXTEEN**

Back from the wilderness

As punishments go, the six-month ban from international cricket served on Herschelle Gibbs could by no means be described as excessively harsh, although it was costly in terms of lost income. He missed a tour of Sri Lanka and one-day tournaments in Australia, Singapore and Kenya as well as the start of the international season in South Africa.

He enjoyed being back with his provincial team-mates at Western Province but his form did not suggest that he would be an automatic selection for the national side once he had served the term of his ban. By the standards of an established international cricketer, his scores for Western Province in four four-day matches and seven one-day games were ordinary, until he came up against Eastern Province in a day-night match at Newlands on 22 December, 10 days before he became eligible for international selection.

The national players were back in action and Gibbs was reunited with Gary Kirsten at the top of the batting order. Eastern Province were unbeaten and in Mfuneko Ngam and Justin Kemp they had two of the form players of the season. Ngam had made his Test debut two weeks earlier, and he was the fastest bowler in the country, a truly exciting prospect.

A big holiday crowd turned up to see what promised to be an enthralling contest. The talented James Bryant made a century for Eastern Province, who scored a moderately challenging 198 for six. There was a buzz of anticipation during the supper break as spectators looked forward to seeing Ngam, who had been timed at 150km an hour in an earlier match, bowling against Kirsten and Gibbs.

What followed was a partnership described by Kirsten as one of the most memorable he had shared with his younger team-mate. Both players were in outstanding form. Ngam conceded 40 runs in four overs, Garnett Kruger 27 off five, Kemp 28 off four, and the promising Robin Peterson 22 off three. It was batting at its best. Gibbs raced to 90 off 74 balls before he was out 24 runs short of victory. Kirsten, typically, saw it through to the end, making 85 not out.

Kirsten went to Durban to play in the first Test against Sri Lanka. Gibbs stayed in Cape Town and was out for nought in another Standard Bank Cup match against Free State.

It has become a tradition that South Africa play back-to-back Tests in Durban and Cape Town over the festive season, with the Durban game starting on 26 December and the Cape Town match on 2 January. It is also traditional that the squad picked for the Durban Test travels on to Newlands unchanged. However, when Rushdi Magiet announced the players for Kingsmead, he added that the selectors reserved the right to add to the squad for Newlands. Would Gibbs be brought in for the Cape Town Test?

Boeta Dippenaar had been opening the batting in Gibbs's absence. He had not secured his place up to then, although in the rain-hit final Test against New Zealand at the Wanderers in early December he had made a splendid century.

The Kingsmead Test was drawn, largely because the fourth day's play was lost due to rain. Dippenaar made 11 and 22. When the teams prepared to travel to Cape Town on 31 December, it was learnt unofficially, though it was not actually announced, that Dippenaar had been released. He would be going to East London to play in a one-day match for Free State.

New Year's Day is not an occasion on which journalists tend to be up and about early but they were out in force for the South African team's practice on the first morning of 2001, suspecting that Gibbs was about to return from the wilderness. Sure enough, Herschelle Gibbs was at the practice, and Magiet confirmed that he would be in the team the next day. The selectors had been unanimous. 'He has served his time and he is the best man for the job.'

After the practice, Gibbs told the scribes and television crews that he hoped cricketers throughout the world would have learnt from what he described as 'the biggest mistake I've made in my life.

'It is a fresh start and hopefully a much more professional and better one,' he said. 'I've had a lot to think about in the last seven or eight months. I've bided my time but it seems to have taken forever.' Asked if he thought he had learnt a lesson, Gibbs said, 'It's not only me. I don't think all the other cricketers around the world will ever make the same mistake again.'

> 'I've had a lot to think about in the last seven or eight months. I've bided my time but it seems to have taken forever.'

He added that he looked forward to making his return at his home ground. 'It is great to represent my country again, with all the honour, prestige and privilege that goes with it.'

South African captain Shaun Pollock welcomed Gibbs back. 'Herschelle is a class player and he's going to be around a long time. It's obviously been frustrating him. It's great to have him back.'

On a lively pitch, Pollock and Ngam destroyed the Sri Lankan batting, bowling the tourists out for 95. Gibbs was batting before tea but it was not a happy return. He was out in the first over of the innings, trapped leg before second ball for nought by the left-armer, Chaminda Vaas, as he went back in his crease to a ball that swung in.

Despite the early setback, South Africa steamrollered to a record win by an innings and 229 runs. The first run of Gibbs's new international career would have to wait.

There were four one-day internationals before the third and final Test, the first in Paarl. Gibbs unveiled a new number, 00, to be worn on the back of his green one-day shirt. 'I thought I might as well re-start my whole career so that is why I chose it,' he said.

His scores, though, weren't much higher than his number. His nought in the Test was followed by a single in his return to the one-day game. Again he lasted just two balls and again the bowler was Vaas. Dippenaar, having lost his Test place to Gibbs, made 65 and Jacques Kallis hit a century.

The next match, at Newlands, was slightly more productive, but once more Gibbs was outscored by Dippenaar, who made 77 to his 13. Vaas again claimed his wicket, with the help of a diving catch at square leg after Gibbs whipped the ball firmly off his body.

The selectors kept faith with their prodigal son, however, and he made 79 in the penultimate one-day international in Bloemfontein. By Gibbs's standards in one-day games, it was a slow innings, although he could afford to take his time because South Africa had a relatively low target of 207. It took him 79 balls to reach 50 and in all he batted for 112 balls before he was run out.

It was his only good innings of the home international summer. Vaas had him caught at square leg again for three in the final one-day game at the Wanderers and he was caught behind off Nuwan Zoysa, also a left-armer, for a single in the final Test at Centurion. South Africa wrapped up the series with another innings win so there was no second chance to shine.

It could by no means be described as a great season for Gibbs. In seven first-class matches he had not hit a century and his average for the season was 26,33. Nor had he shone in the one-day game.

There was never was any serious doubt, however, that he would be picked for a tour that he had long set his sights on, South Africa's first full visit to the West Indies, which included five Tests and seven one-day internationals. His taste of the Caribbean as a schoolboy nine years earlier had made him hungry for more.

Disappointed with his form after his return from international exile, he set himself an important goal. 'Time was the crucial thing. I said to myself I must be patient in the West Indies. Even if I don't score runs for hours, I must stay at the wicket.'

The tour was to be a career highlight and his adherence to his own injunction proved to be a critical factor. There was only one warm-up match, at the Everest club in Georgetown, Guyana, where the ground is visibly below sea level. Situated close to the sea wall that separates the Guyanan capital from the sea, the ground is several metres below the muddy sea water at the mouth of the mighty Essequibo river, which flows from the heart of the South American jungle. Gibbs made 36 and 28 and had enough time to get used to the slow pitches, which had become the norm in the Caribbean.

The first Test was across the small city of Georgetown, at the Bourda ground, which is surrounded by wooden grandstands. As at all the West Indian Test venues, the match would be accompanied by the throbbing beat of a loud disco system pounding out Caribbean rhythms between overs.

It took the South Africans a while to work out the right length to bowl on a bare, slow surface and the West Indies hurried to 101 for one at lunch on the first day. Thereafter, the cricket became a hard grind, with both teams having to work for their runs in a match that seldom seemed likely to end in anything other than a draw. After failing in the first innings, Gibbs made 83 not out on the final afternoon.

There was another important contribution by Gibbs in the second Test at the Queen's Park Oval in Port-of-Spain, Trinidad. Although he was outshone by Daryll Cullinan, whose 103 and 73 were match-winning efforts, he made 38 and 87. Apart from a first-innings half-century by Jacques Kallis, there was not much to the rest of the South African batting and the West Indies needed only 232 to win.

This should have been a relatively easy target but South Africa won what Pollock later described as 'the most intense Test match I have played in'. The West Indies lost their first five wickets for 51 runs but Carl Hooper and Ramnaresh Sarwan put on 92 for the sixth wicket. The match was in the balance again with tea approaching on the last day, before Sarwan fell victim to a planned tactic, caught at square leg off a mis-timed hook. Gibbs struck a decisive blow after the break, running out Ridley Jacobs, the last of the capable West Indian batsmen. He made a direct hit at the bowler's end, showing lightning reflexes after Hooper called for a leg bye as the ball trickled towards backward point. The last three wickets fell quickly as South Africa secured an important win.

The match provided two significant milestones in the history of Test cricket. Queen's Park Oval became the first ground outside of England or Australia to stage 100 Test matches. The emotional highlight, however, was when Courtney Walsh, the seemingly indestructible West Indian fast bowler, became the first bowler in Test history to take 500 wickets. Kallis was the victim in more ways than one. Umpire Darrell Hair of Australia gave the crucial lbw decision despite a thick edge from Kallis's bat before the ball thudded into his pad.

The third Test, in Barbados, was drawn, but not before another Cullinan century and a West Indian collapse on the final afternoon. The home side crashed to 88 for seven after what had seemed a token declaration left them to bat out a minimum of 28 overs. South Africa managed to bowl 38,4 and it would have been more had it had not been for some shameless time wasting by Dinanath Ramnarine and Mervyn Dillon.

The crucial fourth Test was in Antigua, an island that claims to have 365 beaches, one for each day of the year. One of the most impressive is that which fronts the Jolly Harbour resort, which is about as congenial a place for a cricket team to prepare as can be imagined. A huge expanse of dazzling white sand fringes a bay of turquoise sea. In the distance can be seen the island of Montserrat, which was devastated by the eruption of a volcano in 1997. After the Test, the South Africans would travel to Montserrat by ferry to become the first international team to play there since the disaster.

In the grounds of the resort is a cricket field with the best net pitches the South Africans would practise on in the West Indies. Wives, girlfriends and children had arrived. The West Indies board and the series sponsors, Cable and Wireless, hosted a lavish beach party. The guest of honour was Curtly Ambrose, a famous Antiguan, who had retired from Test cricket seven months earlier. It was a great deal more enjoyable to be socialising with Curtly than facing him on a cricket pitch. A steel band played. This was how cricket tours should be.

The serious business was across the island at the Recreation Ground in St John's, an intimate arena of double-decker stands where the spectators are within whispering distance of the players. Except that whispering is not an option when Chicky, the original cricket DJ, whose antics have been imitated at every other major ground in the Caribbean, is playing his reggae music or exhorting the fans to support the West Indies.

It was at the Recreation Ground where Viv Richards, now Sir Vivian, the greatest of all Antiguan cricketers, made the fastest Test century of all time, scored off 56 balls against England in 1985/86. Such feats would not be possible in the Test match of 2001. Word had reached the South Africans in Barbados that the pitch originally earmarked for the fourth Test would not be used. Instead, the West Indies would be gambling on spin bowling on a rough, uneven and under-prepared adjacent pitch. This would be no Test for the stroke-players.

Surprisingly, Carl Hooper decided to send South Africa in after winning the toss, fearing that the South African bowlers would have been able to exploit some moisture near the surface early in the match. The West Indies had picked two specialist spinners as well as Hooper, who was a handy off-spinner, and only two fast bowlers. Allan Donald was missing from the South African team because of an injured hamstring.

Herschelle Gibbs would play two of the most significant innings of his life in Antigua. In the first, he made 85 in a South African total of 247. He was the only South African able to play with consistent fluency on a treacherous pitch of awkward bounce. It was the third time in the series he had reached the eighties, but a century again proved elusive. He swept at Hooper, was too quick on the shot, and the ball looped off the back of his bat to Ridley Jacobs, the wicketkeeper.

The West Indies replied with 140, failing to show the patience that was needed on such a pitch. Gibbs then played probably the slowest innings of his career. It was early on day three and South Africa had an important lead. With Gary Kirsten out cheaply, it was crucial not to allow the West Indies back into the match. The leg-spinner Ramnarine bowled around the wicket into the rough outside leg-stump, and the batsmen padded him away. Not even Chicky's exhortations could lift the tempo of the day as only 72 runs were scored in 61 overs between lunch and the close of play. Gibbs was there for most of that time, scoring 45 off 195 balls.

'We were batting for time. There was no rush because there was still so much time left. The idea was to try to bat out that day and then push it along the next day.' It was all going according to plan until a ball from Ramnarine kicked off the pitch. Gibbs pulled his bat away and the ball went off his shoulder to slip. 'By that stage they were desperate for a wicket. Ridley Jacobs appealed but I think he was just trying it on.' Unfortunately for Gibbs, the appeal was upheld.

Gibbs and Neil McKenzie's painstaking partnership, during which they eked out 78 runs in 53,2 overs, put important distance between them and their hosts. Pollock was happy with the way they batted. 'The West Indies bowled well and it was difficult to score. There is still a lot of time to go and it looked as though the pitch was difficult for batting.' Pollock was able to set the West Indies a target of 323 in 131 overs. Despite some dazzling but high-risk batting by Brian Lara, who made 91, South Africa won by 82 runs.

The series was won. South Africa were the first side to triumph in the Caribbean since Mark Taylor's Australians won a four-match series 2-1 in 1994/95. Before that, the West Indies had been unbeaten in a home series since 1972/73. Even Steve Waugh's team in 1999/2000 had to be content with a share of the honours.

It was time to celebrate but, as would emerge later in the tour when the 'marijuana incident' hit the headlines, it was yet another occasion in his career that Gibbs's judgment let him down.

The Test was followed by an outing to Montserrat for a game that was notable for the brief return to action of Curtly Ambrose and, on the voyage home, the sight of the great man leaning over the rail and losing his lunch as the sea turned choppy. It was enough to bring at least a wry smile to the face of anyone who had felt even mildly ill at the thought of batting against one of the world's most feared fast bowlers.

Yet another Caribbean paradise lay ahead as the South Africans played a two-day match in Montego Bay, Jamaica. Gibbs was given a game off and although he had to go to the ground to do his share of 12th man duties, he was able to enjoy a few relaxing days. The players were accommodated in six-bedroom units at a golf and beach resort. Each unit had its own pool, but with golf at about $120 a round he didn't take the opportunity to hone his swing. Instead, he had fun zipping around the resort in a golf cart. He also discovered a nightclub that had an unusual feature, a slide leading from the first floor to a swimming pool on the ground level. As he wasn't playing in the game, he could linger.

As tends to happen in a 'dead rubber' match, the South Africans played below their best and were beaten in the fifth Test at Sabina Park in Kingston, which was dominated by the emotion of protracted homage to Courtney Walsh. He had announced that the match, in his home town, would be his final Test.

Gibbs was the leading run-scorer from either side in the series, with 464 runs at an average of 51,55. He had been tough and consistent against good-quality bowling in conditions that required concentration and application.

The West Indies won the first one-day international, also at Sabina Park. Gibbs relished a return to Antigua for the second international, hitting the century that had proved just beyond his grasp in the Test matches. He made a match-winning 104 and shared a record second-wicket stand of 179 with Jacques Kallis. Both players hit sixes that soared out of the small ground into the surrounding streets.

South Africa dominated the one-day series, winning five matches in succession, with Gibbs in irresistible form. He made 46 and 27 in back-to-back matches in Grenada and hammered another glorious century in Barbados.

In Barbados, Gibbs hit a high, even by the standards he had set in the West Indies. First, he cut down the West Indies with two outstanding pieces of fielding. Shivnarine Chanderpaul was run out with a direct hit at the bowler's end from midwicket and Ridley Jacobs went to an astonishing catch, Gibbs diving full length to hold on to the ball millimetres from the turf.

Then, after a third successive 50-plus first-wicket stand with Kirsten, he hit some sublime strokes, hitting three sixes and 11 fours as he made 107 off 132 balls. There was a special pleasure at the after-match awards ceremony. The man who judged him man of the match was his old batting mentor, Desmond Haynes, the former Barbados and West Indies opener. Gibbs paid tribute to Haynes for teaching him so much about batting during his stint with Western Province.

The match marked the first time since the advent of one-day internationals that a touring side in the West Indies had taken the honours in both forms of the game.

Back in South Africa, a proud father had been watching his son on television. Herman Gibbs, not outwardly sentimental, was inspired to write a poem, entitled *Remote Control,* which was later published in an anthology by *poetry.com*.

Back from the wilderness

*Faraway on the islands
where the game is played
lies cricket's paradise
the game is on between
yesterday's heroes and
the rising stars
watched by frantic fans
faraway from the islands
a paternal string ties a
bond between father and son
glued in front of the box
every motion is monitored
some will say father's
talking to the TV as he
wills the son on to a ton
on the islands the son shines
the opposition fades in the glare
back home the smile lights up
a face bearing the scars of
ball-by-ball agony and ecstacy.*

CHAPTER **SEVENTEEN**

Smoking in the West Indies

Like so many scandals, the marijuana-smoking incident in Antigua was made worse by a futile attempt to keep it a secret.

It was on 11 May, more than a month after it happened, that the United Cricket Board announced that six members of the South African squad had admitted smoking the drug in an hotel room as they celebrated their Test series victory on 10 April.

There were five players involved, Paul Adams, Roger Telemachus, André Nel, Justin Kemp and Herschelle Gibbs. The sixth offender was Craig Smith, who had been the team's physiotherapist since their return to international cricket in 1991.

According to a statement issued by the UCB, the six admitted their guilt. 'The Misconduct Committee accepted that this was a one-off incident. The accused all expressed remorse, apologised and gave an assurance that this would not happen again.' They were fined R10 000 each and severely reprimanded. The committee consisted of team manager Goolam Rajah, coach Graham Ford, assistant coach Corrie van Zyl, captain Shaun Pollock and vice-captain Mark Boucher.

Gibbs described how the dope-smoking incident arose. 'After the fourth day's play, we knew we had a good chance of winning. We were sitting in the dressing room, having a drink. One of the guys said, in a joking sort of way, "If we win this Test I am going to have the biggest, fattest zol [marijuana cigarette]." The guys said, "Why not? We'll go with that." '

Never one to take a back seat when mischief was about, Gibbs spoke to the team's local liaison officer, appropriately nicknamed 'Smokey', the next morning. 'Listen, buddy, won't you organise us a few joints for us to smoke after the game?'

'No problem,' said the liaison man.

Quite apart from any other legal, moral or role-model considerations, Gibbs and the fellow smokers were wrong to discuss their planned prank in front of team-mates in the dressing room. Nor was it the place to conduct a transaction for the purchase of an illegal substance. Not surprisingly, some of the senior players were offended. This was not the sort of talk expected in a room in which men were preparing to represent their country on a crucial day during a cricket series.

'Smokey' was true to his word and handed Gibbs 'the stuff' after play. He distributed it to some of his co-conspirators. After several drinks to toast a series victory, one player, not Gibbs, started to roll a marijuana cigarette in the dressing room but was persuaded to put it away.

Back at the Jolly Harbour resort that evening, the 'joints' were rolled and smoked. Three players who had earlier said they would join in decided not to participate. 'It was the first and last time I tried it,' said Gibbs.

He claims he was not aware that marijuana was illegal in Antigua and other Caribbean islands. 'You'd never think so, you can smell it at every ground you go to.'

It was only in Montego Bay, several days later, that there were repercussions. 'It had obviously got out somehow and team management called a meeting. The guilty parties had to stay behind and they asked us exactly what had gone on.'

It has never been clearly established how the incident came to the notice of the team management, though there had been some bad feeling between Cullinan and Roger Telemachus, during an otherwise uneventful two-day match against Jamaica in Montego Bay. Telemachus was fined R1 000 for verbally abusing Cullinan, and another R1 000 because it was his second offence on the tour. He also apologised to Cullinan.

Cullinan later denied he had been the 'whistle blower' but there was no doubt he was one of those upset by the irresponsible attitude of some of his team-mates. Ken Jennings, a sports psychologist who worked closely with Cullinan, strongly criticised the leadership in South African cricket for what he said was mismanagement of the incident.

Dr Jennings said in an interview in the *Sunday Times* later in 2001 that the decision to keep it secret for more than a month meant that innocent players had to cover up an illegal action, with potentially harmful effects on long-term team loyalty.

As a former provincial cricketer, Jennings said he agreed there were some things which should 'stay within the team' but this did not extend to condoning law-breaking. 'It is very dangerous to have a veil of secrecy which has to be drawn over the whole team even though the whole team is not involved in the illegality.'

Gerald Majola, who had succeeded Ali Bacher as chief executive of the UCB, issued a statement to explain the delay. He said the *Sunday Independent* newspaper was set to run a story after a tip-off that allegedly came from a member of the squad who was no longer in the Caribbean. There were so many inaccurracies in their version of the events, he said, that the UCB had no option but to put the record straight.

'They were going to write that three coloured players were caught smoking dagga [marijuana] and were going to be sent home in disgrace until the sports minister Ncgonde Balfour intervened. That is just not true,' Majola said.

'I have taken a lot of criticism for the late release of the story and some people have even indicated that we tried to cover it up. That is also not true, it really isn't. There isn't much point in having committees and recognised processes if you are simply going to ignore them. I have never covered anything up and I never will.' Majola added that he and Rajah were planning to submit separate reports on the incident to the UCB executive committee on completion of the tour.

'I hope nobody would condone what they did but they have been caught, sentenced and punished. They owned up, took responsibility for their actions and apologised. Personally, I think the fine is pretty substantial. It's a lot to pay for a puff. What they did was silly and a consequence of the celebrations after winning a hard Test series. I believe they have paid for their mistake now,' said Majola.

For Gibbs there was further cause for concern. He still had a suspended sentence hanging over him after his nightclub escapade in Cape Town in April

2000. He had paid a fine of R5 000 but an additional R10 000 and a ban for three international matches had been suspended for a year.

Brian Basson, the UCB Director of Cricket Operations, said the new transgression was a similar offence and the suspended part of the sentence would come into effect. It would mean missing two Test matches and a one-day international when South Africa toured Zimbabwe in September 2001. Basson said he had referred the matter to Majola.

However, the UCB disciplinary committee, chaired by Brandon Foot, decided not to enforce the sentence, and to extend the period of suspension by another year on condition that the player underwent an approved programme of mentorship and counselling in the life skills 'necessary for a professional sportsman and role model'.

Gibbs expressed his gratitude in a statement issued on his behalf. 'I believe this is a fair outcome and a constructive way of dealing with the matter. I'm relieved it is over so I can move forward and concentrate on my cricket.'

He was enrolled on a life skills programme at the Sports Science Institute in Newlands, put together by Gill Taylor, coordinator of Maestros of the Future. The six-week course, spread over a two-month period, covered a variety of issues, from media training to substance abuse to counselling by a sports psychologist. Twice a week he spent an hour-and-a-half with Morné du Plessis, the former Springbok rugby captain and one of the founders of the Sports Science Institute.

Gibbs was initially negative about the course. He admits, 'It was like going back to school. I had to get up early in the morning and it was winter. It was quite cold and I didn't enjoy that.'

He said he gained from the course, however. 'What benefited me most were the one-on-ones with Morné. You can't speak to your parents about certain things and there are things you can't discuss with your friends in too much depth. With Morné, I was able to speak about what I had kept inside, things that I had kept to myself for years. I could just release everything.'

Du Plessis' stature and record of achievement beyond rugby made him an ideal mentor figure. 'He was someone I could respect and relate to. We spoke a lot about what I had achieved off the field and what I would still like to achieve.'

Du Plessis is cautious about discussing what he stresses is a confidential relationship but says he also gained from his sessions with the young player. 'I enjoyed his openness and his willingness to share his experiences.'

Although the formal sessions are long concluded, Du Plessis says he stays in regular contact with Gibbs. 'He is fulfilling his potential but the best is yet to come.'

Gill Taylor says she has dealt with some 350 young sports achievers, although usually in much more limited modules than the course which was put together especially for Gibbs. 'There is a great deal of pressure on young sportsmen and women, especially high profile people like Herschelle.'

Gibbs says one of the topics discussed was alcohol. The course identified this as a potential pitfall because, being naturally gregarious, Gibbs tended to find it difficult to say no when he was in social situations. 'I enjoy my alcohol,' he admits. 'Most cricketers enjoy a few beers.' He is unlikely to become a teetotaller but says that the 2002 version of Herschelle Gibbs behaves with more moderation than the previous all-or-nothing party animal.

Shaun Pollock, the South African captain, does not believe in keeping too tight a rein on a free spirit like Gibbs. 'He's a guy who enjoys life. Sometimes he does things he regrets but it is good for a team to have a blend of different characters. Now and again we have to make sure he keeps calm and doesn't mess it up. He's much too valuable a player for us.'

CHAPTER **EIGHTEEN**

The runs flow

In the two years leading up to the 2003 World Cup, Herschelle Gibbs established himself as one of the finest batsmen in the world, averaging above 50 in Test matches and better than 40 in one-day internationals. While the runs were valuable to South Africa's cause, it was the style in which they were made that enthralled spectators.

After a break of more than four months, their longest time away from the game in four years, the South Africans started the 2001/02 season with a tour of Zimbabwe. For the first time, there was more than a single Test match between the neighbouring nations as they played two Tests in addition to three one-day internationals.

It was Gibbs's first Test encounter against Zimbabwe and he thoroughly enjoyed the experience. After Shaun Pollock won the toss, Gibbs and Gary Kirsten made the best possible use of a perfect batting pitch at the Harare Sports Club, scoring at more than five runs an over as they took the total to 142 at lunch on the first day. The tally included 28 boundaries in as many overs, Gibbs hitting 15 fours and a six as he raced to 77. Zimbabwe's pace bowlers were seen off without any difficulty. When Ray Price, the left-arm spinner, entered the attack early in the second hour, Gibbs skipped down the pitch and hit him for four and six over mid-on.

Before Harare, Gibbs had played in 28 Test matches but had not added to the back-to-back hundreds he made in New Zealand more than two years earlier.

His third century came in the eighth over after lunch as the runs continued to flow, although he had a scare on 97 when Heath Streak, the Zimbabwe captain, narrowly missed the stumps as Kirsten called for a quick single.

It was a glorious exhibition of batting. The long-standing South African Test record for the first wicket seemed set to be broken until Gibbs tried to nudge Travis Friend to third man but edged the ball into his stumps. He had made 147 off 164 balls and hit 28 fours and two sixes. The partnership was worth 256, only four short of the mark established by Bruce Mitchell and Jack Siedle against England at Newlands in 1930/31.

Gary Kirsten, who had been a doubtful starter after injuring his neck before the tour, went on to make his third Test double century and Jacques Kallis helped himself to a hundred as South Africa made 600 for three before Pollock declared. South Africa seemed set for an innings win when they bowled out Zimbabwe for 286 and had them reeling at 25 for three in the second innings. Andy Flower, the Zimbabwe wicketkeeper and left-handed batsman, led a remarkable fightback that took the match into the fifth day. Flower, who was last man out for 142 in the first innings, made 199 not out in the second.

Gibbs was unable to go onto the field on the final day because of a back spasm, a problem that would recur later in his career, and did not bat in the second innings as South Africa were set to make 78 to win.

The second Test in Bulawayo was drawn after unseasonal rain washed out the second day's play. Gibbs seemed set for another century before he was caught behind for 74. He effectively gave himself out, as it did not look as though umpire John Hampshire was going to raise his finger, but Gibbs set off for the dressing room. It was a rare moment of sportsmanship in an era in which players around the world tend to wait for the umpire's decision. 'Walking is a matter of opinion,' he said. 'I thought it was a blatant nick. There was not much point in hanging around.'

Perhaps the cricketing gods approved. On the same ground, six days later, Gibbs played one of his most spectacular innings, thrashing South Africa's fastest limited overs century after being dropped by wicketkeeper Flower off Friend when he had four. He reached his hundred off 84 balls and went on to score 125 off 112 deliveries with a series of thrilling strokes, some of them almost outrageously audacious. It set South Africa on the way to 363 for three, the country's highest total and the fifth highest in one-day international history.

Another dashing innings followed as he made 69 in the second one-day international in Harare, reaching 50 off 36 balls, and he finished a highly successful tour by making 39 off 31 balls in the third game.

Gibbs was in such good form that it seemed almost too easy for him, yet his record in the triangular one-day series that followed, between South Africa, India and Kenya, was no more than moderate as he averaged just over 30, with a single half-century against Kenya. There were some enjoyable vignettes and he scored at close to a run a ball through the series but there were perhaps too many extravagant strokes. When he did play cautiously, though, he made just 21 in an opening stand of 80 with Kirsten that laid the foundation for a comfortable six-wicket win over India in the final in Durban.

The big runs returned in the Test series against India. The first match of what was scheduled to be a three-Test series was a treat for connoisseurs of attacking strokeplay. Sachin Tendulkar and the hard-hitting debutant, Virender Sehwag, made centuries for India, while Gibbs made a sparkling 107 for South Africa.

On the *Sunday Times* website, the author wrote:

> When he is batting as well as he has done for most of this season, there is hardly a batsman in the world who can match Herschelle Gibbs for style and flair.
>
> The point was underlined in Bloemfontein on Sunday when Gibbs made a splendid 107 against India. Those fortunate enough to have watched the first two days of the first Test have enjoyed a feast of batting.
>
> Sachin Tendulkar on day one, Herschelle Gibbs on day two. They both made outstanding hundreds and it is a tribute to Gibbs that his innings at least matched that of the Indian master for entertainment value.
>
> Gibbs played some breathtaking strokes, driving through the off-side with immaculate timing, while his leg-side play is of a range to make setting a field a challenge. He has perfected a wristy flick-pull which sends the ball rocketing to square leg, he glances fine with effortless placement and pulls with meaty power.

> It was a savage pull for six off Zaheer Khan which brought up his century off 140 balls. He had another six, also pulled off Khan, and 15 fours.
> So consummate has been the display of skill by Gibbs this season that it is difficult to accept that it was only his fourth Test century, and his first in South Africa.

The player himself admitted that he had to temper the attacking approach he had adopted in the one-day series. 'I've been wanting to hit it over the top and it may have become a bad habit.' He added that he had resisted putting pressure on himself by refusing to think about the significance of scoring a first Test century on home soil. 'Every hundred is a milestone. Some guys put a bit more pressure on themselves when they are getting near to a century. It's just another ball and hopefully another scoring shot.'

Gibbs was critical of the way the South African bowlers had failed to bowl the right line to the Indian batsmen in the first innings, allowing the tourists to score 379 at a rate of almost four an over, but there was a much-improved performance in the second innings, with Shaun Pollock bowling superbly.

South Africa romped to a nine-wicket win, with Pollock claiming the man-of-the-match award ahead of the successful batsmen by taking his first 10-wicket match haul in a Test.

The second Test, in Port Elizabeth, will be remembered largely for the controversy over the disciplinary action taken against six Indian players by Mike Denness, the former England captain, who was the match referee.

Before the match descended into acrimony and recriminations, there was a memorable innings by Herschelle Gibbs.

South Africa were sent in on a green pitch. 'Looking at the wicket in the morning, we knew it wasn't going to be easy,' said Gibbs. 'Luckily there wasn't much pace but there was lateral movement and a lot of bounce.'

It was a pitch that proved difficult for all the batsmen with the exception of Gibbs. While his team-mates struggled, particularly against the experienced Indian opening bowler, Javagal Srinath, Gibbs hit some stunning drives through the covers. A key to his innings was his shot selection.

On the first day he scored 155 not out in a total of 237 for five. It was his third Test century in five innings. Seldom has a day been dominated so much by one man. On the second morning, after the early dismissal of Shaun

Pollock, Gibbs found an attacking partner in Mark Boucher, who went for his shots in a stand of 80.

Gibbs went to 194 and a double century seemed assured. Sachin Tendulkar came on for his first over of the match, and Gibbs pulled a short ball dangerously close to mid-on. He got away with the shot, however, and scored two to go to 196. Tendulkar, bowling slow-paced seamers, sent down another short-pitched delivery, this time outside the off-stump. Following his Bloemfontein maxim of 'another ball, another scoring shot', Gibbs leant back to punch it away. But he failed to time it properly, slicing a catch to backward point.

Afterwards, he claimed he was not too distressed about falling so close to a double hundred. Statistics were not hugely important. His main responsibility, he said, was to make a contribution to the team effort and to provide entertainment for the public. He was delighted, though, that his batting had improved so much. He dared to mention that he thought he was growing up as a cricketer. 'Some batsmen mature earlier than others. I have tightened up a lot and become a better opener. My balance and shot selection are better. Batting with Gary has helped a lot.'

> 'Some batsmen mature earlier than others. I have tightened up a lot and become a better opener. My balance and shot selection are better. Batting with Gary has helped a lot.'

The value of the innings was underlined when India were bowled out for 201 in reply to South Africa's 362. In the second innings, Gibbs hit three boundaries but no other scoring strokes before being bowled by Ajit Agarkar. South Africa went on to build what seemed a match-winning position before rain washed out most of the fourth day's play.

The long rain breaks proved fertile breeding grounds for rumour and gossip as it became known that Denness had taken disciplinary steps against Sachin Tendulkar, as well as other Indian players. Tendulkar, it emerged, was suspected of ball-tampering. By the time it was confirmed that six players had been called before Denness, the large Indian media contingent was seething.

Before the final day's play, it was announced that Sehwag had been suspended for one match for excessive appealing, intimidating an umpire and using abusive language during the third day's play. Tendulkar was fined 75 percent of his match fee for interfering with the condition of the ball while bowling. Indian captain Sourav Ganguly was given a suspended ban of one Test and two one-day internationals for failing to control his players. Harbhajan Singh, Shiv Sunder Das and Deep Dasgupta were fined 75 percent of their match fees and given suspended one-match bans for showing dissent and attempting to intimidate the umpire by charging.

In isolation, each of the sentences handed down by Denness might have been justifiable, but to have taken action against more than half the Indian team seemed totally at odds with the general conduct of the game. There had been excessive appealing on the third day, when fielders were clustered around the bat, and television pictures certainly seemed to show that Tendulkar was paying undue attention to the seam of the ball. It had not been a day, though, during which proceedings had at any stage threatened to get out of hand.

This was the same Denness who had failed to take any action against time-wasting by West Indian players in Bridgetown earlier in the year, which had been clearly against the spirit of the game, if not downright cheating. Not for the first time, observers were left to wonder how men who had been players at the pinnacle of the game could be so inconsistent and appear to have so limited a concept of fairness and natural justice. If there was good from the incident, it was that it made inevitable the appointment of a smaller panel of full-time match referees and the drawing up of a far more specific code of conduct, with prescribed penalties.

It was an unhappy incident which should have ended there. What happened next was an even more disappointing episode. The Indian board took up the case on behalf of their players and demanded that Denness be removed as match referee, threatening that if this action was not taken, their team would not play in the third Test at Centurion later in the week. The United Cricket Board, instead of insisting that the Indians fulfil their contract, on threat of legal action if they didn't, meekly bowed to the pressure and asked Denness to stand down. Denness refused, and the UCB announced he would be barred from the match referee's position at the ground. The International Cricket Council, quite properly, announced that if their appointed officials were not allowed to carry out their duties, they would withdraw official Test match status from the game.

Time has done nothing to justify the UCB's actions. It was a blow to the ethics of the game and to the players, who were robbed of a scheduled Test match. Both the Indian and South African boards said they would seek to have the match reinstated as a Test but their efforts were fatally undermined when Shaun Pollock asked to address the media after the first day's play and said the players did not regard it as a proper Test match. Nor was it, although there was some entertaining cricket, which included 59 by Gibbs and centuries by Pollock and Jacques Kallis.

Within a matter of days, the Indian series was consigned to the past as the most important phase of the summer began. South Africa had a chance to dethrone Australia, the official world Test champions, during three Tests in Australia and another three at home. If either series was drawn, South Africa would take the crown because of their better record against other countries.

CHAPTER **NINETEEN**

Outsmarted and outplayed in Australia

South Africa's tour of Australia in 2001/02 was a disastrous campaign in almost all aspects. Poor planning and weak management left the South Africans woefully under-prepared to meet the challenges of Australia, both on and off the field. Herschelle Gibbs set out on his second tour of the world's strongest cricket nation with his confidence high but, like most of his team-mates, he returned disappointed.

The South Africans arrived in Perth while Australia were completing a three-Test series against New Zealand that was to prove a rare blip on the Australian record. With some luck, thanks to rain, and with much spirit, New Zealand shared the series. They had clearly done their homework, particularly in the way their batsmen played against Glenn McGrath and Shane Warne.

By contrast, the South Africans appeared to have done almost no planning for this most important series. This was one situation where the old sporting dictum of taking one match at a time did not hold true. The very fact that the tour of Australia started almost immediately after the Indian series ended should have been reason enough to have set up a task team specifically to prepare for the clash with the champions.

Management meekly failed to insist that the players meet their obligations to the Australian and South African media. A planned media session, set up by the Australian board in consultation with their South African counterparts, was cancelled because the players had not been properly briefed. The tourists were on the back foot in the propaganda war that is an inevitable part of any tour of Australia.

Such matters were not the immediate concern of Herschelle Gibbs. His job was to counteract the new-ball threat of Glenn McGrath and Jason Gillespie. His series started promisingly as he made 78 in the first Test in Adelaide, putting on 87 for the first wicket with Kirsten in reply to the Australians' total of 439. Playing against Australia, however, is not like taking on any other country. One moment of weakness can turn a match or a series. Having batted so well, he went dancing down the wicket to Shane Warne, who slid the ball down the leg-side for Gilchrist to make an easy stumping.

South Africa were all out 65 runs behind but seemed likely to earn a draw, with only two days and three overs remaining. However, Matthew Hayden hit an aggressive century and Australia were able to declare their second innings with 12 overs remaining on the fourth day.

Disastrously, both Gibbs and Kirsten were out before the close, Gibbs to a bat-pad catch at short leg off McGrath, and South Africa collapsed on the final day, losing by 246 runs. It was to prove the closest of the three contests.

Gibbs asserts that a change of team strategy complicated his tour. 'I went to Australia with a lot of confidence and I started the series well enough with that 78 in the first innings. There wasn't much I could do about the ball I got in the second innings. After that there was a change of approach and there was a feeling that we should fight fire with fire.'

Part of the firepower was seen as being in the Gibbs bat. It was decided he should be more aggressive, taking on the Australian bowlers from the start as Hayden and Justin Langer were doing to the South Africans.

It was not a strategy that could be employed in the first innings of the second Test in Melbourne after South Africa were sent in on a grey day. Rain delayed the start and only 11 overs were possible before lunch. The floodlights were on when play resumed in the afternoon and just 14 deliveries were sent down before rain fell again. When play got under way again in mid-afternoon, Gibbs was squared up by McGrath and caught at third slip.

Gibbs's highest score in his remaining innings of the series was 32 as South Africa were comprehensively outplayed in both Melbourne and Sydney. Some of the shots he played, notably a wild slash against McGrath in the second innings in Melbourne, were not worthy of a world-class player. A century against New South Wales in a four-day match between the first and second Tests was his only highlight in the rest of the first-class part of the tour.

Gibbs himself does not complain about the tactical changes but it seems most unfortunate that he felt under pressure to force the pace.

Gibbs himself does not complain about the tactical changes but it seems most unfortunate that he felt under pressure to force the pace. A man capable of striking the ball so crisply and able to hit such a high percentage of boundaries should, if anything, be encouraged to show prudence against bowlers as good as Australia's. His successes in the previous year had come largely as a result of playing within himself and disciplining himself to be patient. Because of the way he plays, any major innings would almost certainly have been scored at a good rate.

There was another, unspoken factor, that of interference from officialdom, possibly provoked by the government. Gibbs was not part of the team management and he rightly does not want to comment on such matters but he made an oblique reference to the problem. 'The selectors obviously had a few complications. From a player's point of view, it's hard enough playing against Australia, all you want to do is to be able to concentrate just on your cricket.'

Journalists on the tour first became aware of the issue as persistent rumours circulated that pressure was being exerted on the tour selectors to keep picking Makhaya Ntini, the only black African member of the side, even though he had been struggling to find his best form. He was, in fact, dropped from the last two Tests before coming back in the one-day series with some excellent bowling.

Rumours of off-field problems became reality when the third Test started on the worst possible note. Percy Sonn used his right of veto as President of the UCB after the tour selectors picked Jacques Rudolph ahead of the out-of-form Lance Klusener, who had gone home to see his pregnant wife. Sonn said the principle of giving opportunities to players from disadvantaged backgrounds, in a series that had already been decided, had not been met. The selectors reconvened and Justin Ontong played instead. It was the second time Rudolph had been picked to play in a Test match but failed to earn his cap, his previous selection for the Test team having been for the match at Centurion, rendered unofficial on account of the Denness affair.

Although it was a chastening series for Gibbs, he says playing against Australia is 'the ultimate' for any Test player. 'They have set the benchmark, and the challenge for everyone else is to get to that level.'

Australia's aggressive cricket puts pressure on opponents. 'Whether they are batting or bowling, they attack you right from the start. They also apply a lot of psychological pressure. Against other teams, you can make mistakes and get away with them, but not against Australia. One mistake could cost you the match.'

A triangular one-day series against Australia and New Zealand proved a much happier venture for the South Africans. Although they could only beat Australia once in four games, they defeated the New Zealanders three times. The Kiwis had three wins against Australia and the round robin series ended with all three teams tied on four wins. A crucial extra bonus point put South Africa on top of the log and New Zealand squeezed out Australia because of their record in the head-to-head games.

'That was really strange,' says Gibbs. 'We found it quite easy to beat New Zealand but somehow they seemed to be able to play well against the Aussies. Thank goodness we got that bonus point.'

South Africa comfortably beat New Zealand 2-0 in the best-of-three final, though it was not an especially successful series for Gibbs, despite an innings of 89 against New Zealand in Adelaide.

Hopes that South Africa might put up a better show in the return Test series on home soil were quickly dashed. Pollock had to withdraw from the first Test at the Wanderers because of a side strain and Ontong, who had shown plenty of character on his Test debut considering the circumstances in which he was selected, was ruled out because of an injured hamstring. Australia made a massive 652 for seven declared, only two runs short of the all-time highest total scored against South Africa, by England in the 'Timeless Test' in Durban in 1938/39. Hayden and Damien Martyn made centuries and Adam Gilchrist flayed the bowlers for a sensational double century off 212 balls, the fastest at that time in Test history.

South Africa's reply was disastrous. Kirsten went early. Gibbs and Ashwell Prince, who had replaced the injured Ontong, put on 40 for the second wicket before Gibbs was trapped lbw by Warne. 'Ashwell and I were the only guys who looked like building an innings,' he says. His own 34 and Prince's 49 were hardly enough to make a serious dent on the Australian juggernaut, however, and South Africa were bowled out for 159. Gibbs again batted competently in the second innings, making 47 before being stumped off Warne in similar fashion to his dismissal in Adelaide. He shared another useful stand with Prince that contributed 69, more than half the dismal total of 133. Australia's victory by an innings and 360 runs was South Africa's heaviest defeat in history. 'We were blown away. It was a good wicket but we just couldn't put the runs on the board and build the partnerships we needed,' said Gibbs.

There were four changes to the team for the second Test at Newlands. One of the planned changes was the inclusion of Daryll Cullinan, who made 86 for South Africa A against the tourists in a match between the Tests. Cullinan demanded a contract from the UCB and when he did not get one he withdrew from the team. He was replaced by Graeme Smith, and joining Smith as new caps were all-rounder Andrew Hall and fast bowler Dewald Pretorius, while left-arm spinner Paul Adams was recalled.

'We had a really good look at ourselves,' says Gibbs. 'We had to find a way to turn it around.' As a batsman, he identified as a major problem the fact that the batting was not consistent enough. 'The name of the game is to put partnerships together, although that is not so easy against a side like Australia.'

For the first time in five matches, South Africa won the toss but the advantage was quickly wrested away as the first six wickets fell for 92 runs. Spirited batting by Hall, Boucher and Adams saw South Africa go beyond 200 but another magnificent innings by Gilchrist ensured a comfortable lead for Australia. South Africa then produced their most solid batting of the two series, scoring 473 in their second innings to set Australia a target of 331. Gibbs made 39 in an opening stand of 84 with Kirsten. Australia ended up winning the match by four wickets but South Africa were encouraged by their fighting performance.

'We took a lot of confidence from the Newlands game going into the third Test,' says Gibbs. It showed as South Africa gained a notable victory, achieving a fourth innings target of 335, a record for South Africa and the ninth highest in history. It was an outstanding match for Gibbs, who was South Africa's top scorer with 51 in the first innings and 104 in the second. He regards the century as one of his most important innings. 'I still rate my 85 against England at the Wanderers in 1999/2000 as my best from a technical point of view, but in terms of the quality of bowling and the context of the game, Durban was a vital innings for me.'

South Africa slipped back into losing ways in the one-day series that followed. Australia won 5-1 with one match tied. Gibbs had a poor series.

Inevitably, there were scapegoats for South Africa's disastrous season. Graham Ford, the coach, and Craig Smith, the physiotherapist, were fired. After a brainstorming session organised by Gerald Majola, the chief executive, a national cricket committee was established, which included several prominent former players. The first task of the committee was to recommend new national selectors. The only survivor from Rushdi Magiet's panel was Haroon Lorgat. The new convenor was Omar Henry, who played for South Africa in the 1992 World Cup and became the oldest man to make his Test debut for South Africa when he played against India in 1992/93 at the age of 40 years 295 days.

Eric Simons, who had been Gibbs's first room-mate when the teenager played for Western Province, was appointed coach.

Gibbs was offered a chance to take up a short-term English county contract with Leicestershire during 2002 but decided it would be better for his cricket to have an extended break before the all-important 2002/03 season.

Thus it was a refreshed player who launched his summer by hitting 114 against Pakistan in the first international match played at a new stadium in Tangier, Morocco. The rest of the triangular tournament was less successful for him. South Africa were beaten in the final by Sri Lanka.

The next big assignment was the ICC Champions Trophy in Colombo, Sri Lanka, effectively a dress rehearsal for the World Cup, although in completely different conditions.

Simons used the time in Colombo to talk to individual players. Simons, skipper Pollock and assistant coach Corrie van Zyl told Gibbs that he was one of the best players in the world. 'It was a very flattering comment.' An hour-long pep talk had him eager to perform. He made a century in a practice match against New Zealand and, after failing in the first match of the tournament against the West Indies, made another century against Kenya. Then he played a magnificent innings in the semi-final against India. He had struggled to cope with the heat in the Kenya match and had to retire with heat exhaustion against India after scoring 116 off 119 balls.

When he was helped from the field, South Africa were 192 for one and needed 70 runs off 13 overs with nine wickets in hand. Disappointingly, they fell 10 runs short.

> Eight days later he equalled a world record shared by Zaheer Abbas and Saeed Anwar, both of Pakistan, when he made his third consecutive one-day international century...

Eight days later he equalled a world record shared by Zaheer Abbas and Saeed Anwar, both of Pakistan, when he made his third consecutive one-day international century, against Bangladesh in Potchefstroom. He mauled the weak Bangladeshi attack, hitting a career-best 153 off 130 balls. He was thinking of a possible double century when, with 39 balls of the innings remaining, he was caught at deep backward square leg.

When Bangladesh were restricted to 154 for nine in the next match in Benoni, it seemed his chance of scoring a record fourth successive hundred had gone. Once more, though, he turned in a turbo-charged performance as he thrashed 97 not out off 66 balls. With six needed to win and his own score on 96, he was on strike at the beginning of an over from Alok Kapali, a leg-spinner. In an apparent repeat of Pat Symcox to Nathan Astle in New Zealand four seasons earlier, Kapali fired the ball down the leg-side for what counted as five wides. Gibbs might have waited a few more balls to see if an opportunity to hit a four would arise but two balls later he hit to long-on and ran. The ball was cut off by a fielder and only one run counted, completing the win. 'I thought he might have bowled another wide so I went for it as soon as possible,' he said.

The centuries were coming thick and fast. After missing out in the first Test against Bangladesh, where he was out for 41, he made 114 in the second Test in Potchefstroom before being carelessly run out, failing to ground his bat in time. He then hit a double century in a SuperSport Series game against KwaZulu-Natal. 'It was one of the best innings I have seen,' said Peter Kirsten, his Western Province coach and boyhood hero.

Gibbs missed the first Test against Sri Lanka because of a back spasm and was run out again in the second Test at Centurion after making 92. Again it was unnecessary. He set off for a risky single, was sent back by Jacques Kallis, and slipped in mid-pitch as he turned.

Like all self-respecting batsmen, Gibbs prizes Test runs highly but, he says, in the 2002/03 season 'the main focus is on one-day cricket because of the World Cup'. A one-day tune-up hundred was recorded as his century in Kimberley clinched the series against Sri Lanka.

Herschelle hit a peak in his last international innings before the 2003 World Cup when he made a magnificent 228 in the second Test against Pakistan at Newlands. At last he was able to do justice to his talents in front of the Newlands faithful. The emotion he felt was obvious when he raised his bat and acknowledged the whole crowd after reaching his century and his double century.

He and Graeme Smith put on 368 for the first wicket, the highest partnership of all time for South Africa. He and Jacques Kallis set the second wicket partnership record of 315 unbeaten against New Zealand in Christchurch in 1998/99. There have been only four partnerships of more than 300 in South African Test history and Gibbs has been involved in two of them.

It was an innings which took Gibbs to new levels of achievement. With his eighth Test century he drew level with Bruce Mitchell, with only Gary Kirsten (16), Daryll Cullinan (14), Jacques Kallis (11) and Dudley Nourse (nine) ahead of him. On 159 he reached 3 000 runs in Tests, only the sixth South African to do so. He joined Pollock, Dudley Nourse and Gary Kirsten as players who have scored two or more Test double centuries. He scored his 200 off 211 balls, the second-fastest of all time and one ball fewer than Adam Gilchrist needed in his sensational innings for Australia against South Africa at the Wanderers the previous season. He beat Graeme Pollock's 209 against Australia in 1996/67, the previous highest Test score at Newlands.

The victim of what seemed a poor decision, given out caught at slip off Saqlain Mushtaq, the off-spinner, when the ball seemed to have looped off his pad without touching his bat, he was disappointed not to have gone on to become the first South African to score a triple century in a Test. It was evidence of how he has raised his sights.

Going into the 2003 World Cup, his season's tally already included five one-day hundreds and two Test Centuries, including a double hundred. If the best was still to come, the world could look forward to a treat.

CHAPTER **TWENTY**

A career in progress

Although his is a career in progress, Herschelle Gibbs has had a more eventful life than many cricketers who have been playing for much longer. He has survived scandals and indiscretions. He has had exceptional highs and depressing lows. He has not been the wisest of young men but he believes he has learned from his experiences.

Perhaps most importantly, in his late twenties and in what should be the prime of a batsman's life, he has started to believe in himself.

His talent is not in doubt. Almost every cricketer interviewed for this book rates him among the most gifted players they have seen.

Among those who believe he needs stand back for no-one in the world in terms of pure ability are his captain, Shaun Pollock, and the national coach, Eric Simons.

'He is an extraordinary cricketer,' says Pollock. 'He has always been right up there as a talented ball player. He has really taken a step up in the last few years and is playing with a lot more confidence and commitment. What I admire about him is the way he has dealt with issues off the field that could have affected his career. He has shown he is a big man by putting those things behind him.'

Simons believes that Gibbs is 'in a league of his own' but that he needs to be convinced that he is exceptional. 'What surprised me when we sat down in Colombo was that he seemed amazed when we told him we thought he was one of the best in the world. It made me think that as much as we may admire people, we often don't tell them about it.'

According to Simons, Gibbs is a player who needs to set his own goals. 'His biggest challenge is himself. He has the ability to get into a zone where nobody is going to get him out. He needs to put mechanisms in place where he gets into that zone more often.'

It is a message that Gibbs seems to be taking to heart. 'Quite a lot of people seem to believe I have the ability but it is only now that I feel I've worked out how to play. Why it's taken so long I'm not sure. There have been days when I have felt good but technically I was not equipped, and other days where my shot selection was appalling.

'If I had to make one criticism of myself it would be that I never really gave myself a chance to play myself in. But you have to make mistakes to learn. I feel I have wasted some years but I don't think I could have had a different mindset. I didn't really know how to build an innings.

'I think I'm there now. My technique is much better than it was a few years ago. My head is in a much better position and my balance is good. The main thing for me is to play within myself and stay nice and tight.'

For a player who as recently as late 2001 claimed that averages were not important to him, he has become more aware that careers are measured in results. He would like to build his Test batting average up to 50, which would put him in a small and exclusive bracket.

'I need to increase my hundreds tally. I'd like to get to 15 or 16 in the next three years or so, be it in Test matches or one-day games. Obviously, if I do that my average is going to go up. There are not a lot of guys outside Australia and India who average in the high 40s or 50s as an opening batsman in Test cricket. I know that if I play as I am at the moment I am capable of ending with an average of 50.'

After the series against Pakistan in 2002/03 he had scored eight Test and 11 one-day hundreds, with six of the Test centuries and eight of those in one-day internationals scored in the previous two years. This put his goals well within reach.

A career in progress

Gary Kirsten, so often his opening partner, feels that Gibbs's career is only just taking off. 'He's got a long way to go. He could be playing for another seven or eight years.'

Gibbs agrees. 'The average international batsman gets to his prime at about the age of 28. Tendulkar is an exception and Lara seems to have gone the other way, he's not nearly as good a player as he was when he was younger. But Steve Waugh took a long time to get his first hundred. After his first 20 Tests his average was less than 30, then he built it up to more than 50. You should get better the longer you play.'

He also has a quiet desire to score a double century in a one-day international. The current world record of 194 is held by Saeed Anwar of Pakistan. 'I have never batted through a full innings in a one-day game. That is something I want to do. When I made that 153 against Bangladesh I realised that a double century was on if I could bat for 50 overs.'

He may be more mature than he was before being led into temptation by Hansie Cronjé, or when he was getting into late-night scrapes, and he may have more belief in himself than he did until recently, but his basic approach to batting has not changed greatly down the years.

'I visualise quite a lot, imagining myself facing this bowler or that bowler, but I don't think too deeply about it. As long as I know that I've done my hours and practised playing tight the day before, I'm happy. It's something I have done all my life. When I was at school I spent so much time visualising how I would play at the weekend that I didn't get my grades in class.'

Asked to single out some of the best players he has encountered, he named three batsmen that 'I would want to go and watch' and three bowlers who he reckons are masters of their craft.

He describes them in his own words:

Brian Lara (West Indies): He's probably the most talented of the lot. He plays some incredible shots even though he gets into some strange body positions. He hasn't performed as well as he did when he was younger but he's still a player who can win matches. He hits it with such ease and flair.

Sachin Tendulkar (India): He can play shots everywhere. On the sub-continent he is by far the best in the world but he's a good player in any conditions. He's awkward to bowl to because he's a short guy and the bowlers have to bowl different lengths to him. He's got really good hands and times the ball well.

Daryll Cullinan (South Africa): I rate Daryll right up there with the best. He's so correct and he always seems to have so much time to play the ball.

Glenn McGrath (Australia): He's not the quickest in the world but he is so accurate. He has a good action and gets good bounce. He bowls you a half-volley once a summer. You have to be very tight technically to play against him and you have to be able to take advantage if he gives you any half-chance to score.

Shane Warne (Australia): I don't usually have a problem playing spinners but he is probably the best leg-spinner ever. He doesn't bowl with as many variations as he used to but he hardly ever bowls a bad ball. Like the rest of the Australians, psychologically he's always at you, trying to get you to lose your concentration.

Wasim Akram (Pakistan): I can only imagine what he must have been like when he was younger and bowling quicker than he does these days. He bowls left-arm off a short run. His arm comes over very quickly and he doesn't really have a delivery stride, so you pick up the ball late. He can make it swing both ways. His stock ball swings in and the other ball goes across you. I try to pick it up by the line the ball starts on.

Gibbs also has a healthy respect for Shoaib Akhtar and Brett Lee, the two fastest bowlers in the world. 'They are good for the game because people come to watch pure pace. As a batsman it gets the adrenaline going. You've got to be awake when you face them.'

The youngster who admitted to being afraid of fast bowling has become an adult who has to handle the likes of Akhtar and Lee, operating with a hard, shiny new ball. There is no longer a fear factor. 'It's a challenge. Once you are in and your feet are moving it becomes second nature to handle the pace. Where it's difficult is if there is uneven bounce and you are not sure whether you are going to have to play the ball or if you are going to be able to duck under it.'

Although they are dissimilar in style and personality, Gibbs admires Steve Waugh, the Australian captain. 'He has had an incredible career. He has such a never-say-die attitude. He epitomises mental strength.'

Whether or not Gibbs will in time be rated alongside the people he regards as the best in their fields, only time will tell. One is inclined to agree with Eric Simons that he himself holds the key.

Career record

All details as at 6 January 2003

First-class career

Competition	M	Inns	NO	Runs	HS	Avg	100	50	Ct
Test	43	72	3	3 069	228	44,47	8	11	31
SuperSport Series ("A Section")	37	65	1	2 259	203	35,29	7	5	27
UCB Bowl ("B Section")	16	26	3	1 166	152*	50,69	2	9	11
Other first-class	29	49	2	2 603	200*	55,38	6	15	22
Grand totals	**125**	**212**	**9**	**9 097**	**228**	**44,81**	**23**	**40**	**91**

Bowling: He has taken three wickets for 74 runs (avg 24,66) in 22 overs in first-class cricket, with a best of two for 14.

Limited Overs career

Competition	M	Inns	NO	Runs	HS	Avg	SR	100	50	Ct
World Cup	9	9	0	341	101	37,88	73,01	1	2	2
Other Limited Overs Internationals	108	108	7	3 488	153	34,53	82,16	10	12	51
All Limited Overs Internationals	117	117	7	3 829	153	34,80	81,26	11	14	53
Standard Bank Cup	64	57	6	1 670	110*	32,74	70,54*	3	10	34
Total Power Series	5	5	2	66	20	22,00	–	0	0	1
All Domestic Limited Overs	69	62	8	1 736	110*	32,14	70,54*	3	10	35
Other Limited Overs	14	13	0	382	69	29,38	70,84*	0	4	8
Grand totals	**200**	**192**	**15**	**5 947**	**153**	**33,59**	**77,37***	**14**	**28**	**96**

* Strike-rates are based on matches where details of balls faced are available. An asterisk indicates that details of balls faced are not available for all matches. Note: Standard Bank Cup includes the Benson & Hedges Series.

Bowling: He has taken two wickets for 57 runs (avg 28,50) in 11 overs in Limited Overs cricket, with a best of one for 16.

Test career

By series

Season	Against	Where	M	Inns	NO	Runs	HS	Avg	SR	100	50	Ct
1996/97	India	India	2	4	0	62	31	15,50	30,39	0	0	1
1996/97	India	South Africa	1	2	0	25	25	12,50	43,85	0	0	0
1996/97	Australia	South Africa	1	2	0	38	31	19,00	44,18	0	0	0
1997/98	Australia	Australia	2	4	0	94	54	23,50	31,54	0	1	1
1997/98	Pakistan	South Africa	1	1	0	4	4	4,00	44,44	0	0	1
1998/99	West Indies	South Africa	4	8	0	210	51	26,25	53,16	0	1	5
1998/99	New Zealand	New Zealand	3	4	1	365	211*	121,66	45,39	2	0	1
1999/00	England	South Africa	5	7	0	203	85	29,00	41,85	0	1	2
1999/00	India	India	2	3	0	97	47	32,33	51,59	0	0	3
2000/01	Sri Lanka	South Africa	2	2	0	1	1	0,50	7,69	0	0	3
2000/01	West Indies	West Indies	5	10	1	464	87	51,55	35,99	0	4	2
2001/02	Zimbabwe	Zimbabwe	2	2	0	221	147	110,50	75,94	1	1	1
2001/02	India	South Africa	2	4	0	316	196	79,00	59,62	2	0	2
2001/02	Australia	Australia	3	6	0	164	78	27,33	40,79	0	1	0
2001/02	Australia	South Africa	3	6	0	287	104	47,83	57,28	1	1	2
2002/03	Bangladesh	South Africa	2	2	0	155	114	77,50	62,00	1	0	4
2002/03	Sri Lanka	South Africa	1	2	0	99	92	49,50	42,48	0	1	0
2002/03	Pakistan	South Africa	2	3	1	264	228	132,00	93,61	1	0	1
Totals			43	72	3	3 069	228	44,47	48,58	8	11	29

Against each opponent

Against	M	Inns	NO	Runs	HS	Avg	SR	100	50	Ct
Australia	9	18	0	583	104	32,38	45,29	1	3	3
Bangladesh	2	2	0	155	114	77,50	62,00	1	0	4
England	5	7	0	203	85	29,00	41,85	0	1	2
India	7	13	0	500	196	38,46	51,07	2	0	6
New Zealand	3	4	1	365	211*	121,66	45,39	2	0	1
Pakistan	3	4	1	268	228	89,33	92,09	1	0	4
Sri Lanka	3	4	0	100	92	25,00	40,65	0	1	3
West Indies	9	18	1	674	87	39,64	40,02	0	5	7
Zimbabwe	2	2	0	221	147	110,50	75,94	1	1	1

Centuries

Season	Against	Venue	Runs	Mins	Balls	Fours	Sixes
1998/99	New Zealand	Christchurch	211*	659	468	23	3
1998/99	New Zealand	Wellington	120	316	250	16	0
2001/02	Zimbabwe	Harare	147	213	164	28	2
2001/02	India	Bloemfontein	107	191	145	16	2
2001/02	India	Port Elizabeth	196	442	354	25	1
2001/02	Australia	Durban	104	296	198	15	0
2002/03	Bangladesh	Potchefstroom	114	214	190	17	2
2002/03	Pakistan	Cape Town	228	381	240	29	6

Limited Overs International career

By year

Year	M	Inns	NO	Runs	HS	Avg	SR	100	50	Ct
1996	3	3	0	83	35	27,66	70,94	0	0	1
1997	8	8	0	149	33	18,62	70,95	0	0	3
1998	6	6	0	60	33	10,00	56,07	0	0	5
1999	22	22	2	805	125	40,25	73,65	2	4	6
2000	20	20	2	576	111	32,00	79,12	1	4	4
2001	21	21	0	846	125	40,28	86,76	3	3	14
2002	37	37	3	1 310	153	38,52	88,39	5	3	20
Totals	117	117	7	3 829	153	34,80	81,26	11	14	53

Against each opponent

Against	M	Inns	NO	Runs	HS	Avg	SR	100	50	Ct
Australia	23	23	0	473	101	20,56	72,99	1	0	7
Bangladesh	3	3	1	265	153	132,50	126,79	1	1	2
England	5	5	0	104	60	20,80	56,83	0	1	2
India	17	17	2	771	116*	51,40	87,81	2	3	6
Kenya	6	6	0	277	116	46,16	94,21	1	1	5
New Zealand	15	15	1	437	91	31,21	70,37	0	3	9
Pakistan	12	12	1	288	114	26,18	80,44	1	2	5
Sri Lanka	15	15	1	333	108*	23,78	76,90	1	1	8
West Indies	13	13	0	495	125	38,07	75,80	3	0	7
Zimbabwe	8	8	1	386	125	55,14	88,73	1	2	2

Centuries

Season	Against	Venue	Runs	Mins	Balls	Fours	Sixes
1998/99	West Indies	Port Elizabeth	125	191	146	9	0
1999	Australia	Leeds	101	185	134	10	1
1999/00	India	Kochi	111	165	127	11	2
2000/01	West Indies	St John's	104	155	141	8	3
2000/01	West Indies	Bridgetown	107	138	132	12	3
2001/02	Zimbabwe	Bulawayo	125	151	112	15	2
2002	Pakistan	Tangier	114	181	130	8	3
2002/03	Kenya	Colombo-RPS	116	159	126	12	3
2002/03	India	Colombo-RPS	116 ri	160	119	16	0
2002/03	Bangladesh	Potchefstroom	153	181	130	17	3
2002/03	Sri Lanka	Kimberley	108*	139	92	14	3

Miscellaneous

- Gibbs is the youngest player to appear in first-class cricket for Western Province, against Northern Transvaal in Cape Town in 1990/91, aged 16 years and 306 days.
- His 200* and 171 for South Africa against India at Nagpur in 1996/97 is the closest anyone has got to emulating Arthur Fagg's unique feat of two double centuries in the same first-class match.
- He is one of three players to have scored three consecutive Limited Overs International centuries:

Name	Season	Scores
Zaheer Abbas (Pak)	1982/83	118 v Ind (Multan), 105 v Ind (Lahore) & 113 v Ind (Karachi)
Saeed Anwar (Pak)	1993/94	107 v SL (Sharjah), 131 v WI (Sharjah) & 111 v SL (Sharjah)
HH Gibbs (SA)	2002/03	116 v Ken (Colombo-RPS), 116 Rtd ill v Ind (Colombo-RPS) & 153 v Ban (Potchefstroom)

Career record

- He is currently the sixth highest Test run-scorer and the sixth highest Limited Overs International run-scorer for South Africa:

South Africa: leading Test run-scorers

Name	M	Inns	NO	Runs	HS	Avg	100	50
G Kirsten	89	155	12	6 133	275	42,88	16	29
DJ Cullinan	70	115	12	4 554	275*	44,21	14	20
JH Kallis	66	107	18	4 486	189*	50,40	11	25
WJ Cronjé	68	111	9	3 714	135	36,41	6	23
B Mitchell	42	80	9	3 471	189*	48,88	8	21
HH Gibbs	43	72	3	3 069	228	44,47	8	11

South Africa: leading Limited Overs International run-scorers

Name	M	Inns	NO	Runs	HS	Avg	SR	100	50
G Kirsten	179	179	16	6 612	188*	40,56	71,62	13	42
JN Rhodes	243	219	51	5 933	121	35,31	81,09	2	33
JH Kallis	168	162	28	5 902	113*	44,04	69,95	8	42
WJ Cronjé	188	175	31	5 565	112	38,64	76,51	2	39
DJ Cullinan	138	133	16	3 860	124	32,99	70,39	3	23
HH Gibbs	117	117	7	3 829	153	34,80	81,26	11	14
L Klusener	149	121	44	3 290	103*	42,72	90,08	2	18
AC Hudson	89	88	1	2 559	161	29,41	64,47	2	18
SM Pollock	180	118	42	1 822	75	23,97	82,36	0	7
MV Boucher	137	95	24	1 691	70	23,81	77,64	0	13

- He has formed an effective opening pair with Gary Kirsten. They have the highest aggregate of runs in opening partnerships for South Africa in both Tests and Limited Overs Internationals:

Competition	Parts	Unb	Runs	Best	Avg	100	50
Tests	52	0	2 303	256	44,28	5	11
Limited Overs Ints	63	3	2 539	235	42,31	7	12

- Of the 25 times he has reached 50 in Limited Overs Internationals, he has gone on to make a century 11 times. This is currently the highest percentage of scores over 50 converted into centuries in Limited Overs Internationals:

Highest conversion rates in Limited Overs Internationals

Name	LOIs	Over 50	Over 100	Perc
HH Gibbs (SA)	117	25	11	44,00
Salim Elahi (Pak)	36	10	4	40,00
SR Tendulkar (Ind)	300	89	33	37,07
DI Gower (Eng)	114	19	7	36,84
Zaheer Abbas (Pak)	62	20	7	35,00
V Sehwag (Ind)	54	12	4	33,33
ME Trescothick (Eng)	50	13	4	30,76
Saeed Anwar (Pak)	242	62	19	30,64
GR Marsh (Aus)	117	31	9	29,03
NJ Astle (NZ)	166	43	12	27,90

(Qualification: 10 scores over 50)

Bibliography

Alfred, Luke: *Lifting the Covers* (Spearhead, Cape Town, 2001)
Allie, Mogamad: *More than a Game* (Western Province Cricket Association, Cape Town, 2000)
Atherton, Mike: *Opening Up* (Hodder & Stoughton, London, 2002)
Bryden, Colin: *Return of the Prodigal* (Jonathan Ball/Sunday Times, Johannesburg, 1992)
Crowley, Brian: *Currie Cup Story* (Don Nelson, Cape Town, 1973)
Crowley, Brian: *Cricket's Exiles* (Don Nelson, Cape Town, 1983)
Donald, Allan: *White Lightning* (CollinsWillow, London, 1999)
Gouws, Deon: *...And Nothing But The Truth* (Zebra, Cape Town, 2000)
Hartman, Rodney: *Hansie and the Boys* (Zebra, Sandton, 1997)
Hartman, Rodney: *A year on...Hansie and the Boys* (Zebra, Halfway House, 1998)
James, CLR: *Beyond a Boundary* (Stanley Paul, London, 1963)
Odendaal, André: *Cricket in Isolation* (André Odendaal, Cape Town, 1997)
Omond, Roger: *The Apartheid Handbook* (Penguin, London, 1985)
Warne, Shane: *My Autobiography* (Coronet, London, 2001)
Waugh, Steve: *No Regrets, a Captain's Diary* (HarperSports, Sydney, 1999)
Woolmer, Bob: *Woolmer on Cricket* (Virgin, London, 2000)
Wisden Cricketers' Almanack 1997-2002
Protea/Mutual & Federal South African Cricket Annual 1990-2002

Index

A
Ackerman, HD 15, 16, 55, 56, 154
Ackerman, Hylton 13, 25, 51-52
Adams, Paul 58, 102, 172
Ambrose, Curtly 169
Aronstam, Marlon 130
Atherton, Mike 129
Avendale 14, 20

B
Bacher, Dr Ali 42, 102, 144-145, 147, 148, 150, 155
Bey, Basil 30-31, 32, 34, 160-161
Bojé, Nicky 40, 144-145, 147, 150
Boome, Selborne 31, 34, 161
Bosch, Tertius 25, 27
Botha, Naas 29-30
Boucher, Mark 101, 135, 150, 152, 153
Bradman, Sir Donald 94

C
Cape Argus 23, 34, 36, 90
Cape Times 22, 23, 30, 153
Cassim, Hamid 'Banjo' 130-131, 135
Centurion Test (vs England 1999/00) 128-130
Chawla, Sanjeev 'Sanjay' 130-131, 135, 136, 141, 145, 148

Commins, Donné 4, 151, 152
Commins, John 4, 23, 59-61
Commins, Kevin 52-53
Craven Week 29, 30, 32
Crayenstein, Clinton 64
Cronjé, Bertha 144, 160
Cronjé, Hansie
  Batting with Gibbs in Nagpur 141-142
  Breaking umpires' door 96
  Death in air crash 160
  Dispute with Ali Bacher over quota 108-109
  Influence over players 157-161
  Losing temper in India 68
  Match-fixing scandal and suspension 144-156
  Meeting with Mukesh Gupta 75
  Meeting with Sanjay Chawla 131
  Offers to South African players 135-139
  Offer to 'throw' game in Mumbai 78-85
  Test 'deal' at Centurion 128-130
Crookes, Derek 79-83, 153
Cullinan, Daryll 24, 66, 71, 80, 81, 82, 153, 173-174, 196

D
Du Plessis, Morné 175-176

F
Fish, Mark 35
Fitzgerald, Mike 137-138, 151, 152
Fleck, Robbie 32, 161
Fletcher, Duncan 50, 55, 56, 57, 58, 59, 60
Ford, Graham 136
Fuller, Liesl 46, 62-64
Fuller, Rashad 63-64

G
Gardener, John 154
Gauntlett, Jeremy 152
Gibbs, Barbara 6-11, 64
Gibbs, Herman 5, 6-16, 22, 33, 35, 53-55, 170-171
Gibbs, Herschelle
  Athletics 35-36
  Becomes a father 62-64
  Bishops (Diocesan College) 16-17, 18-23, 27-32, 39, 41, 45
  Events at Nagpur on 1999/00 tour 137-142
  First century in Test cricket 112-113
  First-class debut 23
  First day at school 6
  First match aged eight 13
  Hansie Cronjé offer in Mumbai 78-85
  International series:

206

Index

Australia to SA (1996/97) 87-90
Australia to SA (2001/02) 187-189
Bangladesh to SA (2002/03) 190-191
Commonwealth Games (Malaysia, 1998/99) 100-101
England to SA (1999/00) 127-132
India to SA (1996/97) 86-89
India to SA (2001/02) 179-183
Pakistan to SA (1997/98) 97-98
Pakistan to SA (2002/03) 191-192
SA A to England (1996) 59-61
SA A to Sri Lanka (1997/98) 98-99
SA to Australia (1997/98) 91-96
SA to Australia (2001/02) 184-187
SA to India (1996/97) 67-85
SA to India (1999/00) 133-143
SA to Kenya (1996/97) 65-67
SA to Kenya (1999/00) 127
SA to Morocco (2002/03) 189
SA to New Zealand (1998/99) 110-114
SA to Sri Lanka (2002/03) 189-190
SA to West Indies (2000/01) 165-171
SA to Zimbabwe (2001/02) 177-179
SA Under 19 to West Indies (1996) 41-45,
Sri Lanka to SA (2000/01) 163-165
Sri Lanka to SA (2002/03) 191
West Indies to SA (1998/99) 101-110
World Cup (1999) 115-125
Life-skills course 175-176
Maiden Castle Cup century 55
Maiden first-class century 48
Marijuana-smoking incident 172-175
Match-fixing allegations and King Commission 144-156
Nuffield Week 20, 24, 39-40, 46-47
One-day international debut 66
Opens batting in one-day games 58-59
Relationship with Hansie Cronjé 157-161
Return to international cricket 163-164
Rugby career 29-34
SA record partnership with Smith 191
SA Schools 40
SA Test record with Kallis 112-113
Selected against West Indies 103
Selected for South Africa 61
Soccer career 34-35
Suspended by United Cricket Board 155
Test debut 71
Three successive one-day international centuries 190
Under 13 provincial week 15
Gibbs, Lucinda 8, 10-12, 36-37
Green, Clifford 145, 148, 150
Greig, Tony 140

H

Harrison, Richard 150
Haynes, Desmond 55, 56
Hudson, Andrew 80, 81, 83
Hunte, Conrad 42

I

International Cricket Council (ICC) 28, 85, 155

J

Jackman, Robin 25, 27, 52, 53
Jennings, Dr Ken 174

K

Kallis, Jacques 46, 55, 56, 57, 58, 135
Kapil Dev 136
Kemp, Justin 172
Keohane, Mark 34
King Commission 79, 83, 130-132, 135, 136, 137-143, 147, 148, 150, 151, 152-156
King, Judge Edwin 157
King, Mervyn 154
Kirsten, Gary 80, 81, 104, 113, 128, 136-137, 141, 149, 195
Kirsten, Noel 13
Kirsten, Peter 13, 14, 20, 34, 191
Klusener, Lance 124-125, 135, 145

Krige, Corné 32
Kuiper, Adrian 19
Kuper, Michael 155

L

Lara, Brian 195
Leary, Stuart 13, 15, 19
Lee, Brett 196

M

Majola, Gerald 174
Malik Qayyum, Judge 84
Mandela, Nelson 102
Matthews, Craig 154
May, Tim 49
McGlew, Jackie 42, 43
McGrath, Glenn 196
McMillan, Brian 53, 68, 80, 161
Mohammad Azharuddin 75
Montgomery, Percy 32-33
Morris, Richard 25, 51
Mukesh 'MK' Gupta 75, 76, 70
Muzzell, Robbie 82

N

National Sports Council 102
Nel, André 172
Nicky Oppenheimer XI 45, 49, 58
Noakes, Professor Tim 157-158
Norton, Grant 20, 21, 22, 28, 52, 161
Ntini, Makhaya 102

O

Octagon 4, 151
Owen-Smith, Michael 56-57

P

Pfuhl, Gavin 22, 23, 24-25
Pollock, Graeme 23-24
Pollock, Peter 114
Pollock, Shaun 40, 164, 176, 193
Pringle, Meyrick 43

R

Rajah, Goolam 145, 149, 150
Rapport 53
Reid, John 73
Retief, Dan 33
Richardson, Dave 79-80, 81, 82
Richardson, Keith 39-40, 46-47, 48
Roberts, Gwyneth 54-55, 58, 63
Rygersdal Club 35

S

Sacos (South African Council on Sport) 10, 34-35
SA Cricket Annual 23
SA Cricket Board 40
SA Sports Illustrated 103-104
Shoaib Akhtar 117, 196
Shuttleworth, Mark 17
Simons, Eric 27, 189, 194
Smith, Craig 172
Smith, Graeme 191
Sonn, Percy 147, 148, 186-187
St Joseph's College 6, 12, 13, 14, 16
Strydom, Pieter 135, 144, 145, 146, 149, 150, 151, 154, 155, 157
Sunday Independent 174
Sunday Telegraph 122, 123
Sunday Times 56, 84, 147, 174, 179
Symcox, Pat 83, 111, 153

T

Telemachus, Roger 172
Tendulkar, Sachin 45, 181, 195
The Mercury 147
Tshwete, Steve 102
Tuigamala, Va'aiga 33
Turner, Arthur 154

U

United Cricket Board of South Africa (UCB) 28, 85, 102, 155
Upton, Paddy 68

V

Van Zyl, Corrie 189
Viljoen, Deon 23-24
Villager Rugby Club 33
Von Hoesslin, Dave 31

W

Wallis-Brown, Melvyn 18-19, 21, 22, 52-53
Walsh, Courtney 104, 169
Warne, Shane 84, 120-121, 123, 196
Wasim Akram 196
Waugh, Mark 84
Waugh, Steve 101, 120-121, 196
White, Raymond 110, 130
Wilkinson, Bronwyn 145, 148, 150, 151
Williams, Henry 138, 139, 142, 146, 150, 151, 152, 153-154, 155, 156
Wisden 60, 69
Woolmer, Bob 14, 61, 70, 73, 79, 82-83, 89, 103, 104, 106, 110, 111, 118-119, 120, 121, 122, 158-159
World Cup (1999) 115-125

Y

Yorkshire club 12, 16, 35
You magazine 62
Young Cavaliers 12, 14-15